Global Issues

GLOBAL

A Cross-Cultural Perspective

ISSUES

SHIRLEY A. FEDORAK

UNIVERSITY OF TORONTO PRESS

Library and Archives Canada Cataloguing in Publication

Fedorak, Shirley, author
          Global issues : a cross-cultural perspective / Shirley A. Fedorak.

Includes bibliographical references and index.
Issued in print and electronic formats.
ISBN 978-1-4426-0773-6 (bound).—ISBN 978-1-4426-0596-1 (pbk.).
—ISBN 978-1-4426-0597-8 (pdf). —ISBN 978-1-4426-0598-5 (epub)

          1. Social problems. 2. Social conflict. 3. Social prediction.
4. Culture and globalization. 5. Civilization, Modern--21st century. I. Title.

HN18.3.F43   2013   361.1   C2013-904792-1 C2013-904793-X

We welcome comments and suggestions regarding any aspect of our publications—please feel free to contact us at news@utphighereducation.com or visit our Internet site at www.utppublishing.com.

North America
5201 Dufferin Street
North York, Ontario, Canada, M3H 5T8

2250 Military Road
Tonawanda, New York, USA, 14150

ORDERS PHONE: 1–800–565–9523
ORDERS FAX: 1–800–221–9985
ORDERS E-MAIL: utpbooks@utpress.utoronto.ca

UK, Ireland, and continental Europe
NBN International
Estover Road, Plymouth, PL6 7PY, UK
ORDERS PHONE: 44 (0) 1752 202301
ORDERS FAX: 44 (0) 1752 202333
ORDERS E-MAIL:
enquiries@nbninternational.com

Every effort has been made to contact copyright holders; in the event of an error or omission, please notify the publisher.

This book is printed on paper containing 100% post-consumer fibre.

The University of Toronto Press acknowledges the financial support for its publishing activities of the Government of Canada through the Canada Book Fund.

Printed in Canada

To my students, who have asked these questions.

CONTENTS

ILLUSTRATIONS

FIGURES

MAPS

TABLES

AUTHOR PROFILE

Shirley A. Fedorak taught socio-cultural anthropology and archaeology at the University of Saskatchewan for 16 years. In the 1990s she worked on several curriculum projects, including "People in Their World: A Study of First Nations Peoples on the Plains," sponsored by the Saskatoon Public School Board. She has also written and developed multimedia courses in anthropology and archaeology for the University of Saskatchewan's Extension Division.

In addition to serving as lead author for the first, second, and third Canadian editions of William A. Haviland's *Cultural Anthropology* (2002, 2005, 2009), Shirley Fedorak has co-authored a Canadian supplement for archaeology and biological anthropology courses, *Canadian Perspectives on Archaeology and Biological Anthropology* (2002), and the first Canadian edition of William A. Haviland's *Human Evolution and Prehistory* (2005). Her most recent publications include *Windows on the World: Case Studies in Anthropology* (2006), *Anthropology Matters!* (2007), *Pop Culture: The Culture of Everyday Life* (2009), and *Anthropology Matters*, 2nd ed. (2013).

After living in Cairo, Egypt, for five years, where she taught social sciences at Cairo American College, she now lives in Lake Chapala, Mexico, where she continues to write.

Shirley Fedorak considers preparing students for global citizenship one of her most important goals as an educator: "No matter what the discipline, it should be one where students actually learn about what it means to be citizens of the world."

ACKNOWLEDGEMENTS

Over the years, when students approached me with a concern, or searched for the answers to troubling questions, it became increasingly apparent to me that social sciences are more than academic disciplines. Therefore, I wish to extend my heartfelt thanks to my university students, who have grappled with these difficult questions and have turned to global studies for at least part of their answers. I also wish to thank my students at Cairo American College, who taught me a great deal about Egyptian culture, language, and people. Their refreshing perspectives on life have enriched my understanding of what it means to be a global citizen in the twenty-first century, regardless of place of origin. I am especially grateful to Yasmin Shawky, Johnathan Shimabuku, and Sohyun Kim for their insights into what it means to be a Third Culture Kid. I would also like to thank the teachers at Cairo American College who have assisted me in various ways with the preparation of this book, with a special thank-you to Beau Cain, Jocelyn Popinchalk, and Dr. Heba Farouk. Thank you to my daughter-in-law Fang Lian (Rachel) and son Kristopher for their insights into the one-child policy in China, and to my son Cory for his computer expertise.

I am grateful to Anne Brackenbury, Executive Editor for University of Toronto Press, for recognizing the value of this text. Her enthusiasm and willingness to let me find the direction this book would take are appreciated, as is all the help that freelance assistant Ashley Rayner, Beate Schwirtlich, and copyeditor Martin Boyne have provided.

And finally, I would like to thank my husband, Rob. Over the years he has played the role of sounding board, editorial critic, bibliographer, librarian, subject specialist, and instructional designer during my writing projects. I wish to thank him for his encouragement, support, and careful scrutiny of this edition.

TO THE INSTRUCTOR

Many instructors use global issues to prepare students for their future roles as global citizens. To that end, *Global Issues: A Cross-Cultural Perspective* provides instructors and students with several avenues for considering issues of importance in today's global society: critical analysis of socially relevant and often controversial issues that influence people and societies; cross-cultural comparison of globalization forces at work; the role of local cultures in understanding current global issues; and exploration of the value of global citizenship when considering solutions to global issues. These discussions may also prepare students to meet people who are "different" than they are – who speak a different language, or who look, believe, and behave differently.

The topics addressed in *Global Issues* challenge students to re-evaluate their media-shaped positions and may reduce or eliminate ill-conceived stereotypes and assumptions about "others." Several key concepts, including globalization, identity, cultural relativism, human rights, cultural imperialism, culture change, and various forms of conflict, provide interrelated themes running through *Global Issues*.

PEDAGOGICAL VALUE

Written primarily for first- and second-year university students, *Global Issues* is designed to supplement introductory textbooks dedicated to international, development, and global studies, human geography, political and legal studies, and socio-cultural anthropology. *Global Issues* links concepts commonly discussed in these disciplines to contemporary issues and practices:

- gender stratification and *purdah*;
- cultural relativism and female circumcision;
- cultural imperialism and international aid;
- human rights and birthrates;
- linguistics and language revitalization;
- transnational flow and body image;
- equality and same-sex marriage;
- socio-political reform and social media;
- identity and global nomads;
- political economy and food security;
- ethnopolitics and ethnic conflict;

- globalization and human migration; and
- militarism and global conflict.

Global Issues addresses socially relevant issues that are often controversial or that present an ethical challenge. The spotlight is often on local cultures and how they operate within a "globalized world," and how the processes of globalization affect day-to-day lives. *Global Issues* also takes a critical perspective when examining issues such as food security and American militarism. Each of these topics is designed to generate discussion among students interested in human issues within a global context.

Global Issues offers students the opportunity for cross-cultural comparative studies as they examine interpretations of human rights in the practice of *purdah*, female circumcision, and population growth, or when investigating the underlying reasons for ethnic and religious intolerance. Global variations in the ideal body image, the political power of social media, the socio-economic impact of NGOs in developing countries, human migration, and the dynamics of same-sex marriage also lend themselves to a comparative approach.

Although strongly influenced by an anthropological perspective, this investigation of global issues is not an isolated endeavour. The knowledge and expertise of scholars from history, political science, social justice, international studies, development studies, economics, sociology, human geography, indigenous studies, linguistics, environmental studies, media studies, education, medicine, food studies, agriculture, and gender studies allow students to gain a broader understanding of the questions posed in *Global Issues*. For an insider's view, each chapter offers personal narratives from people directly affected or from experts in a relevant field. For example, Sierra Leone anthropologist Fuambai Ahmadu was circumcised as an adult; she is therefore able to offer both an anthropological and participatory perspective. At times the insights of my students are presented in this work; they are not trained scientists, nor do they have much experience "out in the real world," but what they do possess is a sense of clarity not yet clouded with confusing and conflicting theory. Their candour is often refreshing and eye-opening.

Global Issues complements the subjects covered in social-science textbooks. Instructors may assign readings from *Global Issues* that correspond to the topics covered in class. Some of the topics, such as body image and Third Culture Kids, were chosen because of their interest quotient for students. Other topics were chosen because of their current social or political significance, such as the debate concerning same-sex marriage, or the influence of social media on socio-economic and political revolutions. Some topics, such as language revitalization and food security, were chosen to encourage students to examine a subject seldom considered by young people. Several of the topics, in particular female circumcision, same-sex marriage, and ethnic conflict, were specifically chosen because they are not usually covered in a global studies textbook, yet they are directly linked to cultural imperialism and questions of human rights and global citizenship.

Instructors may draw on a variety of instructional tools to expand students' comprehension of the topics presented in *Global Issues*. The Questions for Consideration and Classroom Activities in each chapter are designed to encourage critical thinking and group discussions, and will challenge students to apply the knowledge they have gained to compare, analyze, and interpret the material. The questions may also guide students in identifying the major themes and concepts found in each chapter. Websites and online lesson plans for instructors will engage students in participatory activities. Many of the chapters also include maps to assist students in placing the study groups in geographical context. The Suggested Readings in each chapter offer students the opportunity to investigate the subject matter in greater detail and from several viewpoints. Bolded terms throughout the text highlight key concepts that are then defined in the Glossary at the end of the text.

ORGANIZATION OF THE TEXT

Global Issues is divided into an introduction, three main sections with issue-related questions, and a conclusion. Although there is a great deal of overlap between sections, Part One contains four chapters with the underlying theme of cultural imperialism and human rights, Part Two contains five diverse chapters that address culture change and changing identities from several perspectives, and Part Three has four chapters that discuss conflict caused by economic, political, and social factors. A basic template is followed in each chapter, including a list of key terms, an introduction, a discussion of the issue, and a conclusion.

In Part One, "Cultural Imperialism and Human Rights," two controversial cultural practices and two interrelated issues are examined within the broader context of cultural imperialism, human rights, and the processes of globalization.

We begin with a cross-cultural comparison of differing, and often contradictory, perspectives on *purdah* and wearing *hijab* in Chapter 1, "*Purdah*: Is the practice of female seclusion and wearing *hijab* oppressive to women or an expression of their identity?" The voices of women who do and who do not wear *hijab* are a major component of this discussion. This chapter is designed to dispel some of the misconceptions that people in the West hold regarding the status of women in Muslim nations, while also addressing the volatile nature of gender stratification and oppression.

Chapter 2, "Female Circumcision: Is this practice a violation of human rights or a cherished cultural tradition?", lends itself to a discussion of the problems with maintaining a neutral, culturally relativistic stance while addressing contentious practices that outsiders classify as human-rights abuses. The political, socio-economic, and historical factors that contribute to the persistence of female circumcision are explored. This discussion offers a forum for the voices of women who value this custom, as well as those who oppose it. With such a sensitive topic, viewing it through the lens of anthropology may assist students in critically assessing the ethics of Western interference in this custom.

Chapter 3, "International Aid: What benefits do NGOs provide developing countries, and how can their presence generate new challenges?", provides an opportunity to critically assess the impact of NGOs on developing nations, using Haiti as our case study. This chapter provides students with information on the nature of aid, the problems inherent in foreign aid, whether disaster relief or humanitarian aid, and the legitimacy of aid agencies that moves beyond the usual Western self-congratulatory tone.

Chapter 4, "Population Growth: Is the world over-populated, and should governments have the right to control birthrates?", questions the prevailing notion that the world has too many people, especially in developing countries, and that this is the main reason for natural-resource depletion and social unrest. It also calls into question the agendas of developed nations and global institutions (e.g., the United Nations) for advocating population control. Students are provided with perspectives from both sides of this debate with the ultimate goal of critically assessing whether the world is over-populated or over-consumed.

Part Two, "Culture Change and Changing Identities," links culture change and changing identities to social reform and questions of personal and national identity in our increasingly globalized world. Here, too, the force of cultural imperialism is addressed.

We begin with an investigation of language loss and the role of linguists and speech communities in preserving endangered languages in Chapter 5, "Heritage Languages: Are they an endangered species?" There are between 6,000 and 7,000 extant languages in the world today, many in imminent danger of extinction, especially if they are indigenous or heritage languages. Indeed, linguist Nicholas Ostler (2001) warns that we are losing two languages a month. Some will not be saved, but others, through the efforts of speech communities and dedicated linguists, may be revitalized or at the very least preserved for future generations. This chapter exposes students to the cultural meaning of language and its importance to identity, the implications of language loss, and ongoing efforts to preserve and revitalize endangered languages.

Chapter 6, "Body Image: How does body image affect identity and status, and how has the transnational flow of Western ideals of beauty impacted other cultures?", provides an opportunity to investigate the flow of Western ideals, in this case, the ideal body, to the rest of the world. For a very different view on beauty, the concept of fatness as symbolic capital among the Tuareg of Nigeria is explored, as is the role of body-modification practices in engendering identities among queer, cyberpunk, and Modern Primitive subcultures. The value of cross-cultural comparisons and the power of the transnational flow of ideas are reinforced in this chapter.

Chapter 7, "Same-Sex Marriage: What are the socio-economic, religious, and political implications of same-sex marriage and changing family structure?", is an examination of how the institution of same-sex marriage is viewed and defined cross-culturally. Three opposing schools of thought – social conservative, critical feminist/queer, and gay and lesbian assimilationalist – are featured in this chapter. This discussion may help students make some sense of the debate over same-sex marriage, and provides evidence of how cultural values, practices, and identities are constantly changing, and that the concept of "traditional" has many meanings.

Chapter 8, "Social Media: What is its role in socio-political revolution?", addresses the power of social media in spearheading socio-economic and political protest. This topic is particularly timely given the Arab Spring and ongoing revolutions in the Middle East; however, students should recognize that the use of social media continues to evolve.

Chapter 9, "Global Nomads: Do Third Culture Kids own a national identity?", addresses the impact of living abroad, especially for young people, who are often called Third Culture Kids (TCKs). TCKs are youth who blend elements from all of the cultures they have lived in to create a third culture. As a consequence, they see the world and those around them in a different light than their monoculture peers. TCKs have been largely invisible, yet understanding their world is becoming important because they attend universities in North America or Europe, thereby adding their unique perspectives to the college experience. Their lives and the challenges they face when searching for their identity is the focus of this chapter. TCKs may also represent a microcosm of a much larger question: are globalization processes and the ever-increasing transnational community threatening national identity?

Part Three, "Economic, Political, and Social Conflict," examines various local and global crises and conflicts. As with the previous sections, cultural imperialism, human rights, and globalization processes provide a backdrop for these discussions.

Many reasons are given for the prevalence of world hunger. Chapter 10, "Food Security: What are the economic and political determinants of food security and the global implications of world hunger?", is a critical analysis of food security issues that often runs counter to prevailing assumptions that market-driven agriculture is the most productive method of feeding local and global populations. Indeed, the role of global institutions, such as the International Monetary Fund (IMF), and the ongoing process of displacing small-scale farmers with large agribusinesses are probed from a highly critical perspective. This chapter encourages students to peer beneath the surface of world hunger and begin to understand the real reasons why so many people are hungry.

Ethnic and religious intolerance is rampant the world over. In Chapter 11, "Ethnic Conflicts: What are the underlying reasons and the consequences of these conflicts?", the economic, political, social, and religious reasons behind ethnic conflict are addressed through the ongoing conflict in Darfur. Ethnic conflict creates human victims known as refugees; their hardships and the communities and social networks that have evolved in refugee camps are explored through the personal narratives of refugees. This discussion reinforces the fact that cultural institutions are integrated, and that we cannot be informed about complex issues without understanding the interconnections within systems of culture.

The mass migration of people fleeing economic servitude, political instability, environmental degradation, or religious intolerance has increased dramatically in recent decades, often causing conflict and dissension in host countries. In Chapter 12, "Human Migration: What are the socio-economic and political implications of the transnational flow of people?", human migration is situated within the context of globalization processes as we explore discrimination in France, the sex trade in Thailand, and human trafficking in Canada. This chapter offers students an opportunity to consider the conflicts, inequities, and challenges that immigrants face, and may help them develop more empathy for their plight and admiration for their strength and courage.

Chapter 13, "Global Conflict: Is the world safer because of military intervention, and what are the consequences of militarism?", closes *Global Issues*. This is an examination of militarism and just war ideologies, and the consequences of major powers intervening in the conflicts of other nations. As the most powerful promoter of Western imperialism and militarism, the United States is the major focus in this chapter.

Obviously, the questions posed in *Global Issues* will not be answered in any definitive way, but they are probed, analyzed, and critiqued to the point where readers should possess a broader, more balanced sense of these issues. *Global Issues* was written for anyone interested in the study of humankind and the issues that have meaning for people from many walks of life. This is not a theoretical discourse; rather, *Global Issues* challenges readers to rise above their current level of understanding – to think outside and beyond the box.

INTRODUCTION

Key Terms: climate change, cultural diversity, cultural imperialism, cultural relativism, culture, culture change, development, gender inequality, global citizenship, global economy, global issues, globalization, human rights, modernization

Why should we study global issues? This is a question I have been asked on numerous occasions, often by students who have had little experience with the world outside their own community. As an instructor, I have asked my students a similar question: "Why should we understand the world beyond our borders?" The answer to this question is the subject of *Global Issues: A Cross-Cultural Perspective*.

WHAT IS GLOBAL CITIZENSHIP?

One of the themes running throughout *Global Issues* is global citizenship and its role in creating global communities. **Global citizenship** is the sense that every person belongs to a larger system, beyond family, community, and country. It also means taking responsibility for protecting and respecting our natural and human resources. To become global citizens we need to understand and question the issues that impact all of us, or conversely, affect only a few. In support of this need to understand, *Global Issues* critically examines socio-economic, political, and cultural issues, including food security, same-sex marriage, *purdah*, female circumcision, language loss, human migration, ethnic and global conflict, humanitarian aid, and population growth. *Global Issues* also features topics of special interest to young adults on the cusp of becoming global citizens, such as the influence of social media, body image, and facing the challenges of being global nomads.

Students, the audience for this book, live in a world mired in conflict and socio-economic inequalities. Through rapidly changing forms of media they are exposed to human problems and contentious issues at home and abroad that cause them great concern, and they know that in the very near future they will have to step into that world and make some sense of it. *Global Issues* addresses some of their concerns, and exposes the false notions of gender, racial, and cultural superiority.

GLOBAL ISSUES AND KEY CONCEPTS

Social scientists from many fields have gathered detailed information on global issues, often putting this knowledge to practical use to solve or alleviate societal problems that humans face. This may evoke images of scientists marching into a crisis situation and saving the day, yet more often it is their knowledge and insights that are of value when addressing the concerns of humankind. In *Global Issues* we will explore some of these concerns, drawing on the expertise of disciplines such as political science, history, global studies, anthropology, and economics. This requires an understanding of several key concepts, including globalization, global economy, and development; climate change; culture, cultural diversity, and culture change; cultural imperialism; cultural relativism and human rights; and conflict.

Global issues are those concerns that require the cooperation of all nations to resolve. Many of these issues are interconnected, and often one type of global issue is responsible for causing other global concerns. This is particularly true of climate change, which has had a profound effect on food security, impacted the availability of natural resources, and greatly reduced biodiversity. **Climate change** refers to long-term changes in weather patterns. Climate change is threatening our global well-being by generating extreme weather events and creating water shortages. Climate change has also reduced agricultural production, resulting in more poverty and hunger, further exacerbating economic and gender inequalities, and forcing mass migration of humans from many developing countries. Energy consumption, the over-consumption of resources, and ultimately the release of greenhouse gases into the atmosphere have been identified as the main reasons for climate change (ClimateChangeConnection 2013). Therefore, climate change is not just a developing-nation problem – it is everyone's problem. This fact began entering public discourse in North America after Hurricane Sandy devastated the New York and New Jersey areas in 2012.

Globalization, which evolved out of colonialism, is the integration and transnational flow of financial resources (e.g., markets, trade goods, production), people (e.g., international migration, tourism), and information (e.g., ideas, fashion, culture, education) (Bhargava 2006). Globalization has played an important role in creating widespread inequities, over-consumption of natural resources, increasing poverty and growing food insecurity, as well as social unrest, international and ethnic conflicts, and forced migration of people in search of economic and political security. On the other hand, the transnational flow of ideas, mainly via the Internet, has empowered people to demand socio-economic change. This became evident during the Arab Spring uprisings in the Middle East in 2011 and 2013, when revolutionaries used social media to call the people to action. Global communication has also assisted in advocacy for gay rights and gender equality. Thus, the sharing of information and increasing awareness of international affairs have encouraged global citizenship.

International trade, production chains (e.g., assembly of various parts of an automobile in several countries), international financial markets, and the sharing of technologies and scientific knowledge – all globalization processes – have created a growing interdependence of people and societies (Bhargava 2006), and a **global economy** that is both stronger and more vulnerable – as witnessed in the collapse of global markets that began in 2008, and in the enormous debt load and near-bankruptcy of many countries that were exacerbated by this global financial crisis. The Internet has also brought to light the standard of living in developed countries and fuelled a desire among people in developing nations to enjoy the same consumer opportunities. This raises the questions of whether there are enough resources, and what impact over-consumption has on food security.

Globalization processes have also threatened traditional cultures. Haviland, Fedorak, and Lee (2009: 34) define **culture** as "the shared ideals, values, and beliefs that people use to interpret, experience, and generate behaviour," or in other words, "the whole way of life." Anthropologist Clifford Geertz (1973: 362), on the other hand, defined culture as a system of meanings that are embodied by symbols that are unique to each culture, and a culture's social structure as "economic, political, and social relations among individuals and groups." Obviously, culture is a dynamic force that can be defined in many ways.

Cultural diversity is a hallmark of human existence and is as important to our survival as genetic variation: just as species are threatened with extinction if they lose their genetic diversity, the human species is threatened if it loses its ability to respond to varying environments and situations. Each local culture or society determines the most effective way of making a living, given its circumstances. Globalization processes now jeopardize these traditional subsistence modes; for example, market-driven agribusinesses are forcing small-scale farmers off their land. In our globalized society, cultural diversity is increasingly threatened. Linguistic diversity is threatened by the prevalence and power of English and by the influence of developed nations that question the value of preserving heritage languages. Those involved in preserving endangered languages recognize the importance of linguistic diversity and the cultural knowledge reflected in these languages, yet many of the extant languages of today are in danger of disappearing.

Customs and traditions that outsiders view as unjust, such as female circumcision and *purdah*, are also threatened. Organizations and activists from the developed world are attempting to eradicate these practices, labelling them violations of human rights. Failure to recognize that there are other world views, other ways of living, presents the very real danger of **cultural imperialism** – promoting one nation's values, beliefs, and behaviour over all others. This is particularly prevalent in the West, where economic, political, religious, and military power has been used to "blackmail" other nations into adopting Western values and **modernization**. In fact, modernization usually refers to making others over in the Western image.

Development projects are ostensibly designed to improve the way people live; however, many **development** projects have been accused of imperialistic goals, including foreign investment and humanitarian aid. Development usually contains an element of modernization, such as moving toward an international market economy, and often means that developing countries become beholden to international institutions such as the World Bank for technological and financial assistance.

Although **culture change** is an inevitable and natural process, the speed at which it occurs and whether it is voluntary often determines its benefits or harm. This is why the goals of NGOs or the advocates of population control and the eradication of traditional cultural practices are so conflicting: change in society is inevitable, but outside forces implementing these changes can have a profound effect on the well-being of members of these societies and often originate from questionable ethics. *Global Issues* champions the value of cultural diversity and consistently promotes the worth of other world views and other ways of living.

To mitigate the loss of cultural traditions and beliefs, global citizens need to understand other cultures through their practices, values, and world view – what Overing (1985) calls the moral universe, or in other words, understanding a cultural group based on how the people understand themselves and the world around them. This approach, known as **cultural relativism**, acknowledges that the way "others" see the world is as valid as the way we see the world. This is particularly important when we are examining sensitive subjects such as family size and population growth. A culturally relativistic perspective does not set out to disprove anyone's beliefs or traditions; rather, the goal is to understand the reasons behind these practices within the context of that culture. Indeed, Clifford Geertz

(1984: 265) suggested that cultural relativism helps humans rise above provincialism and become true global citizens.

Cultural relativism is a contentious philosophy because of conflicting ideals and human-rights issues. Nor has a consensus ever been reached as to what cultural relativism actually means. Simply put, cultural relativism is the belief that all cultures are equally valid in their own right. This suggests, for some, that the beliefs and traditions of cultural groups must be accepted, regardless of whether they fit into our idea of acceptable behaviour. For others, the issue of human rights and equality supersedes cultural traditions: if a practice has the potential to harm, either physically or emotionally, then it should be stopped, regardless of its cultural value or historical context. The concept of cultural relativism elicits fear in some people because it calls into question, and may even reject, their own sense of right and wrong. Much of this fear can be traced to misunderstanding the basic tenets of cultural relativism: it is not that all ideas are true, but rather that all ideas deserve consideration. Cultural relativism is not about "anything goes"; it is about *respect* – respect for other ways of living, believing, and practising, and respect for the rights of all cultural groups to self-determination.

Human rights is also a vague, contradictory, and often misused term. On its most basic level, human rights refers to "reasonable demands for personal security and basic well-being" (Messer 1993: 222). Depending on the agency or organization, human rights may also include political and civil rights, socio-economic and cultural rights, development rights, and indigenous rights. However, what is or is not considered a human right differs from one local culture to another and often appears contradictory. For example, why is there opposition to same-sex couples who want the same right to marry as heterosexual couples in nations that purport equal rights for all? Why is male circumcision acceptable in the West, while female circumcision is labelled a violation of human rights? Why is it acceptable for wealthy nations to consume 80 per cent of the world's resources, yet demand that developing nations reduce their population numbers and promote low birthrates among couples regardless of their wishes? Although at times it is extremely difficult, all reflective people need to strike a balance between cultural relativism and human rights. In these debates, the role of social scientists is to serve as a conduit for voices that would otherwise go unheard.

Women's rights are indelibly linked to human rights and increasing attention is being paid to women in development and international affairs. Yet critics suggest that efforts to improve the lives of women have been symbolic rather than substantive, and that globalization has led to the "feminization of poverty" (Shah 2012). One reliable indicator of gender inequality is a sex ratio imbalance that is due to patriarchy and cultural preference for sons, as seen in several countries, including the two most powerful emerging markets, India and China. Without empowering women – through education, employment opportunities, and changing social norms that recognize the value of girls and women – development goals will continue to be a challenge. Although **gender inequality** has been at the forefront of discourse on global issues, little sustainable success has been achieved, partly due to neoliberal institutions such as the World Bank and International Monetary Fund, which tout development projects for private profit, a concept that so far has done little to better conditions for women.

A cornerstone of *Global Issues* is **conflict** (cultural, ethnic, economic, political, and so on). Although there are many forms of conflict, international conflict and militarism within the major powers is a consuming global issue that links directly to economic, political, and cultural imperialism.

As should be evident by now, we will be discussing some rather complex and controversial topics in *Global Issues*. The goal of this text is not to solve these problems, but to investigate them from a multidisciplinary perspective, and to challenge stereotypical assumptions, while searching out the reasons behind these assumptions. Throughout *Global Issues* we will consider the question, "Why do we need to know?"

Part One

CULTURAL IMPERIALISM
AND HUMAN RIGHTS

When is helping considered interference? When is encouraging a shift to more Westernized values and lifestyles considered cultural imperialism? What is a basic human right, and are these rights embraced or even understood in the same way by all people? The complex nature of these two concepts is reflected in Part One, "Cultural Imperialism and Human Rights."

Cultural imperialism, in its simplest form, refers to promoting one nation's values, beliefs, and behaviour over those of other nations. Cultural imperialism can take on many guises, some of which have a beneficial or humanitarian goal, at least on the surface, but also create problems and challenges for local cultures. Since culture is integrated, when one part of a culture (e.g., religious beliefs) is changed through outside influences, other systems of a culture (e.g., social status, economic security) may also be affected. This will become evident in the four topics chosen for Part One, which highlight the problems created when highly valued local practices and ways of living face harsh criticism and even eradication by outsiders. The role of cultural imperialism in attempts to end these traditions, under the guise of human rights, is a strong theme running throughout the first section of *Global Issues* and indeed the entire book.

In Chapter 1, "*Purdah*: Is the practice of female seclusion and wearing *hijab* oppressive to women or an expression of their identity?", the role of these traditions in reinforcing beliefs and announcing cultural, religious, and personal identity is considered from a cross-cultural perspective. In Chapter 2, "Female Circumcision: Is this practice a violation of human rights or a cherished cultural tradition?", the ancient custom of altering female genitalia to make a woman more desirable and marriageable, thereby increasing her status and economic security within a local culture, is examined. Western opposition to this practice and the cultural imperialism evident in movements to stop it are a major focus of this chapter.

The impact of international aid on local cultures and attempts to reduce birthrates in developing nations also reflect cultural imperialism, despite promoting human rights and equality for all. In Chapter 3, "International Aid: What benefits do NGOs provide developing countries, and how can their presence generate new challenges?", the question of cultural imperialism and human rights becomes even more clouded. Humanitarian aid, disaster relief, and development projects to improve an economy all appear beneficial. Yet questions increasingly arise regarding the true efficacy and benefits of these endeavours, or whether they are also instruments of cultural imperialism. Also, reducing birthrates to improve the standard of living of families in developing nations appears to be sound logic. Yet in Chapter 4, "Population Growth: Is the world over-populated, and should governments have the right to control birthrates?", the question of whether high birthrates result in poverty and depletion of global resources or if over-consumption by developed nations is the real culprit is critically examined.

Part One, then, demonstrates the local and international links between cultural imperialism at work and the challenges of supporting human-rights efforts in local cultures without harming those cultures' right to self-determination. The stage is also set for Part Two, where culture change and changing identities also face imperialistic attitudes.

Chapter 1

Purdah : Is the Practice of Female Seclusion and Wearing *Hijab* Oppressive to Women or an Expression of Their Identity?

Key Terms: cultural imperialism, discrimination, gender stratification, *hijab*, human rights, oppression, patriarchal society, *purdah*

INTRODUCTION

When a woman is covered, men cannot judge her by her appearance but are forced to evaluate her by her personality, character, and morals. "The *hijab* is not a responsibility, it's a right given to me by my Creator who knows us best. It's a benefit to me, so why not? It's something every woman should strive to get and should want." A North American Muslim woman who chooses to veil, quoted in Barr, Clark, & Marsh (n.d.).

The image of an Afghan woman hurrying through the streets draped from head to toe in voluminous folds of thick blue cloth, with not even her eyes visible, resonates among Westerners. These women are wearing *hijab*, a full body covering, and observing the ancient custom of *purdah* or female seclusion. To Westerners, *purdah* and *hijab* are symbols of female subjugation and oppression, tangible evidence that women in Muslim societies are treated like second-class citizens, forever submissive and secluded from the public eye. But is this an accurate assessment, or a remnant of colonialist perceptions of all things non-Western? Do women who follow *purdah* and wear *hijab* consider themselves oppressed, and what, if any, differences are there in the way the practices of *purdah* and *hijab* are viewed and applied from one culture to another?

In this chapter we will address gender stratification through the age-old practices of *purdah* and *hijab*, or what is commonly called veiling.[1] We will explore human sexuality as it pertains to these practices, as well as the historical, religious, and socio-cultural implications of *purdah* and *hijab*. Since *purdah* is both religious and cultural, the degree to which they are practised and their meaning(s) often vary, depending on differing internal and external factors, including religious piety, socio-economic class, familial expectations,

---

1 Veiling is the term Muslims use when referring to wearing a head scarf.

3

political agendas, and cultural mores. For this reason we will cross-culturally examine the practice in Palestine, Iran, and Afghanistan, as well as more briefly in countries such as Egypt. As people from Muslim states migrate to other countries, the issue of human rights and *purdah*, and the meaning of *choice* itself, becomes more complex. We will consider the challenges faced by people who wish to continue *purdah* and *hijab* while those around them disapprove.

Anthropologists, as well as other social scientists, have grown increasingly conscious of a new voice in the study of humankind – that of the people being studied. In this case, the thoughts of women who follow *purdah* and wear various forms of *hijab*, as well as women who choose not to wear *hijab*, will be heard, as it is their interpretation that is most relevant. Internet sources are drawn upon extensively, since it is here, rather than in academic papers, that Muslim women have found a timely and effective forum for expressing their views on the experience and meaning of *purdah* and *hijab*.

An insider's (or emic) perspective from social scientists also lends an added dimension to the study of *purdah*. For example, Homa Hoodfar is a Canadian anthropologist of Iranian descent who has focused her research on the experience of veiled Muslim women. She draws on historical accounts and anthropological data, as well as her personal perspective as a Muslim woman, to understand the practice. Finally, this chapter not only considers whether *purdah* and *hijab* are oppressive but also examines the *perception* of oppression that many Westerners hold.

THE NATURE OF *PURDAH* AND *HIJAB*

Just as the concept of gender is a cultural construct, so is gender stratification culturally defined. **Gender stratification** refers to inequality between men and women, based on their access to wealth and resources, power and self-determination, and the prestige and status afforded to each gender. Thus, the social and political positions that women hold in a culture, the economic independence they are able to achieve, and the decision-making power they have over their own lives and bodies are all indicators of gender equality, or the lack thereof. Some degree of female gender stratification exists in all modern-day societies; the question here is whether *purdah* exemplifies a form of gender stratification.

The Persian word *purdah* means curtain (Khan 1999); it can also mean screen or veil (Arnett 2001). Most people associate *purdah* with clothing that covers a woman; this is really veiling or *hijab* (see below), while *purdah* is a more general term for the seclusion of women, whether beneath concealing clothing or isolation in their homes. Although people outside the Muslim faith and culture may view *purdah* as repressive, to many Muslims, following *purdah* symbolizes the importance of feminine modesty and purity, and reflects positively on the family. These women are following the Qur'an (24: 30–31), which states: "And say to the believing women that they should lower their gaze and guard their modesty; and that they should not display their beauty and ornaments except what must ordinarily appear thereof; that they should draw their veils over their bosoms and not display their beauty except to their husbands."

The modest covering of a woman's head and body is known as **hijab** or veiling. *Hijab* comes from the Arabic word *hajaba*, meaning to hide or conceal from view (Ali n.d.). If a woman does not wear her veil in the presence of a man then she considers him kin (MacLeod 1991). Besides modestly covering a woman's body, the clothing must be loose and shapeless, and opaque so as not to draw attention.[2] To many women, *hijab* is the truest expression of being Muslim.

Many cultural groups practise *hijab*, although the form of *hijab* adopted varies considerably. Azerbaijani women wear a head scarf to cover their hair, while women of the Rashaayda Bedouin wear a married woman's mask. The Indian *sari*, Sudanese *tobah*, Iraqi *abbayah*, Turkish *yashmak*, North African *djellabah* and *haik*, and Egyptian *milaya* (Fernea & Fernea 2000; Hoodfar 2003) are also tangible expressions of cultural practices that hold deeply rooted meanings in each of these societies.

The practice of veiling is not unknown in Western society. A common example is the white veil covering a bride during a Christian wedding ceremony, symbolizing chastity and purity. Until the 1960s, women were required to cover their heads when in Catholic churches. Other cultural groups, including Hutterites, Amish, and Canadian Doukhobors, traditionally wore head scarves as a symbol of modesty and tradition. Catholic nuns also wear habits that exemplify a form of *purdah* and *hijab*.

So why do some Muslim women wear *hijab*? According to Hoodfar (1993:3), "veiling is a lived experience." Wearing *hijab*, or even a simple head scarf, identifies a woman as a socially active Muslim, reflects her solidarity with other Muslims, and publicly proclaims her identity as a Muslim. *Hijab* expresses spirituality, personal dignity, and sexual integrity. *Hijab* has also become a symbol of Muslim women's struggles for gender and ethnic justice when they publicly announce their Muslim identity in countries such as the United States. For some women, wearing *hijab* empowers them and enables them to challenge stereotypes about Muslims. According to Islamic scholar Wadid Ahmed, American Muslim women are able to integrate Islam with American social and political activism by wearing *hijab* (cited in Paulsell 2011).

"Women from Pakistan ... [wore] comfortable *salwar kameez* — silky tunics drifting low over billowing pants with long shawls of matching fabric tossed loosely over their heads. Saudi women trod carefully behind their husbands, peering from behind gauzy face veils and 360-degree black cloaks that made them look, as Guy de Maupassant once wrote, 'like death out for a walk.' Afghan women also wore 360-degree coverings, called chadris — colourful crinkly shrouds with an oblong of embroidered lattice work over the eyes. Women from Dubai wore stiff, birdlike masks of black and gold that beaked over the nose." Eyewitness account by journalist Geraldine Brooks (1994: 21) at the Cairo airport.

Ensuring that females remain sexually pure until marriage and faithful to their husbands after marriage is the most common reason given for *purdah* (Khan 1999). Muslim clergy believe that Muslim women should wear *hijab* to protect their virtue and help men control their sexual appetites. In Egypt, women cover their bodies to ward off sexual harassment in the streets (Martin 2010). In Afghanistan, the *chaadaree* veil completely covers a woman's head, thereby protecting men from distraction as they go about their religious and social duties (Hughes 2007). Furthermore, some Muslim women living in the West feel that wearing *hijab* isolates them from the Western tendency to objectify women. Observing *purdah* is also a symbol of the Muslim world's rejection of Western morals and political ideology; therefore, wearing *hijab* has become politicized. Indeed, women in Egypt have worn *hijab* to express their Muslim identity, but also to reject former president Hosni Mubarak's ties with the West, in particular the United States (Hughes 2007).

---

2 In Cairo young women wear form-fitting tunics that are colour-coordinated with their *hijab*. They wear blue jeans beneath the tunics.

FIGURE 1.1 WOMEN WEARING *HIJAB*

From a religious perspective, the Qur'an appears to sanction female seclusion: "And when you ask his wives for anything, ask it of them from behind a curtain (*hejjab*). That is purer for your hearts and their hearts." According to the Qur'an, then, *purdah* is considered a code of behaviour that sustains a woman's privacy, protects her reputation, and prevents sexual exploitation (Geissinger 2000). However, some Muslim women see the *hijab* as a submission to their God and faith, not to men (Bullock 2001). Fernea and Fernea (2000: 239) call the *hijab* "portable seclusion" that enables a woman to affect an aura of respectability and religious piety, thereby bringing honour to her family. Despite the religious link to *hijab* and *purdah*, however, the Qur'an does not specifically recommend veiling or seclusion (Mernissi 1991).

Purdah also serves to maintain control over wealth and property (de Souza 2004). Women are the mothers of sons who will inherit property and wealth from the patriarch; the paternity of these sons must therefore be ensured. Consequently, veiling has strong socio-economic implications, since "the more economic rights women have had, the more their sexuality has been subject to control through the development of complex social institutions" (Hoodfar 2003: 6). Thus, in some states, *purdah* is deemed more important for the wealthy upper classes who have property to protect than for the poorer lower classes. *Purdah*, then, becomes a symbol of status – only wealthy women can afford to practise *purdah*, while women who must work to help support their families find it difficult to practise.[3]

Although *purdah* requires women to wear concealing clothing when they leave the house, it also refers to female seclusion, or what Young (1996) calls segregation of the sexes.

---

3 In Egypt, women wear their *hijab* at work, or if they are domestics, they change into "working clothes" and remove their *hijab* once in their employer's residence.

This segregation is practised among the Rashaayda Bedouin, who recognize private domestic spaces for women and open public spaces for men. In some cases, *purdah* has been used to keep women from participating in socio-economic and political life. Among the Yusufzai Pakhtun of the Swat Valley in northeast Pakistan, women remain secluded inside domestic compounds, leaving only to attend weddings, funerals, and circumcision rituals. If they do leave their homes, they must be accompanied by other women or a male family member (Lindholm & Lindholm 2000). This practice ensures that women spend most of their lives within the domestic sphere and are unable to obtain employment or an education, or to participate in other activities within their community.

THE HISTORY OF *PURDAH* AND *HIJAB*

The origin of *purdah* remains unclear, although it may have developed in ancient Persia. Regardless of its origin, *purdah* was practised long before the beginning of Islam (Nashat 1988). In fact, *purdah* did not spread to the Middle East until the Arab conquest of the region in the seventh century. Ancient Babylonian women were masked and chaperoned by a male relative when they left the house. They were also segregated in a separate part of the household. Similarly, respectable Assyrian women were hidden behind screens in their houses (Arnett 2001), while prostitutes were forbidden from veiling (Keddie & Baron 1991). Evidence of *purdah* and *hijab* has also been found in classical Greece, Byzantium, Persia, and India among the Rajput caste (Women in World History Curriculum 2011). In Assyrian, Greco-Roman, and Byzantine cultures and in the pre-Islamic empire in Persia, *purdah* was a mark of prestige and status, and in India, *purdah* was practised as early as 100 BCE to protect royal women from unwanted gazes (Khan 1999). Records suggest that the practice of *hijab* began in Islamic society after Mohammad's wives were insulted (Fernea & Fernea 2000).

By the eighth century, female seclusion was well entrenched in Persia and the Eastern Mediterranean among the upper classes (Khan 1999), but not until the reign of the Safavids (1501–1722) did the veil emerge as a symbol of status among Muslim ruling classes and elite in Persia and the Ottoman Empire (1357–1924) (Hoodfar 2003). In India, *purdah* was followed even during colonial rule. Indeed, most of the negative perceptions that Westerners have regarding the veil originated during colonial periods when veiling was cited as an example of Muslim "backwardness" (Hoodfar 1993). This perceived subjugation of women in turn justified colonialism. However, colonialism did not better the position of Muslim women. In India, they lost their right to inherit property and wealth, and to maintain control over income they earned, bringing the economic rights of Muslim women more in line with Hindu and British women of the time. In essence, colonial rule destroyed the matrilineal societies of southern India (Khan 1999).

In the late nineteenth and early twentieth centuries, liberals and intellectuals pushed for an end to *hijab* and *purdah*. Following the 1923 international feminist meeting in Rome, Islamic feminists in Egypt publicly de-veiled (Hoodfar 1993). Despite Islamic feminism labelling the veil a symbol of oppression in the early twentieth century, especially in Egypt, Iran, and Turkey, by the latter half of the century this ideology was revisited. As the twentieth century progressed, *hijab* enjoyed a revival, especially in areas where people felt that Islam was being

"... although Egyptian women of low income classes never veiled their faces and wore more dresses which did not prevent movement, they nevertheless regarded the upper-class veil as an ideal. It was not ideology which prevented them from taking 'the veil'; rather it was the lack of economic possibilities." (Hoodfar 1989: 21).

threatened by Western influence. *Hijab* became a symbol of religious piety, cultural identity, and feminine virtue.

Today, *hijab* is compulsory in Saudi Arabia and Iran, and expected in countries such as Egypt, Algeria, Kuwait, and Palestine. In other Muslim countries, conditions remain volatile, with some segments advocating *hijab*, while others have rejected the custom. Women find themselves at the centre of this debate, often enduring harassment and discrimination whether they wear *hijab* or not, depending on the current political and ideological atmosphere. Thus, *purdah* and *hijab* are dynamic practices. Indeed, Hoodfar (1993: 5) argues that "in Muslim cultures the veil's functions and social significance have varied tremendously, particularly during times of a rapid social change."

PURDAH AND *HIJAB* AS OPPRESSION

Those outside the Muslim world often think that Muslim women occupy a subordinate position in Middle Eastern countries (Cohen & Peery 2006) and that *hijab* is a symbol of this supposed **oppression**. However, we should question whether oppression and subjugation are a reality for Muslim women. Indeed, a recent resurgence of the *hijab* has been noted among educated Muslim women who wish to announce their faith and traditions: "Young Muslim women are reclaiming the *hijab*, reinterpreting it in light of its original purpose – to give back to women ultimate control of their own bodies" (Mustafa n.d.: 1).

To understand how Muslim women outside the confines of a Muslim country view the veil, Read and Bartkowski (2000) conducted a study of two dozen Muslim women living in Austin, Texas. Half of these women wore the veil and the other half were unveiled. They found that the unveiled women viewed *hijab* as a mechanism for the patriarchal domination of women: "The veil is used to control women" (408). Both groups felt that *hijab* was directly related to men's sexuality and lack of control: "Men can't control themselves, so they make women veil" (408).

Many of the unveiled respondents sought to weaken the link between *hijab* and religion: "Women are made to believe that the veil is religious. In reality, it's all political" (408). However, some narratives from veiled women indicate that they do wear *hijab* for religious reasons: "I wear the *hijab* because the Qur'an says it's better" (403). Another woman believed that "the veil represents submission to God" (403). *Hijab* can also be a cultural marker – a statement of a Muslim's ethnic and cultural distinctiveness: "The veil differentiates Muslim women from other women. When you see a woman in hijab, you know she's Muslim" (404). Even the unveiled women considered *hijab* an important cultural marker: "Some Muslim women need the veil to identify them with the Muslim culture" (409).

Although veiled women in this study did not explicitly discuss the idea that men's sexual activities must be controlled, they did allude to the problem: "If the veil did not exist, many evil things would happen. Boys would mix with girls, which will result in evil things" (404). The sense of female distinctiveness was articulated by one woman: "Women are like diamonds; they are so precious. They should not be revealed to everyone – just to their husbands and close kin" (404). Contrary to the Western perspective that *hijab* restricts women, the veiled women in Read and Bartkowski's (2000) study felt that the veil liberated them. To these women, then, *hijab* has overlapping religious, gendered, and ethnic significance.

"Women who wear the hijab are not excluded from society. They are freer to move around in society because of it." A North American Muslim woman, quoted in Read & Bartkowski (2000: 405).

Opponents view *purdah* as oppressive, depriving women of **human rights** such as education, economic independence, and participation in community life. They see *purdah* as a way to marginalize and subjugate women. Interestingly, some feminist writers on *hijab* suggest that women are veiled to mute their sexual desires and their potential danger to men (Bonvillain 1998), while women who wear *hijab* believe it is men's sexual desires that are controlled. Opponents also point out that *hijab* originated before Islam and outside the Middle East, that using religious scripture to support wearing *hijab* is false reasoning, and that interpretations of the scriptures and *hadiths*[4] are highly questionable.

A common rationale for *hijab* is the sense of anonymity. "Wearing the *hijab* has given me freedom from constant attention to my physical self," says Canadian-born Muslim Naheed Mustafa (n.d.: n.p.) who began wearing a head scarf at the age of 21. While others tend to see her as a terrorist or an oppressed woman, she feels liberated – free from un-wanted sexual advances and the body politics of Western "gender games." Empirical evidence suggests that men interact differently with women wearing *hijab*. Supporters of *purdah* also suggest that seclusion can offer women protection and safe haven, a place where they can relax and enjoy their favourite activities.

Although the discussion thus far has taken a positive perspective toward *purdah* and *hijab*, in the following cultural examples you will see that they can also be used as a vehicle of control over women and children, as well as to fulfill political and religious agendas.

> According to one female informant, "Women have been exploited so much, and men make such silly fools of themselves over women, that I really think it is a good thing for men, that women wear hijab." (Bullock 2001: 2).

PALESTINE

During the *intifada*[5] of the 1980s in Gaza, Hamas extremists attempted to impose *hijab* on Palestinian women (Hammami 1990). These women, who had enjoyed relative freedom to choose whether to wear *hijab*, now found their dress code under increasing scrutiny and pressure to conform to the Hamas interpretation of *hijab*. Although *hijab* was common among older Palestinian peasant women, many educated urban women had given up wearing any form of *hijab* by the 1950s (Hammami 1990). Even those wearing *hijab* considered it a symbol of group identity, not a genderized restriction. For some, *hijab* was a symbol of resistance to Israeli occupation in Gaza. Regardless of how the *hijab* was viewed, most Palestinian women were against forced imposition of *hijab*.

The Hamas, however, sought to restore *hijab* as part of a movement to return to a moral and social order closer to their interpretations of Islam. Hamas considered *hijab* a reflection of traditional Islamic piety and political affiliation. Women who refused became targets for attacks by youths who threw stones at them and shouted verbal abuse. The original religious and modesty aspects of *hijab* seemed lost, and *hijab* became a sign of a woman's political commitment to the *intifada*. As one woman said, "It [the *hijab*] is not an issue for me. … In my community [Abassan] it's natural to wear it. The problem is when little boys, including my son, feel they have the right to tell me to wear it" (Hammami 1990: 26).

---

4 Sayings or anecdotes about Muhammad.
5 Intifada symbolizes the Palestinian uprising against Israeli occupation of Palestinian territory.

In May 1988, hooligans, acting under the auspice of Hamas, broke into a school and demanded that the girls wear the *hijab*, and in September of that year a group of males attacked girls at the Ahmad Shawqi school in Gaza City for not covering their heads (Hammami 1990). When the attacks on women spread to Jerusalem, the Unified National Leadership of the Uprising (UNLU) political leaders in Gaza came to the aid of Palestinian women. After a particularly ugly incident in which two women were harassed and accused of being collaborators, the UNLU condemned the attacks in a statement, and the attacks stopped for a time (Hammami 1990). Unfortunately, in 1990 Hamas resumed the *hijab* campaign with a vengeance, but now they were advocating full body coverage. Hamas also issued orders that women were to have a male relative with them when leaving the house. Hamas has even advocated for the imposition of Sharia law, with particular attention to Islamic dress code, and in February 2011, women's hairstyling by men was banned in Gaza (Cunningham 2010). Obviously in Palestine, *hijab* is being used as an instrument of oppression, "a direct disciplining of women's bodies for political ends" (Hammami 1990: 25).

Palestinian women resisting the pressure to wear *hijab* are not necessarily against the practice, but they want the right to choose. They also resist the patriarchal control that Hamas has been trying to wield, and fear that *hijab* is only a first step in an offensive against Palestinian women's rights. In 2013, the majority of Palestinian women wear *hijab*, but those who do not experience social pressure to conform, and some women have even been arrested. As an example of how extreme this pressure can become, female students at Al-Azhar University, although a far less conservative institution than some of the universities in Gaza, must wear the *hijab* in order to receive their graduation certificate (Saldanha 2010).

IRAN

The story of women and *hijab* in Iran has taken a convoluted path that differs dramatically depending on socio-economic class. The veil was banned by Reza Shah Pahlevi in 1936 (Talvi 2002) as part of the Women's Awakening and the Shah's plan to modernize Iran. For modern urban Iranian women, this project opened up educational and employment opportunities – if they gave up their veils (Amin 2002). Following the project's failure, urban women experienced a backlash from men; some unveiled women were even attacked by religious extremists.

For lower- and middle-class Iranian women, banning the veil created scandal and great inconvenience. These women were socialized from birth to see the veil as the only respectable way to dress, and they did not want to appear in the streets "naked" (Hoodfar 1993: 10). Where they had previously shopped and built social support networks in the neighbourhood, they now stayed at home – too embarrassed to appear in public without their *hijab*. Since many of their husbands were away working, they were reduced to begging male relatives and neighbours to perform public tasks for them.

There were also economic implications. Moderate families no longer allowed their daughters to attend school if they could not wear *hijab*. Young women who used to attend carpet-making workshops to earn some independent income now stayed at home. Some resorted to making carpets at home, but their male relatives had to sell them, thereby gaining control over the women's productive strategies and income. The women also lost their only avenue for socializing with neighbours. Thus, this new law created a culture of dependency among middle- and lower-class conservative women and led to further seclusion and isolation of women in Iranian society.

By the 1960s and 1970s, Iranian women under the rule of the Shah enjoyed a degree of independence. They received educations and worked in traditionally male professions. However, this does not mean that Iranian women were free from oppression. Those who veiled were arrested and their veils forcibly removed, at least until dress codes became more open and women were allowed to wear the veil if they so chose. In the 1970s, the political atmosphere changed and Iranian women began wearing the *chador* (black, loose-fitting robes). When the Shah was deposed in 1979 and the Islamic Revolution swept the country, the *chador* became compulsory, and women were once again punished – this time for *not* wearing *hijab* (Talvi 2002). Under the Ayatollah Khomeini, religious and cultural fundamentalism forced women to veil and take on more traditional gender roles. Women were seen as pivotal to changing Iran's moral code, and those who resisted were mocked and called "unchaste painted dolls" (Women in World History Curriculum 2011). Witnesses recounted the terror of executions by public stoning of women who broke the strict laws of Islamic appearance and conduct (Talvi 2002).

When Middle Eastern studies professor Faegheh Shirazi visited her home country of Iran in 1997, graffiti slogans such as "Death to the improperly veiled woman" covered the walls of buildings, reminding her that *hijab* was not only a cultural and religious custom to Iranians, but an ideology that permeated every aspect of their lives. Propaganda on the virtues of the veil was everywhere: television programs, newspaper and magazine articles and advertisements, and even stamps had the word *hijab* inscribed on the lower left corner (Shirazi 2001).

> "Some Western feminists have such strong opinions about the veil that they are totally incapable of seeing the women who wear them, much less their reasons for doing so." (Hoodfar 1993: 14)

Although wearing the *hijab* has been the custom in several periods of Iranian history, in modern Iran choice is no longer an issue. This suggests that currently *hijab* is an instrument of gender oppression in Iran, and a symbol of the degradation of women's rights. However, we should not construe from the above that Iranian women are passive, powerless pawns in the regime. Women have ways of exerting power; for example, if a man outside the family argues with a woman, she may insult him by dropping her veil, indicating that she does not consider him a real man (Hoodfar 1991). Resistance against the veil is also common through small gestures, such as leaving strands of hair free. These acts of defiance "develop [women's] identities specifically for the reason that they are forbidden; and enables them to construct their identities against the torturous rituals governing what they are forced to wear, how they are expected to act, the gestures they have to control, the daily struggle against arbitrary rules and restrictions" (Shilandari 2010: n.p.).

AFGHANISTAN

The image of an Afghan woman scurrying through the streets, completely concealed beneath a blue *burqa*, is difficult for Westerners to reconcile with their sense of personal freedom and human rights. When they were in public spaces, Afghan women under the control of the Taliban had to be concealed beneath a form of *burqa* known as a *chadri*. Only close family members – husbands, children, fathers, and siblings – and other women were allowed to see a woman without her *chadri*. Afghan women were also forbidden to work outside the home or to pursue an education. Feminists liken the lives of Afghan women under the rule of the Taliban to "gender apartheid" (Geissinger 2000).

Resurgence of the *hijab* began in the 1970s; the Taliban simply made the custom a law. Since the overthrow of the Taliban, women have returned to school and university and have assumed professional positions. Yet their lives are far from peaceful or safe; warlords who have traditionally practised ethnically motivated rape are now in positions of power sanctioned by the United States. Thus, many Afghan women continue to wear the *chadri*, partly for safety, and partly because of the historical and cultural significance of *purdah*. To the men, women are socially immature and likely to behave irresponsibly, so to protect the family honour, strict regulation of *purdah* is necessary. Thus, social and familial pressures continue to perpetuate the practice of *purdah* among Afghani women.

The purpose of the *burqa* is ostensibly to silence or make women invisible. It has served to do both in Afghanistan; however, international development consultant Michelle Risinger (2012) sees a transformation of the *chadri* taking place, from a symbol of oppression to a means of resistance and empowerment. Afghani women, in their resistance to Taliban culture[6] and its proponents, have learned to use the *chadri* for concealment and protection (Boone 2010). Women's resistance movements, including the Revolutionary Association of the Women of Afghanistan, run orphanages and women's literacy classes, and raise awareness of women's rights among Afghani women. They are also suspected of organizing public demonstrations against a law that gave Shia males "the right to demand sex from their wives while denying them basic rights" (Boone 2010: n.p.). Thus, although self-determination for Afghani women is a distant dream, there are women within the country who are working toward that goal.

WESTERN PERCEPTIONS OF *PURDAH* AND MUSLIM WOMEN

Since September 11, 2001, Muslims in North America have found themselves under a new and intense scrutiny – what Alan Lebleigez, a European Union parliament member, has called Islamaphobia (Bishr n.d.). **Discrimination** against, and harassment of, women dressed in *hijab* in countries such as Canada has shocked the Muslim community and re-iterated their status as that of the "Other." *Purdah* has become symbolic of this otherness.

In response to what is a form of **cultural imperialism**, Muslims are re-asserting their identity, including wearing *hijab*. However, *hijab* makes Westerners feel uncomfortable because, with it, women seem to become invisible, and a negative image of *purdah* and *hijab* is still very evident in the West (Bullock 2001). Canada has also banned face veils at citizenship oath ceremonies and is considering banning them in schools, hospitals, and government buildings (BBC News 2011). Muslim women have been accosted by other Canadians and accused of bringing "backwardness" to Canada. Even some Muslim women have decried the *hijab*, wanting Muslims to modernize. However, forcing a woman to conform to Canadian ideals of dress and give up a symbol of her Muslim identity is a form of discrimination and is as oppressive as forcing a woman to wear *hijab*.

Readers might ask how something like this could happen in a multicultural country like Canada. The answer lies in the uneasy truce between religion and the secularization of Canadian institutions. Culturally, Westerners have not moved beyond the image of *hijab* as oppressive. They continue to express concern that women who wear *hijab* must have been

---

6 Although United States troops drove the Taliban out of Kabul, the cultural environment the Taliban created still exists.

pressured or coerced into doing so by male relatives or religious leaders. Despite Canada's official multiculturalism policy, when it comes to *hijab*, there is a sense that Muslims should comply with Western behaviour.

In March 2004, France banned conspicuous religious symbols and attire in schools – children were no longer allowed to wear Islamic head scarves, Christian crosses, Jewish skull caps, or Sikh turbans (IRNA 2005). Yet the real target was Muslim veiling. According to the Stasis Commission, created by former French president Jacques Chirac to examine the principle of secularity, the veil is a rejection of *mixité* – coeducation and the mixing of the sexes (Debré 2003). Banning the veil in France meant that Muslim girls could no longer attend coeducational schools. Full face veils were also banned in Belgium in 2010, setting off a firestorm of debate, especially since so few women actually wear them.[7] Amnesty International has condemned the Belgian law, calling it "an attack on religious freedom" (Hasan 2010: 22). Some states in Germany have passed similar legislation. Muslim women and supporters protested this move, demanding their religious freedom. In fact, human-rights activists and some European Union parliament members are demanding that EU countries respect the freedom of faith and dress (Islamonline.net).

In Turkey, where veiling is not encouraged, educated urban women are returning to *hijab*, reflecting a renewed interest in their religion and culture, and a desire to publicly affirm their Muslim identity and physically announce resistance to Western domination. This return to traditional Islamic dress has been met with opposition. In Turkey, head scarves have been banned from educational institutions and state offices, and young women have been arrested for wearing head scarves to class (Geissinger 2000). Women have also been expelled from government positions. In Uzbekistan, men with beards and women with scarves have been harassed and arrested. In Cameroon, veils are banned in state-subsidized schools; this ban has been blamed for the establishment of private Islamic schools (van Santen 2010). These acts of discrimination have been justified as a way to stamp out fundamentalism and terrorism.

Debate among Islamic groups continues to rage today. Some groups, such as the Women's Action Forum (WAF) in Pakistan, actively reject attempts to impose *hijab* on women, while the women's mosque movement in Egypt aims to return the veil to a symbol of religious piety rather than religico-cultural identity (Mahmood 2003). According to Hajja Nur, a mosque teacher, Egyptian women "understand forms of bodily practice (such as veiling) to not simply express the self but also shape the self that they are supposed to signify" (Mahmood 2003: 843). European activists have demonstrated at state buildings to demand religious freedom of expression. At a Wayne State University protest in the United States, scarves became a weapon against ignorance and a symbol of solidarity (Capeloto 2004). Non-Muslim women

"'Take those clothes off, you don't have to wear that. You're in Canada now,' shouted the elderly lady [...] Normally I would have replied with something witty, but being in a state of shock, all I could come up with was, 'I know where I am.'
'Then take them off. You make me feel hot!'
'I'm wearing this by choice,' I replied.
'No you're not. You're being controlled. You're being controlled by males!'
Her striking words ... caught me off-guard. I felt certain that this woman was not just repeating an old stereotype. This was what she really believed!" (Zahedi n.d.).

"If I don't stand up for Muslim women's right to wear *hijab* when they want to, who's going to stand up for me when I'm attacked?" A non-Muslim supporter, quoted in Capeloto (2004: 1).

---

7 Full face veils are worn only by the most conservative of Muslim sects.

donned the scarves alongside Muslim women in defence of a growing worldwide campaign to show support for the right to wear *hijab*.

CONCLUSION

The practice of *purdah* is a complicated issue. *Hijab* represents three major tenets in a Muslim woman's life: religious faith and adherence to religious commandments; cultural and personal identity representing status, class, kinship, and culture membership; and political consciousness and activism. Although the custom is often symptomatic of a patriarchal society, it is also a way for women to affirm their religious beliefs and their respectability. In many ways, wearing *hijab* is a liberating practice – de-emphasizing the beauty and sexuality of a woman, and drawing attention to her self-worth.

Veiling is certainly a dynamic cultural practice with myriad meanings. Unfortunately, much of the literature takes a negative and rather limited stance on *purdah*, whether the history of the custom is being examined or contemporary practices discussed. It is only when we ask the women themselves what *purdah* means to them and why they choose to continue wearing *hijab* that we learn there are many facets to the issue. The changing meanings of *hijab* and *purdah* are above all symbolic of the way in which beliefs can transform through time and region.

Fernandez (2009) suggests that Western concern for Muslim women is merely a shield for anti-Muslim sentiment. She also warns that focusing on gender equality issues such as veiling is facilitating the institutionalization of Islamaphobia. Within the broader scope of geopolitics, the controversy surrounding Muslim women and the veil coincides with Europe's retreat from multiculturalism as concepts such as civil integration of immigrant communities are gaining ground (Mullally 2011).

There is an enormous difference between voluntarily adopting *hijab* and being forced to wear it. Although shrouded in religious dogma, *purdah* and *hijab* are far more a political issue. The three cultural examples in this chapter exemplify this point: in Palestine, Iran, and Afghanistan, the political agendas of Hamas, the Iranian regime, and the Taliban exploit *purdah* as one of many forms of control. The *hijab* is just one symptom of a repressive society. The key here seems to be that of choice: if a woman chooses to wear *hijab*, then that is her will. However, if the practice is forced on her, whether it be through insidious social pressure, familial demands, or overt threats of punishment, then it is oppressive, no matter the country. With regards to female seclusion, the issues are more clouded. It appears that women obey seclusionary rules to keep peace with parents, husbands, and religious leaders. Choice does not appear to play a significant role in the equation. Does this mean that secluded women are oppressed – victims of gender exclusion and inequality? Only these women can answer that, and they have not yet spoken.

The issue should not be whether women are wearing *hijab*, nor should they be stigmatized for doing so. Rather, the issue should be whether they have access to the same resources and opportunities as men. Obviously, many women choose to wear the *hijab*. The reasons for this choice are numerous, and to a certain extent they may be connected to oppression, but not the oppression of the veil – rather the oppression of societies that fail to offer women equal status and treatment. A woman who feels safer covered in folds of cloth so that men will not leer at her or make unwanted advances is being oppressed by men, not the veil. A woman who feels she will be taken seriously as a human being with something to offer the community only if she is anonymously hidden behind concealing clothing is being oppressed by societal views, not the veil. A woman who must hide under a *burqa* to attend school or a women's rights rally is being oppressed by political factions, not the veil. This type of oppression is worldwide, and is as serious an issue in the West as anywhere else in the world.

QUESTIONS FOR CONSIDERATION AND CLASSROOM ACTIVITIES

1. As a global citizen, where do you stand on the issue of *purdah* and *hijab*? Do you consider it oppressive to force young Muslim women to remove their head scarves or other religious symbols? Why or why not? Are students free to wear religious symbols at your institution? Would you stand up for their right to do so?
2. Research the meaning of *purdah* to Muslims, and then compare it to the meaning held by most Westerners. How are these views influenced by cultural environments, media, and body politics?
3. Choose two or three countries and investigate whether and why wearing *hijab* has increased or decreased.
4. Ultimately, this chapter was about gender stratification, although readers should recognize that this oppression does not come from *purdah*, but rather that *purdah* is a symptom of global female oppression. Examine your own society. How are women limited in their economic, social, and political opportunities, or restricted by the attitudes of society?
5. Although this chapter focused on female *purdah*, in some cultures there are male *purdah* rules as well. Identify *purdah* requirements for men in Egypt, Pakistan, and Sudan.
6. Debate question: Is *purdah* oppressive? Choose a country and argue your side based on the reality of that country.

SUGGESTED READINGS

Heath, J. (Ed.). (2008). *The veil: Women writers on its history, lore, and politics.* Berkeley: University of California Press.

A collection of 21 essays that provide valuable discourse on the multiple meanings of veiling, through the voices of women. These essays cross time, space, and culture. A must-read book for anyone interested in current women's and human issues.

Shirazi, F. (2001). *The veil unveiled: The hijab in modern culture.* Gainesville: University of Florida Press.

This book is an engrossing, non-academic treatment of *purdah* and the *hijab* that actually examines *hijab* as part of everyday or popular culture. Shirazi attempts to dispel some stereotypes about Muslim women without resorting to theoretical perspectives, which makes this book a refreshing read for everyone.

Chapter 2

Female Circumcision: Is This Practice a Violation of Human Rights or a Cherished Cultural Tradition?

Key Terms: cultural imperialism, cultural relativism, development and modernization approach, engaged anthropology, ethical dilemma, female circumcision, human rights, rite of passage, ritual, universalism

---

INTRODUCTION

"Protecting the rights of a minority of women who oppose the practice is a legitimate and noble cause ... mounting an international campaign to coerce 80 million African women to give up their tradition is unjustified." (Ahmadu 2000: 45).

Perhaps no other cultural practice has raised the ire of the international community more than female circumcision. Feminist and human rights groups, medical practitioners, religious and political organizations, the media, and many others have voiced their opposition to this ancient practice. Yet some anthropologists believe we must look beyond the "shock" value of female circumcision to understand the deeply rooted and divergent reasons behind this practice. We must ask what meaning(s) female circumcision holds for individuals and local cultures and why this ritual is so persistent, despite global condemnation. Only then will we begin to understand female circumcision through the eyes of its followers. This does not mean that anthropologists condone female circumcision, nor does it mean they champion the rights of cultural groups to continue the practice. Rather, we cannot understand the cultural meanings behind this ritual without *listening* to why people practise female circumcision, what the ceremony accomplishes in their eyes, and why it is important in their everyday lives. Only then can anthropologists offer an informed opinion, and as anthropologist Dave Smith states: "It's fine to want to help people, but you need to wait to be asked" (Erickson et al. 2001: n.p.).

The practice of female circumcision represents an **ethical dilemma** for anthropologists and other social scientists who grapple with the intellectual, emotional, and moral issues attached to female circumcision. Some anthropologists, including feminist anthropologists, view the practice as oppressive and symptomatic of a male-dominated, patriarchal society. Others believe that outsiders, including anthropologists, have no business interfering with this ancient cultural practice. Both of these perspectives are one-dimensional and have prevented anthropologists from becoming fully involved in what Howell (2010: S269) refers to as **engaged anthropology.** According to Low and Merry (2010: S214), engaged anthropology ranges "from basic commitment to our informants, to sharing and support with the communities with which we work, to teaching and public education, to social critique in academic and public forums, to more commonly understood forms of engagement such as collaboration, advocacy, and activism." With an issue as sensitive as female circumcision, not to become engaged makes anthropology or any social science somewhat irrelevant (Martinez 2005: 31).

What many social scientists advocate is the freedom of cultural groups to choose this practice or not, without pressure from outsiders. However, the word *choice* is a vague term that often fails to recognize that the girls and their families may not have much in the way of a choice if they are to meet the social expectations of their community and avoid ostracism if they refuse to follow group norms. As far as group choice is concerned, the issue becomes even more complex – who in the group makes the decision? Are the women of the community equal decision makers or is tradition established by men? Are opponents to the ruling hierarchy silenced, or do all members have a say in group decisions? There does appear to be some community autonomy. When I discussed this issue with my male students from Nigeria, they pointed out that their village no longer practises female circumcision, while the village down the road still does.

Janice Boddy (1982) is one anthropologist who looked beyond her own biases to understand the cultural meanings and value of female circumcision. In northern Sudan, 98 per cent of the women are circumcised. Boddy knew her responsibility was to the Sudanese women – to tell their story in their words. Not surprisingly, Boddy's perspective has drawn the wrath of feminists bent on eradicating the practice. However, the issue here is respect – having enough respect for these women to listen to their point of view and attempt to understand the importance of female circumcision to their physical, spiritual, and cultural identity (Blackburn-Evans 2002).

"Ultimately, the thing I try to do in my research as well as in my teaching is to emphasize the need to really explore what it is we're trying to understand — from as many angles as possible — so that we're informed of the complexities." Janice Boddy, quoted in Blackburn-Evans (2002: 1).

In this chapter we will enter the debate surrounding female circumcision and the politics of reproduction, a debate that often pits cultural relativism against universalism. **Cultural relativism** holds that every culture is equally valid and should not be judged against other cultures, while **universalism** suggests there are universal human rights that must be followed, regardless of culture or tradition. Anthropologists tend to focus on protecting and supporting cultural groups, rather than promoting Western values. Thus, they have much to offer to the discourse as they investigate the political, socio-economic, and historical factors that contribute to the persistence of female circumcision. The controversy surrounding female circumcision, the opposition to this practice, and the reasons behind this opposition will also be addressed.

To offer insight into the complexity of this issue, several personal narratives are presented. Readers should note that while it is easy to find people who hold negative views on female circumcision, giving voice to people who support this practice is more challenging. The reasons for this one-sided debate are many: the researchers, usually of Western origin, may be unconsciously showing their bias by seeking out those who reject female circumcision; those who practise female circumcision may be less willing to speak out for fear of reprisals from government officials or condemnation from the interviewer; or they may feel no need to justify their customs to outsiders.

DEFINITION OF FEMALE CIRCUMCISION

Female circumcision is the ritual cutting, removal, or altering of external genitalia. The procedure is performed by traditional or government-trained midwives living in the community. Although popular media tends to lump all forms of female circumcision together, there are several types; the choice of which type is practised is influenced by differing socio-cultural, political, and historical contexts (Shell-Duncan 2001: 2). The least invasive procedure is sunna circumcision, where only the clitoral prepuce (hood) is removed (Gordon 1991). The second and most common type of circumcision is known as excision or clitoridectomy, where part or all of the clitoris is removed, as well as part or all of the labia minora, the inner lips of the vulva. Pharaonic circumcision involves the complete removal of the clitoris, labia minora, and most or all of the labia majora, the outer lips of the vulva. In pharaonic circumcision, the cut edges are then stitched together, leaving a small opening for urine and menstrual flow. This stitching is known as infibulation. Before intercourse, an infibulated woman may have to be cut open, then re-infibulated after the birth of her child. The type of circumcision performed is determined by the underlying reasons for the procedure, as is the age at which circumcision is performed. The most common times are soon after birth, before puberty, at the onset of puberty, just before marriage, in the seventh month of a first pregnancy, or after the first birth (Mackie 2000).

Historically, colonial efforts to eradicate the practice met with stiff resistance. Indeed, such efforts, predicated on a notion of moral superiority, often served to further entrench the practice (Martinez 2005: 33). In northern Sudan in the late 1940s, the British colonial government passed a law that prohibited pharaonic circumcision (Abusharaf 2006: 209). Because of their desire to eradicate female circumcision, the British established themselves as authority figures in family matters and ultimately reinforced male dominance in Sudanese society by encouraging "colonial surveillance and the policing of women by their male relatives under the direction of colonial authorities" (Abusharaf 2006: 219). They were horrified that women had control over circumcision – what they called female sadism – but the real problem stemmed from the power of Sudanese women to make decisions, something that contradicted the male-centred society of early-twentieth-century Britain. The end result was that the power and authority of Sudanese women in cultural and ritual life were weakened.

The British ignored the importance of female circumcision to Sudanese ethnic and gender identity, and instead labelled it a "crime against humanity" (Abusharaf 2006: 216). They even sought a Muslim *fatwa*[1] to lend credibility to their legislation.[2] The British

> "There is an unfortunate and perturbing silence among African women intellectuals who have experienced initiation and 'circumcision.' This is understandable, given the venomous tone of the debate and unswerving demand that a definitive stance be taken — evidently, if one is educated — *against* the practice." (Ahmadu 2000: 283)

> "In their attempt to outlaw customs the European rulers considered cruel, it was not the concern with indigenous suffering that dominated their thinking, but the desire to impose what they considered civilized standards of justice and humanity on a subject population, that is, the desire to create new subjects." (Asad 1996: 1091)

---

1 Religious decree or opinion.

2 In 2010, Muslim clerics and scholars in Mauritania declared a *fatwa* against female circumcision, even though 72 per cent of Mauritanian women are circumcised.

attempts to legislate (Western) morality was viewed as an attack on Sudanese identity and self-determination that led to what Abusharaf (2006) calls cultural wars between British colonial authorities and northern Sudanese society, and a surge in Sudanese cultural nationalism: women's bodies became synonymous with nation.

THE NATURE OF FEMALE CIRCUMCISION

Female circumcision is an ancient and widespread **ritual**, although in some nations, for example in Chad, the Sara people only adopted clitoridectomies 30 years ago (Leonard 2000). The World Health Organization (WHO) estimates that 130 million females living in 28 countries have been circumcised at a rate of two million per year (Rahlenbeck, Mekonnen, & Melkamu 2010: 867). It is practised extensively in Africa, and in some regions of Indonesia, Malaysia, and the Arabian peninsula. The practice has also found its way to North America with immigrants from these regions. Toubia and Izette (1998) point out that 85 per cent of all circumcisions involve sunna circumcision or clitoridectomies, while infibulation is practised mainly in Somalia, Sudan, northeastern Kenya, Eritrea, parts of Mali, and a small region in northern Nigeria. In Djibouti, Mali, Egypt, and Somalia, the practice is nearly universal, while in other countries, such as Tanzania, Uganda, and Niger, fewer than 20 per cent of the women are circumcised. Female circumcision appears to be declining in some regions (e.g., Kenya), while in others it is spreading (e.g., southern Chad). However, statistics on the extent of the practice are unreliable, since much of the data is anecdotal and government-released statistics are often questionable.

The origin of female circumcision is lost in time, although the practice is at least 3,000 years old. Mackie (2000) believes that female circumcision began in ancient Sudan, where it ensured fidelity and paternity. The practice may have developed independently in several regions of sub-Saharan Africa in tandem with male circumcision, beginning as puberty or

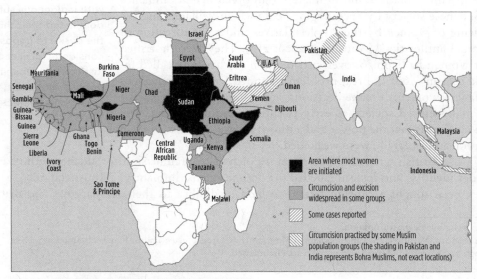

MAP 2.1 COUNTRIES PRACTISING FEMALE CIRCUMCISION

TABLE 2.1   COUNTRIES WHERE FEMALE CIRCUMCISION IS DOCUMENTED[1]

COUNTRY	PREVALENCE	YEAR	TYPE[2]
Benin	16.8%	2001	excision
Burkina Faso	72.5%	2005	excision
Cameroon	1.4%	2004	clitoridectomy, excision
Central African Republic	2.5%	2005	clitoridectomy, excision
Chad	44.9%	2004	excision, infibulation
Côte d'Ivoire	41.9%	2005	excision
Djibouti	93.1%	2006	excision, infibulation
Egypt	95.8%	2005	excision, clitoridectomy
Eritrea	88.7%	2002	excision, clitoridectomy, infibulation
Ethiopia	74.3%	2005	clitoridectomy, excision
The Gambia	78.3%	2005	excision, infibulation
Ghana	3.8%	2005	excision
Guinea	95.6%	2005	clitoridectomy, excision, infibulation
Guinea Bissau	44.5%	2005	clitoridectomy, excision
Kenya	32.2%	2003	clitoridectomy, excision, infibulation
Liberia	45%		excision
Mali	91.6%	2001	clitoridectomy, excision, infibulation
Mauritania	71.3%	2001	clitoridectomy, excision
Niger	2.2%	2006	excision
Nigeria	19%	2003	clitoridectomy, excision, infibulation
Senegal	28.2%	2005	excision
Sierra Leone	94%	2005	excision
Somalia	97.9%	2005	infibulation
Sudan (Northern)	80%	2000	excision, infibulation
Tanzania	14.6%	2004	excision, infibulation
Togo	5.8%	2005	excision
Uganda	0.6%	2006	clitoridectomy, excision
Yemen	22.6%	1997	< no information >

1 World Health Organization (2008), *Eliminating female genital mutilation: An interagency statement.* http://www.who.int/reproductivehealth/publications/fgm/9789241596442/en/. These estimates were derived from national survey data (the Demographic and Health Survey [DHS] published by Macro, or the Multiple Cluster Indicator Surveys [MKS] published by UNICEF).

2 Type of female circumcision was taken from Amnesty International (1997), *Female genital mutilation in Africa: Information by country.* http://www.amnesty.org/en/library/info/ACT77/007/1997/en.
Colombia, Democratic Republic of Congo, India, Indonesia, Iraq, Israel, Malaysia, Oman, Peru, Sri Lanka, and the United Arab Emirates also practise female circumcision, but statistics are unavailable.

initiation rites. Boddy (1982: 685) points out that knowing this "custom's remote historical origin [does not] contribute to our understanding of its present significance." Nevertheless, for those who value this practice, but find themselves continually having to justify it, an ancient origin may be significant.

HEALTH RISKS ASSOCIATED WITH FEMALE CIRCUMCISION

Any discussion of female circumcision would be incomplete without consideration of the potential health risks and complications. These health risks are used as medical justification for eradicating the practice, although much of the information on complications is dated, originating with British colonial medical practitioners in the 1930s and 1940s (Shell-Duncan & Hernlund 2000). These "facts" are often not supported by the experiences of women in communities that practise female circumcision, and the view that female circumcision is a pathological practice given the risks to health and even life has not resonated with people who practise female circumcision. Gruenbaum (1982) notes that medical complications have little relevance for changing or ending the practice. Most of the problems described are the result of bungled infibulations, not the far more common and less invasive clitoridectomy or sunna circumcision. In other words, we need to view Western propaganda against female circumcision with caution.[3]

Female circumcision is usually performed without anaesthetic. In some cultures, such as the Mandinga of Guinea-Bissau, the ability to bear pain with courage and fortitude is an important part of the ceremony, bringing honour to the girl and her family (Johnson 2000). For the Gikuyu of Kenya, the pain from circumcision is ritualized, and it is considered one marker on the path to adulthood (Moruzzi 2005). However, in areas where medical services are available, anaesthetic may be used, as well as antibiotics to prevent infection, and if infibulation is practised, catgut or silk sutures are used rather than the more traditional thorns.

The actual prevalence of complications is difficult to assess; circumcised women are often unwilling to seek medical care, or they may not associate their medical problems with circumcision. Shortly after the procedure, some women have experienced hemorrhaging, pain, local and systemic infections, shock, and in extreme cases, death. Young girls may refuse to urinate for fear of stinging, which can lead to urinary tract infections. Infections at the wound site are also common. Infibulation may lead to chronic complications, such as difficulties in passing urine and menstrual flow, renal failure or septicaemia from untreated urinary tract infections, and serious pelvic infections that may cause infertility. The inelasticity of the scar tissue may prolong labour and delivery, risking the life of infant and mother. Despite the possibility of problems, Obermeyer (2003) determined, through an intensive review of the literature, that medical complications are the exception rather than the rule.[4] Female circumcision may also cause psychological injury, although this is impossible to assess. Indeed, Gruenbaum (2000) found that circumcised women remembered the pain and fear, but refused to dwell on it, and even laughed about it.

Boddy (1982) looked beyond the medical issues that consume Western activists, and instead focused on the social role that female circumcision plays in the lives of Sudanese women. To the Sudanese, this is a time of celebration – gift giving, feasting, and visiting with well-wishers. The identity of women as sexual beings is downplayed and their role as future mothers of men is emphasized. Lutkekaus and Roscoe (1995) agree: the Sudanese believe that circumcision marks a transition from an androgynous childhood into a distinct female gender. Thus, female circumcision is an integral part of Sudanese gender identity. This is also true among the Kono of Sierra Leone, where female and male circumcision (*bondo*) and other initiation rites are cultural and symbolic processes that celebrate the transition from boyhood and girlhood to manhood and womanhood (Ahmadu quoted in Shweder 2009). The prepuce and foreskin of the penis are associated with femininity, so their removal masculinizes boys; the exposed clitoris represents the male organ, and its removal feminizes girls.

---

3 The proliferation of articles on the evils of female circumcision on the Internet is an example of this one-sided debate.

4 Obermeyer's review, as well as other studies that run counter to the prevailing notions of medical complications, have been largely ignored by Western media (Shweder 2009).

Although decreased sexual pleasure is cited by opponents as a consequence of circumcision, Toubia and Izette (1998) report that up to 90 per cent of infibulated women enjoy sex and experience orgasms. Indeed, interviewees who have been excised claim they enjoy sex and achieve orgasm as much as "intact" women (Londoño-Sulkin 2009: 18). On the other hand, El Dareer (1982) found that up to 50 per cent of his respondents experienced reduced sexual enjoyment. These conflicting statistics add to the debate surrounding female circumcision.

REASONS FOR FEMALE CIRCUMCISION

Given the possibility of complications and the painful nature of the procedure, the question uppermost in readers' minds might be why is female circumcision practised? For what reasons would parents put their daughters through the ordeal and dangers of this procedure? This is where examining female circumcision becomes complex because the issue is hampered by assumptions, Western ideas about human rights, sexuality, and gender equality, and a lack of consensus regarding the practice – what it means, the way it is done, and the value it holds for the people who practise it.

Female circumcision is governed by tradition, religious beliefs, honour, prestige, ethnic identity, gender, aesthetics, and sexuality (Gruenbaum 2005: 435). Although groups or clusters of societies may share similar reasons, for example, a gendered identity marker, other societies and even individuals may have different reasons or multiple motivations for continuing the practice despite mounting pressure to stop.

The most common reason given for female circumcision is to ensure that a young woman remains a virgin until marriage and that any children born of the marriage are the husband's progeny. Among northern Sudanese, circumcised and infibulated women are considered a preferred marriage choice that will increase family honour (Gruenbaum 2000). Although women contribute significantly to the household economy, they gain most of their economic security from their husbands (e.g., access to land and livestock), and in old age from their sons. Thus, female circumcision may ensure socio-economic well-being for a woman, and it is often her only path to social status, acceptance, and security. The question needs to be asked, then: If women gain economic independence, through education and employment, will female circumcision decrease in frequency?

For many groups, the answer would be no, since maintaining an age-old tradition is the underlying reason. The practice continues because the women do not want to break with their grandmothers' tradition (Hernlund 2000). A bond of solidarity is forged between generations of women when everyone has undergone the ritual. Female circumcision, then, is often viewed as a **rite of passage**, symbolizing the passing from girlhood to womanhood. Once circumcised, a girl is considered pure, clean, and womanly, and her status increases (Althaus 1997). Indeed, among the Sudanese, pharaonic circumcision reinforces class distinctions and is a symbol of northern Sudanese ethnic and class identity that distinguishes them from other Sudanese.

"Of course, I shall have them circumcised exactly as their parents, grandparents, and sisters were circumcised. This is our custom, our boys and girls must get circumcised. We don't want our girls to be like men. Men derive pleasure only from circumcised women. Both my older girls were circumcised at the age of 6. A woman circumcised them at home, before circumcision it was I who told them, 'We want to celebrate your circumcision, have a feast and prepare you a chicken.'" Fatma, an Egyptian mother quoted in Assaad (1980: 13).

Various beliefs, whether substantiated or not, influence the prevalence of female circumcision. The Yoruba believe that if the clitoris touches the baby's head during birth, it will die; therefore, the Yoruba practise female circumcision to ensure the survival of their children (Orubuloye, Caldwell & Caldwell 2000). In addition, clitoridectomies and sunna circumcision are believed to reduce a woman's sexual desire, preventing her from becoming sexually active before marriage or seeking extramarital affairs during marriage. Infibulation prevents sexual intercourse outside of marriage and is alleged to increase a man's sexual pleasure. However, Shandall (1967) found that Sudanese men who practised polygyny preferred sex with their uncircumcised wives.

Female circumcision is often associated with Islam. Despite pharaonic circumcision predating Islam by hundreds or even thousands of years, the practice has been incorporated into Islamic beliefs (Gruenbaum 1982). This incorporation ignores the fact that Islamic scholars are adamant that the Qur'an does not promote female circumcision. It also ignores the fact that some form of female circumcision occurs among "Coptic Christians, Ethiopian Jews, traditional spiritualists, and Christian converts" (Moruzzi 2005: 208). Those who link female circumcision with Islam see the practice as a cleansing rite that marks the woman as a Muslim and gives her the right to pray (Johnson 2000). Regardless of whether the connection to Islam is legitimate or not, if people believe that their religion commands it, then it is an important religious practice.

GLOBAL OPPOSITION TO FEMALE CIRCUMCISION

When Hilary Rodham Clinton addressed the 1995 United Nations Fourth World Conference on Women in Beijing, she stated unequivocally: "It is a violation of human rights when young girls are brutalized by the painful and degrading practice of female genital mutilation" (Equality Now 1996: n.p.). Clinton's forceful statement is understandable given that it comes from a woman living in the West where there are strong opinions about **human rights**, especially the right to health and safety. However, this is a Western position and does not take into consideration the way other cultures perceive female circumcision or how they define human rights. The whole issue of human rights, though based on a desire to ensure that everyone, the world over, is free from harm, is a vaguely understood and by no means universally acknowledged concept used to justify "making people over in the Western image" – what Shell-Duncan and Hernlund (2000: 34) label the **development and modernization approach.**

As is obvious from Clinton's statement, the terms we use provide a barometer for attitudes. The politics of names is particularly evident when it comes to female circumcision. In the West, the practice is called "female genital mutilation" to symbolize Western disapproval. However, "mutilation" is a judgemental term and does not belong in an intellectual

"Foreigners from America, from London, who call us bad names, call us primitive and call our circumcision rites genital mutilation. ... It makes us want to do more." Kapchorwa magistrate Albert Laigiya, a Ugandan elder, quoted in Masland (1999: 9).

discussion of this topic. Even when the term "female circumcision" is used, the word "circumcision" is often placed in quotation marks to distinguish it from male circumcision, which is still practised in North America and considered a legitimate custom. Opponents also object to the word circumcision because it detracts from the severity of the procedure. To avoid a judgemental tone, but to separate the practice from male circumcision, some researchers prefer to use the term "female genital cutting."

Opponents of the practice believe that female circumcision "violates a minor child's human right to bodily integrity" (Gruenbaum 2005: 430). Yet to practitioners, female circumcision is not an act of cruelty or child abuse. Indeed, parents who have their daughters circumcised care about their well-being as much as any parents do, so to characterize circumcised women as victims is simplistic and condescending. Whether female circumcision is a violation of human rights depends on how we define the concept of human rights. As some of my more insightful students have pointed out, taking away a woman's right to be circumcised and enjoy higher status in the community, her right to marry well and bear sons, thereby ensuring her security in old age, is in itself an infringement on her human rights.

Female circumcision is often blamed on men and their need to control women. Although some men are purported to prefer circumcised women, this is by no means universal, and the procedure itself is controlled and perpetuated by women. Banning circumcision has not improved the status of women; indeed, it often has the opposite effect, and there is growing evidence that female circumcision actually empowers women, although this is a contested stand. Furthermore, to suggest that these women are submissive and "brainwashed" into thinking circumcision is a good practice is an insult to the intelligence and strength of all women.

Opponents of female circumcision are often accused of **cultural imperialism** – the promotion of Western values, beliefs, and behaviours. Campaigns against female circumcision, funded by the West and often cocooned in development projects, are well entrenched in most African communities, although they have met with limited success. These campaigns have failed because the goal has been to change women's minds about female circumcision with little consideration given to what the practice means to them socially, economically, and culturally. As well, it is naive to assume that education and awareness programs will put an end to the practice once people realize the health risks, and except for isolated cases, practitioners are far more aware of the dangers than outsiders. Toubia (1988) asserts that female circumcision is not a medical problem; rather, it is part of women's social sphere, where cultural pressures (e.g., peer, parental, societal) and marriageability supersede any perceived risks. Furthermore, the suggestion that female circumcision must be eradicated as if it were a disease appears to be a form of medical imperialism.

The most damaging impact of anti-circumcision movements has been to bring to light the pervasiveness of the practice, which, in turn, has resulted in unwanted international attention (Ginsburg 1991), especially since the 1970s when international organizations such as WHO and the United Nations took notice. These movements have outraged women in the countries where female circumcision is practised. Women, such as anthropologist Soheir Morsy, have expressed indignation over Western interference. The paternalistic concept of helping other people – what Morsy (1991) calls "rescue and civilizational missions" – is an attack on their cultural values, and has resulted in silencing and alienating the very women who could bring about change.

"Over the last decade the West has acted as though they have suddenly discovered a dangerous epidemic which they then sensationalized in international women's forums creating a backlash of over-sensitivity in the concerned communities. They have portrayed it as irrefutable evidence of the barbarism and vulgarity of underdeveloped countries ... [and] the primitiveness of Arabs, Muslims, and Africans all in one blow." (Toubia 1988: 101)

"The voices of the many East and West African women who value the practice of genital modification for girls and boys have not been audible in North America and European media accounts of the practice." (Shweder 2009)

Not all opposition to female circumcision comes from Westerners, however. African women's organizations, such as the Inter African Committee Against Harmful Traditional Practices, which was formed in 1984 and now has national committees in more than 20 countries (Althaus 1997). Their mandate has been to bring the harmful effects of the procedure to the attention of African governments in order to ban the practice. Grassroots self-help movements, such as Abandon the Knife in the Pokot community of highland Kenya, struggle to change the community's perception of female circumcision (Al Jazeera English 2011). Most of their efforts focus on convincing parents that allowing their daughters to get an education is of more economic value than cutting followed by marriage for a dowry.

> "What's important is that I become empowered and help myself and people like me. My parents want me to be cut and married off for a dowry. ... Boys and girls are equal ... I can see a flood coming and all you people just want to hold us back. I'm moving forward. I'm heading for the land of milk and honey. My passion for education is driving me. Look for someone else to cut, so long as it's not me." Nancy, a 17-year-old Kenyan from the Pokot community (Al Jazeera English 2011)

Some activists promote the criminalization of female circumcision to counter social pressures to continue the practice. In 1994, for example, a law was passed in Sudan banning female circumcision. It caused a public furor and a backlash that actually increased the incidence of the practice (Shell-Duncan & Hernlund 2000). As an example of how extreme the resistance became, a ban on clitoridectomies in Kenya's Meru District resulted in adolescent girls excising each other (Thomas 2000). Another worry is that legislation may force the practice underground, where sanitation and quality of care are poor. Circumcised women experiencing difficulties might then be unwilling to seek medical assistance for fear of prosecution – similar to young women having illegal abortions in Canada before 1969 – and then refusing to go to a hospital if they became ill after the procedure. Even Amnesty International has acknowledged that efforts to ban female circumcision through legislation have backfired (Amnesty International 1997). Some Western countries have threatened to make international aid conditional on the country's banning of female circumcision. Governments may yield to Western pressure, but if the ban is not enforceable, then it is irrelevant.

> "You simply can't outlaw cultural practices . ... It is not possible to criminalize the entirety of a population, or the entirety of a discrete and insular minority of the population, without methods of mass terror. People have to decide to stop on their own." (Mackie, quoted in *The Economist* 1999: 450)

Both opponents and defenders of female circumcision have raised alarms over efforts to medicalize the procedure (Shell-Duncan, Obiero, & Muruli 2000). If female circumcision became institutionalized – performed in medical institutions by licensed doctors — opponents fear that this would amount to tacit approval that would stymie efforts to eliminate the practice. Others suggest that if medicalization improves the health and saves the lives of women, then it is worth the risk. On the other hand, defenders of female circumcision fear that medicalization would shift control of female circumcision from women in the community to male practitioners in biomedical facilities (Shell-Duncan & Hernlund 2000). The symbolic value of circumcision is also an important factor. Johnson (2000: 230) found that among the Mandinga of Guinea-Bissau, women refused a hospital circumcision because the cutting is "not the same."

Recent efforts to find alternative rituals in the Gambia and Kenya, where the clitoris is only nicked, have met with limited success. Practitioners seem not to value symbolic circumcision in the same way as traditional cutting. Some of the reasons for female circumcision, for example, ensuring chastity, are not served by symbolic circumcision. In North America, where symbolic circumcision would offer immigrants an alternative to more invasive procedures, activists have protested that even symbolic circumcision is oppressive and have effectively shut down the programs with their protests. However, opponents ignore the fact that male circumcision is still performed in North American hospitals and is much more invasive than symbolic circumcision (Coleman 1998). Ironically, many of the reasons for justifying male circumcision in the West are the same as those given for female circumcision: for example, cleanliness, aesthetics, family tradition, and religious beliefs (Ahmadu, quoted in Shweder 2009).

CONCLUSION

Obviously, it is extremely difficult to step outside our Western bias when examining an issue as sensitive as female circumcision. Yet, to comprehend the symbolic complexities of this practice, this is what we must do. Female circumcision holds meaning for millions of people; this cannot be taken away without causing harm equal to or surpassing the perceived harm of circumcision. Female circumcision will not be eradicated if the reasons it is so important and why it continues to be practised despite international condemnation are not understood. Herein lies the challenge: to respect cultural traditions, values, and autonomy while promoting global human rights.

"If they [cutting practices] are to disappear, let it not be as a result of impositions from powerful outsiders with unquestioning faith in their own understandings of personhood, cosmology, and sociality." (Londoño-Sulkin 2009).

Yet cultures are not static; they change to meet changing needs. If the meaning of female circumcision to a community changes, then its value and continued practice would likely change as well. Anthropologist Carolyn Sargent (1991) believes that efforts to change or end this custom must come from within the local cultures, and will happen only when women have opportunities for economic security other than marriage and childbearing. A refreshing example of this is the Senegal-based NGO Tostan, which has established literacy and leadership skills programs and promotes social development, giving women the power to decide for themselves if female circumcision is necessary in their community (Gruenbaum 2005: 438). Rahlenbeck, Mekonnen, and Melkamu (2010: 868) found that among the Oromia of Ethiopia "a woman's feeling of self-empowerment is proportional to the degree to which she takes a stance against the practice." In this study, those with a higher education opposed the practice, as did those who rejected any form of domestic violence as being normal. This runs counter to many upper-class urban families in Egypt, where women tend to have higher education yet the practice is common, even to the point of taking their educated, sophisticated daughters back to traditional villages to have the procedure done. Indeed, in quite a few cases, women of middle and upper classes are more likely to be circumcised than are those from the poorer classes.

Anthropologists have found that the practice is spreading in the face of modernization – often the poorer social classes are adopting infibulations in the hopes that their circumcised daughters will make a good marriage, thereby increasing their status and economic well-being (Leonard 2000). Certainly, Western interference has been met with strong resistance – both from within the cultures that practise female circumcision and from others who resent this Western intrusion.

While hopes for eradication remain high, in reality there is little evidence that female circumcision is on the decline, despite some purported successes. Although Westerners may believe that eradication of female circumcision is a priority, women in developing nations have more serious concerns on their minds – like poverty, childhood diseases and malnutrition, ethnic conflict and war, and a lack of resources due to decades of exploitation by the very Westerners bent on changing their traditions. Young people, such as the women in Pokot, Kenya, appear more amenable to ending the practice than older people; however, this does not mean that as they mature, the members of this generation will continue to reject the custom – honouring the traditions of forbears is a powerful force. Legislation appears ineffective and difficult to enforce, and if the people value the custom, it will continue despite its illegality.

Will female circumcision ever be eradicated? The question itself is controversial because it harkens back to the West's desire to eliminate cultural practices considered wrong, as well as to the political implications of colonialism and imperialism. The issue is incredibly complex because it seems natural, even fundamentally human, to want everyone to enjoy the rights and freedoms enjoyed in the West. Some argue that in the West, human life, individuality, and freedom are honoured, and that other people deserve the same quality of life – a laudable sentiment, but if examined closely, somewhat hollow and based on a sense of cultural superiority and over-dramatization of questionable information. To barge in and demand that people change because outsiders consider these acts cruel and barbaric appears unethical and immoral.

So how do anthropologists reconcile their responsibilities as scientists and researchers with their sense of human rights? Should anthropologists in their role as advocates work to end female circumcision, or should they continue to advocate for the freedom of cultural self-determination? There is no easy answer to issues of body politics. Fuambai S. Ahmadu sums up the politics of reproduction: "There are different and contested views and experiences and ... no one is more right than the other" (Ahmadu, quoted in Shweder 2009: 17).

QUESTIONS FOR CONSIDERATION AND CLASSROOM ACTIVITIES

1. As a global citizen, you possess more knowledge and awareness of this practice and the reasons for its continuance. Therefore, in your opinion, should Westerners attempt to eradicate the practice of female circumcision? If yes, what is the best way to go about ending this practice? If no, why do you feel this way? Create a student blog to open debate on the pros and cons of Westerners interfering with female circumcision.
2. Immigrants to Western countries (e.g., Canada) may wish to continue this practice. How should this issue be addressed in Canada? Consider the implications of the options and address them in your response.
3. In chapter 6, the issue of body image is addressed. How is the practice of female circumcision connected to body image? How is female circumcision similar to North American cosmetic surgery, such as breast implants? How is it different – or is it?
4. Compare female circumcision to male circumcision. How are these procedures alike and how are they different? Create a comparative analysis of reasons given for practising male and female circumcision, and then enter into a class debate. Each group must provide five reasons to justify either female or male circumcision and be able to argue the merits of each reason.

5. The Kenyan woman in Pokot wanted an education and employment opportunities rather than circumcision and marriage. If she, and other young people like her, is successful, how will this change their community – socially, economically, and politically?

6. Imagine an anthropologist from another country studying your community and negatively judging your lifestyle choices (e.g., rodeos, compulsory school attendance for girls, ear piercing, alcohol consumption, androgynous clothing, or unsupervised teen dating). How would you and the rest of your community react? Would this condemnation make you stop these practices? Why or why not?

7. It is extremely difficult to maintain a culturally relativistic stance when confronted with what we perceive to be a harmful cultural practice. How do we reconcile our ideas of right and wrong with the needs of cultural groups for self-determination?

8. Why do you suppose Western media has ignored research that suggests medical complications from female circumcision are overstated and relatively uncommon?

9. "The operation was usually performed by untrained midwives, old and dirty who use the blade of a cut-throat razor or some locally made instrument often blunt and always unsterilized. No injections were given at the time" (Hills-Young 1943: 13). In this quotation, identify the biased language that perpetuates images of horror, fear, disgust, etc. Discuss why these particular words might have been chosen and describe the message they convey. Now try re-writing the quotation, taking out the biased language and using neutral terms to explain the practice, and then discuss how the rewritten statement changes your views.

10. Create a research project that uses the Universal Declaration of Human Rights as the basis for assessing the violation of human rights in female circumcision, and/or the violation of human rights by forcefully eradicating female circumcision.

SUGGESTED READINGS

Barnes, V.L. (1994). *Aman: The story of a Somali girl – as told to Virginia Lee Barnes and Janice Boddy*. **London: Bloomsbury Publishing.**

This book presents the personal account of Aman, a 17-year-old young woman living in Somalia. She describes being circumcised at age eight, and married to a much older man at age 13. By 17, she has endured rape, divorced twice, and had two children, one of whom died. Anthropologists Virginia Barnes and Janice Boddy offer a straightforward, objective account of Aman's life and the patriarchal society in which she lives.

Little, C.M. (2003, Spring). Female genital circumcision: Medical and cultural considerations. *Journal of Cultural Diversity*, *10*(1), 30–34. Medline:12776545

A comprehensive discussion of the medical and cultural implications of female circumcision. Presents a fairly balanced discussion and is easily accessible to students. The site also provides numerous links to related articles.

Chapter 3

International Aid: What Benefits Do NGOs Provide Developing Countries, and How Can Their Presence Generate New Challenges?

Key Terms: advocacy, civil society, cultural imperialism, cultural sensitivity, development, human rights, missionism, modernization, NGOs

INTRODUCTION

"Development aid is a planned economy, even if it doesn't have a plan." Correspondent for Africa, Thilo Thielke (2008: n.p.).

When a massive earthquake struck Port-au-Prince, Haiti, on January 12, 2010, more than 220,000 people were killed, 300,000 injured, and nearly two million displaced (Goyet, Sarmiento, & Grünewald 2011). Hundreds of buildings were reduced to rubble, essential services such as hospitals and schools were destroyed, communication systems shut down, and roads were covered with debris, preventing relief workers and the military from reaching people in need. Humanitarian relief agencies provided food, water, and tents for some of the victims, but in the early days, confusion about who was in control prevented any effective relief. More than a million and a half Haitians moved into makeshift tent cities set up in the parks and streets.

Haiti is home to countless non-government organizations (NGOs); indeed, the small impoverished nation has been called a "republic of NGOs" (Goyet, Sarmiento, & Grünewald 2011). **NGOs** are non-governmental, not-for-profit organizations that provide humanitarian services and development aid to those in need. They gained prominence in the 1990s because of their ability to provide aid in a more economical way than government agencies. The mandates of NGOs vary, from conflict resolution, to educational programming, environmental protection, missionism, and human-rights advocacy. Many NGOs focus on **development**, such as establishing sustainable agricultural projects. NGOs also bring issues before the United Nations, including women's and children's rights, and were involved in the formation of the International Criminal Court (Stephenson 2005). As consultants in the United Nations, NGOs have pushed for resolutions on such issues as disarmament. The International Campaign to Ban Landmines NGO successfully lobbied governments and mobilized states and other NGOs for the Ottawa Convention that was signed in December 1997, and it continues to monitor compliance among the 143 states that signed the treaty (Stephenson 2005).

Despite many beneficial projects, however, NGOs have been criticized, and people – some in positions of power – have raised questions concerning the purpose and usefulness of NGOs. Indeed, the term "NGO industry" alludes to the self-serving ambitions of these organizations, and the transformation of humanitarian aid into big business that employs thousands of aid workers around the world. In Haiti, for example, NGOs have been criticized for their lack of tangible results following the earthquake, and the inefficiency of their service delivery.

Among the most serious accusations is the growing evidence that NGOs and the assistance they provide have created a self-perpetuating culture of dependency in many countries, including Haiti. Indeed, Kenyan economics expert James Shikwati blames international aid policies, along with corrupt rulers, for Africa's poor economic state. He believes that aid from NGOs and others has created corrupt bureaucracies, weakened local markets, destroyed entrepreneurship, and transformed Africans into beggars (Thielke 2005).

"If they really want to fight poverty, they should completely halt development aid and give Africa the opportunity to ensure its own survival. Currently, Africa is like a child that immediately cries for its babysitter when something goes wrong. Africa should stand on its own two feet." Kenyan economist James Shikwati, quoted in Thielke (2005: n.p.)

Academics, too, have problems with the concept of development aid and NGOs. Some social scientists are openly hostile to the interference of NGOs in local communities and their attempts to change the way people live. They recognize the danger in imposing Western ideals on other nations without understanding or respecting the local culture (Ishkanian 2004). Others support NGOs that have the welfare of people and protection of fragile small-scale cultures in mind. They have become involved in development projects to support and assist marginalized groups with whom they are interacting on a local level. Still others have taken it upon themselves to study NGOs and their role in development, and work to mitigate any harmful effects of NGO projects. Consequently, social scientists involved in development projects do so because of their "long-standing concerns with the social and cultural effects of economic change in the less developed areas of the world" (Lewis 2005: n.p.).

In this chapter we will explore the roles of NGOs, their successes and failures, and the challenges that can arise from NGO involvement in developing nations. We will review several NGO projects and the issues that arise from their presence: emergency humanitarian efforts in Pakistan and cultural sensitivity; missionism and cultural imperialism; medical assistance and grassroots health NGOs; and human rights and the politicizing of the family. Our case study is Haiti, a country that currently has more NGO involvement than any other nation in the world, yet it has very little to show for it. Expertise from anthropology, sociology, psychology, social justice, economics, and development studies will be drawn upon to present a critical analysis of the impact of NGOs on developing countries.

THE NATURE OF NGOs AND INTERNATIONAL AID

International development and development aid are complex issues that attract passionate advocates as well as detractors. The concept of development and aid emerged following World War II, when organizations and government agencies sought to provide assistance to developing nations in order to hasten modernization. However, **modernization** should be viewed cautiously, because it generally means making other nations over in the Western image. This is what most NGOs set out to do, although their goals are often couched in terminology such as "sustainable development" (Lewis 2005).

NGOs are often criticized for their lack of accountability, and their questionable connections with donors and sponsors. Their efforts to democratize and create civil societies are almost always at the root of an NGO's mandate, regardless of what other services they provide (Stephenson 2005). Smith (2010: 244) defines **civil society** as "occupying the political space between the individual or household and the state." The concept suggests broad societal participation in the organization of a state from many walks of life, to advance mutual interests. Although proponents believe that civil society is a necessary ingredient for a democratic nation, it is often at odds with local cultural systems (Stephenson 2005).

CHALLENGES FOR NGOs

NGOs face many challenges, some economic, others political or cultural. Funding is an ongoing concern for most NGOs; they have to solicit funding in an increasingly competitive field, and often their sponsors have agendas attached to their financial support. In fact, some NGOs are even created "to order": in other words, to carry out a specific, often politically motivated, mission funded by an interested party (Tishkov 2005). In Armenia, for example, NGOs established in the 1990s were shaped by donor initiatives and funding strategies rather than the needs and concerns of the local people (Ishkanian 2004). One project dealt with domestic violence even though Armenians consider this a private, family matter. That a family matter should be made public alarmed Armenians, especially the women, who saw it as inviting surveillance and humiliation, and as challenging the sacredness of family. Nevertheless, funding poured in and hotlines and crisis shelters were established at the behest of the sponsors. However, the hotline was not a feasible idea because telecommunication services are poor in Armenia, using a phone is expensive, and the poorest and most vulnerable women do not have phones in their homes. According to Armenian law, if a woman leaves her home, she loses access to health care, financial support, and subsidized housing; therefore, shelters were not a viable solution. Plans to train the police force to deal with domestic violence were ill-conceived as well, since calling the corrupt police could open a family to abuse and extortion (Ishkanian 2004). This study exemplifies the failure of an NGO that did not become familiar with the local culture, but instead attempted to impose Western strategies and values where they simply did not work.

NGOs, particularly from the United States and Europe, operate under a pro-democracy directive. This type of work carries with it many challenges and even dangers, exemplified by the problems that NGOs encountered in post-revolutionary Egypt. In February 2012, 43 NGO staff from several countries were arrested and charged with fostering civil and political unrest, and with spying for foreign governments. The National Democratic Institute and the International Republican Institute, two NGOs with close links to the American Congress, promote democracy in Egypt. Such interference would never be tolerated in the United States, yet it is often part of NGO policies in other countries. This case highlights two major criticisms of many NGOs – that they cross the line from providing development aid and step into political interference, and that they are instruments of American foreign policy and propaganda (Spoerri 2012). Swedish anthropologist Steven Sampson (2002), who analyzed NGO activities in the Balkans, suggests that despite some successes, "the most suitable term for Western intervention in the Balkans would be benevolent colonialism."

Critics of NGOs cite **cultural sensitivity** toward the local culture as a matter of great concern. When an earthquake devastated northern Pakistan and Kashmir in October 2004, Pakistani and international aid workers rushed to the region (Wilder & Morris 2008). Once the initial trauma was over, accusations of cultural insensitivity and reports of national and international aid workers not respecting the cultural norms of behaviour began to circulate. Differing standards of conduct held by the people of northern Pakistan and Kashmir and those of national (Pakistani) relief workers was one source of conflict. Indeed, the international staff earned the respect of the locals for dressing and behaving appropriately, the only exception being the Cuban medical workers who wore shorts and T-shirts, tried to procure alcohol, and had men and women sharing tents. The Pakistani aid workers, especially the women, were criticized for interacting with men (talking to them, playing sports) and not wearing appropriate (concealing) clothing. It appears, then, that the national staff was judged under a stricter set of standards than the international staff, and that the national female staff were expected to follow stricter standards of conduct than the national male staff. Ultimately, local leaders were concerned that exposure to liberal Pakistanis and international aid workers' behaviour would influence local Kashmiri women (Wilder & Morris 2008).

These problems could be summed up as ignorance about local customs, a general lack of cultural sensitivity on the part of aid workers, and the inability of aid agencies to properly train their staff. However, the World Health Organization provided a checklist for their staff that suggested disaster situations provided Western agencies with a "window of opportunity for challenging gender inequality" (Wilder & Morris 2008: 2), leading to the suspicion that some of this behaviour was a deliberate attempt to show the northern Pakistani and Kashmiri women how Western men and women interact. This incident lends itself to questioning whether local norms can be respected without compromising aid workers' rights to self-expression and cultural freedom, and suggests the need for culturally sensitive ways of delivering programs that are compatible with the local cultural norms.

Advocacy for children's rights is not a new phenomenon. In 1924 the League of Nations adopted the World Child Welfare Charter's key principles: children have the right "to material, moral and spiritual development, to special help in case of hunger, illness, disability and orphan status, to relief in situations of distress, to protection against economic exploitation, and to an upbringing towards societal responsibility" (Black 1996, quoted in Valentin & Meinert 2009: 24). The right to be protected against discrimination on the basis of race, colour, gender, and language, and the right to name and nationality, were added in 1959. During the 1990s, the legally binding United Nations Convention on the Rights of the Child (CRC) was almost universally ratified (Boyden 1997). The fact that the CRC is legally binding gives a state the right to intervene in another state's affairs if children's rights are being violated. Thus, children's rights became institutionalized, and morality and policy became intertwined. However, as with other aid and development agencies, the CRC is also a political tool that provides Western donors with a legitimate rationale in order to set conditions for receiving aid (Valentin & Meinert 2009).

Some NGOs promote their vision of what constitutes a proper childhood and proper parenting and attempt to legitimize these views through the promotion of universal rights. This returns us to a fundamental question that is addressed several times in this book: "To what extent can and should existing social and cultural practices be respected while still insisting on a set of universally valid rights? [and] Should/can aid be unconditional?" (Valentin & Meinert 2009: 24). Doubtless the goal is to improve the lives of children; however, the Westernized interpretation of children's rights and a "proper" childhood politicizes family under the guise of universal **human rights.** However, socio-economic conditions in many states may prevent children from enjoying so-called universal rights, including the right to education and leisure time. The individualistic, egalitarian view of children in the Convention contradicts generational hierarchies and social structures within many nations that do not separate child from family. Some state governments have responded defiantly to this kind of interference; for example, Vietnamese authorities passed the Child Protection, Care and Education law in 1991, which states that children must show their parents affection and respect, and obey them (Burr 2006).

Uganda provides an example of how standards and ideals from the international community can have a direct impact on issues such as children's rights, and just how difficult determining the right path can be (Valentin & Meinert 2009). The Ugandan government has been in conflict with the Lord's Resistance Army in the north for 25 years. Many Ugandan people live in internally displaced camps, having lost their land, homes, and livelihood. NGOs have criticized the rebel army for turning innocent children into soldiers or sex slaves and the Ugandan government for not protecting the children. NGOs have even taken the Ugandan government to the International Criminal Court. Although these steps may appear the responsible response to a dire situation, in effect NGOs were offering aid while commenting on social policy and practices. Although readers will likely have very negative feelings regarding child soldiers, these NGOs were acting like moral watchdogs in a foreign country. NGOs, then, appear to want to play a role in civilizing, enlightening, and socializing children in the "Western way" without taking into consideration the local situation. To further illustrate this point, albeit not in as dramatic a manner as child soldiers, a Child Rights Education program was organized by the Save the Child Denmark NGO. Workers indoctrinated children, teachers, and parents in children's rights but then had to act as mediators when children began demanding their right to leisure time, although their parents needed them to work for the survival of the family.

Clearly, children endure hardships all over the world due to economic, political, and religious persecution, and some NGOs have done much to ameliorate these harsh conditions, especially in health care. However, at times children have been turned into contested objects for other motives (Pupavac 2000), which is patronizing and reminiscent of early Christian missionism.

MISSIONISM AND NGOs

The subject of religious conversion is controversial; many people decry the destruction of traditional beliefs and the ensuing cultural disruptions, while others feel a moral obligation to bring their beliefs into local cultures as they offer badly needed aid. The aim of early **missionism** was to assimilate non-Western cultures into Western ideology and practices (Cudd 2005). Indeed, missionism has been accused of being an agent of **cultural imperialism,** that ultimately changes a traditional culture. In an historical example of the problems missionism can cause, in the early nineteenth century at Fiske Seminary in Persia, missionaries encouraged Nestorian women to renounce Islamic female seclusion practices (*purdah*; see Chapter 1). These changes to their cultural traditions caused friction between

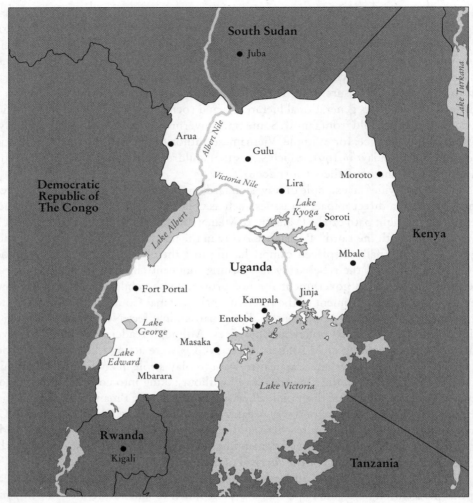

MAP 3.1 UGANDA

Nestorians and the dominant Muslim culture and led to the persecution and eventual decline of the Nestorians (Tomasek 1999).

Medical missionism has given missionaries a great deal of power over people suffering from diseases, but even in the early twentieth century debates raged around the ethics of conversion under the guise of offering medical aid. Some medical missionaries have viewed medical work as merely a tool for evangelization (Macola 2005). The proselytizing can undermine social, cultural, and political authority in the community. On the other hand, there is little doubt that Christian-based organizations have provided desperately needed services to areas of the world stricken with devastating diseases. An excellent example of humanitarian work is that of John Tucker, with the US-based Catholic Markoll Missioners, who has worked in Cambodia since 2001 providing shelters and medical care to children with HIV and AIDS (Fraser 2005).

Missionaries provide international aid, especially after major ecological or natural disasters. In some instances, however, this aid has come with conditions. Following the Indonesian tsunami, American evangelist agencies travelled to India, Indonesia, and Sri Lanka purportedly to offer humanitarian aid but also distributed Christian literature, prompting the US National Council of Churches to protest their behaviour (Baldauf 2005). This tactic, known as "conversion for aid" and involving proselytizing to traumatized people, angered local Christian groups, who feared a backlash in Sri Lanka, a country that already suffers from serious religious tensions (Rohde 2005).

Most missionaries and their sponsoring churches have come to terms with their colonial past. By the mid-twentieth century, development-oriented missionary work – establishing local infrastructures (e.g., building roads and hospitals, digging wells) and providing medical and educational services – became a common strategy, still with the goal of converting the locals to Christianity but with a more humanitarian focus. Today, missionary NGOs assist people in their struggles against repressive regimes and work tirelessly to improve the standard of living of local cultures.

THE CRISIS IN HAITI

Haiti is the poorest country in the Western hemisphere, with the highest rates of infant and maternal mortality, extremely poor nutrition, and the worst HIV/AIDS epidemic in the Americas (Partners in Health 2009–12). When the earthquake struck in 2010, thousands of NGOs already stationed in Haiti, and many more that would soon arrive, sprang into action. Yet, three years later, Haiti and its people remain in dire straits. Nearly half a million people still live in tent refugee camps that do little to protect them from the elements, and many are without toilets or potable water. Even those not in the camps are living in badly damaged houses that need to be torn down. One of the questions being asked is this: Why have the tremendous amounts of aid and the numerous NGOs sent to Haiti not benefitted the people?

According to journalist Reed Lindsay (2010), who is based in Port-au-Prince, the Haitian capital, in the days following the 2010 quake most NGOs, United Nations peacekeepers, and Haitian police were absent from the streets. Survivors set up camps and formed security brigades to ward off looters, while local doctors and nurses established community clinics. Camp committees were also organized to locate the missing-in-action NGOs and procure emergency aid (Lindsay 2010). However, delivery of aid was hampered because the Port-au-Prince airport was blockaded by the United States government – only troop deployments and planes delivering military equipment were allowed to land. Inside the camps, families worked together to earn enough money to survive. Some pooled money to buy a gas-powered generator and then started a cell-phone recharging business, young boys cleaned car windows for tips, and others removed rubble for a mere pittance (Bock 2010). They managed to survive, despite the missing NGOs.

The crisis in Haiti exemplifies the problems and ultimately the failures of NGOs. Zanotti (2010: 20) argues that the lack of democracy, the political unrest, the earthquake, and other excuses are not the reasons for Haiti's problems; rather, NGOs are the root cause. Essentially, international strategies have "promoted NGOs as substitutes for the [Haitian] state." The presence of thousands of NGOs, international peacekeeping units, and multilateral and bilateral aid has eroded the ability of existing state institutions to provide for their citizens, and the country is sinking deeper into dependency on foreign aid. Indeed, Joseph G. Bock (2010), of the Kroc Institute for International Peace Studies at the University of Notre Dame, believes the greatest danger from the aid industry lies in fostering a state of dependency rather than enabling Haitians to help themselves.

Many of the problems with NGOs addressed in this chapter are also evident in Haiti. Indeed, these problems appear to be endemic to the aid industry: 1) poor coordination between agencies leading to ineffective delivery of services; 2) donor/sponsor influence that channels aid into specific economic or political agendas; 3) lack of accountability and exclusion of Haitians from the decision-making process; 4) destruction of local economies; and 5) corruption and misuse of funds (Zanotti 2010). Some of the most recent findings also suggest there is a great deal of cultural insensitivity, ignorance, arrogance, and racism endemic to some NGOs (Panchang 2012). So entrenched are these impediments that the Organization of American States (OAS) special representative to Haiti, Ricardo Seitenfus, was removed from his position for publicly denouncing the United Nations' "imposed occupation" that is "transforming Haitians into prisoners on their own island" (Doucet 2001: n.p.).

"According to international Organization for Migration (IOM) officials, displaced Haitians living in tent camps a year after the earthquake, were 'waiting for houses, cars, helicopters,' ... and 'visas to Canada,' quipped another [TOM official]" (Panchang 2012: n.p.).

John Holmes, a United Nations official in charge of humanitarian aid, has attributed many of the problems with distribution of much-needed resources to "a lack of coordination among international organizations" (Lindsay 2010: 20). This poor coordination resulted in neglect of some regions desperate for relief, while other regions were overwhelmed with redundant NGOs. The aid agencies ignored camp committees and refused to distribute food unless American or United Nations troops were present to protect them. The food distribution often turned into a melee because people were desperate, although many families refused to attend these distributions, unwilling to fight for food despite their hunger.

Other critics point to corporate and business influence that searches for ways to make a profit from the aid industry, or forces NGOs to develop projects because of their profit potential. Indeed, 84 cents of every dollar spent in Haiti is returned to the United States through salaries (Zanotti 2010: 760). Other donations are spent on foreign experts, hotel bills, car rentals, and hotel conferences rather than on the people in need. A recent investigation found that most reconstruction contracts are awarded to American companies, who are getting rich off rebuilding the infrastructure. Thus, Haiti's reconstruction has been "privatized, outsourced, or taken over by foreign NGOs" (Doucet 2011: n.p.).

According to Ruth Derilus, a Haitian aid worker, "There might be a camp with 3000 families and they're trying to distribute 200 items. Of course there are going to be fights.... Some camps have four or five organizations helping them, and none of them seem to be working together. Other camps have received nothing." (Lindsay 2010: 20).

Foreign political institutions with hidden agendas have manipulated aid to support various regimes, and they recently bankrolled and endorsed the election that most Haitians consider illegitimate. Indeed, the most popular political party in Haiti, led by exiled former president Jean-Bertrand Aristide, was excluded from the election. A weak government in Haiti ensures that NGOs and other interested parties can continue to profit from Haiti's crisis (Doucet 2011). Thus, NGOs have taken political processes out of the hands of the Haitian people and their leaders (Zanotti 2010) and turned humanitarian aid into big business.

FIGURE 3.1 HAITIAN TENT CAMP

Haitians have also been excluded from the decision-making process. Local Haitians were banned from meetings where international aid groups discussed strategies for distributing aid. The 12 Haitian members of the Interim Haiti Reconstruction Commission (IHRC), which determines where to use donations, protested to co-chairman Bill Clinton that they are being "completely disconnected from the activities of the IHRC" (Doucet 2011: n.p.). Indeed, the large aid organizations do not reach out to local, community-based organizations at all.

One of the issues repeatedly denounced by Haitians is the destruction of the agricultural industry. Thirty years ago Haitians produced most of their food and enjoyed a diverse diet of "manioc, breadfruit, yams, sweet potatoes, plantains, millet, corn and rice" (Doucet 2011: 21). In 1986, a military junta, backed by Washington, flooded the market with cheap imported rice subsidized by the United States government. These American imports and ongoing food donations have decimated the Haitian agricultural sector. Farmers need assistance in refrigeration and storage technology; instead, NGOs donate more food that continues to impede the sustainability of Haitian agriculture. Farmers are now unable to feed the population, and Haiti has become dependent on imported rice from the United States. The 2010 earthquake has increased this dependency.

"'I don't think there is real co-ordination,' says [Haitian Jesuit priest] Father Kawas. 'We have observed a lot of conflict on the ground in Haiti, conflict for example between Venezuelans and French NGOs, between French NGOs and Cubans, between Americans and Cubans in Haiti.'" (Tran 2013).

"We're going to fight against the way in which they are giving aid ... These meetings of the big foreigners are the ones that will decide our future. We can't be afraid of what they think of us. We need to speak when we're not in agreement." Ruth Derilus, quoted in Lindsay (2010: 21).

Despite the many criticisms of NGOs, there are some NGOs that have been able to effectively provide assistance to the Haitians. These NGOs are locally accountable, internationally connected, and financially independent. They provide services and create economic sustainability without eroding the capacity of the state to provide for Haitians in the future (Zanotti 2010). One example of a successful NGO in Haiti is Partners in Health (PIH), which grew from a small clinic in 1985 into one of the largest NGO health-care providers in Haiti, with facilities that include an infectious-disease centre and a women's health clinic. In 2009, PIH launched the first neonatal intensive care unit (NICU) in Central Haiti, established a Red Cross blood bank, and opened a dozen schools.

"Giving food aid from day to day is fine, but they should help us develop our natural resources for the long term." Community leader Anse Rouge, quoted in Lindsay (2010: 21).

Partners in Health operates in a similar fashion to other successful NGOs. It encourages accountability to the community and is connected to diverse international networks of support, but it remains independent of any sponsors' agendas. PIH ensures the transfer of economic resources and knowledge directly to the community and focuses on the needs of the poor. This holistic model combines academic research with social activism, operating under five principles: access to primary health care, free health care and education for the poor, community partnerships, addressing both social and economic needs, and serving the poor through the public sector (Zanotti 2010: 763). For example, the staff will provide primary health care and medications for the sick, but also food to reduce malnutrition, and money for the family to continue care at home. PIH also provides access to clean water and agricultural programs to feed the poor.

In summary, PIH decisions regarding allocation of services are needs-driven and based on community requests; therefore, the NGO is accountable to the local population and their mandate is not defined by donors or sponsors. For 20 years, PIH has provided free health-care services, advanced a sustainable lifestyle by paying its workers, promoted local food production, created social capital by promoting literacy and professional skills, and encouraged a spirit of solidarity in the community.

CONCLUSION

As we have seen throughout this chapter, the actual roles and purposes of NGOs are often at odds with the real needs of the people. In Haiti, and elsewhere, some NGOs have lost their way and no longer fulfill their humanitarian mandate. Thus, the accountability of NGOs, and whether they represent a new form of cultural imperialism and agents of change, are rightly called into question. Ultimately, NGOs create a catch-22 situation in developing countries. As seen in Haiti, the population desperately needs emergency assistance from large, financially established NGOs. However, development agencies are often charged with promoting Western-style democracy and lifestyle, with little regard for the culture, customs, or economic realities of the nations they "occupy," and for some NGOs, the not-for-profit label is little more than a veneer for hiding enormous financial profits.

Although there is little doubt that some NGOs have successfully launched and completed projects that are of benefit, such as the landmine ban, in most cases their interference and very presence create challenges, not the least of which is increasing dependency on foreign aid. Other issues, such as cultural sensitivity, meddling in private family affairs, destruction of local economies and state institutions, and proselytizing for aid, all suggest that some NGOs may cause more harm than good. To regain their reputations and legitimacy, NGOs will have to return to their original mandate – emergency humanitarian aid – and leave other matters to state institutions, grassroots organizations, and local governments.

Haiti is a prime example of a nation that is more victim than beneficiary of NGO aid. Three years after the quake in Haiti, reconstruction has barely begun. Most of the rubble has not been cleared, streets are still impassable, and half a million people are living in decrepit, dangerous tent camps. Information on what happened to the $2.1 billion raised is conflicting; some say it is almost all spent, while others suggest that much of the money never made it to the streets or to the Haitian people. On the other hand, the successful NGO featured in this chapter, Partners in Health (PIH), has learned that community-based, accountable, needs-driven organization can create sustainable results for the local community. PIH has provided many positive changes, but only because their holistic vision takes the NGO back to grassroots organization. Ultimately, this is the reason why they have been successful when so many others have failed.

QUESTIONS FOR CONSIDERATION AND CLASSROOM ACTIVITIES

1. Research the work of a missionary agency in a country of your choice. What are their goals, and how are they achieving these goals? Are the people benefitting from this missionism and is the aid sustainable (a valid question for any NGO)? How is this work changing the cultural systems of the people? In your opinion, is missionism a worthwhile endeavour?

2. Place yourself in the position of Ugandan parents: authorities from another state have accused your leaders of neglecting the rights of children. NGOs move into your community and begin "educating" you and your parents, as well as teachers and local leaders on what a "proper childhood" means. This advice runs counter to the life you have known. How would you and others in your community react to this interference? What if your leaders have no choice but to obey the new conditions?

3. Choose an NGO and research its work in Haiti. Has it been successful in fulfilling its mandate? What challenges and obstacles has this NGO faced when delivering aid to Haitians? Are there other factors that are keeping the people of Haiti from returning to their normal lives besides inefficient NGOs?

4. The Red Cross is an NGO, and yet very few criticisms are levelled at this organization. Provide a detailed analysis of how the Red Cross provides services in a crisis situation that are different from other NGOs.

5. Review the definition of civil society. Is your country a civil society? Why or why not?

6. If NGOs cause so much harm, why don't the leaders of nations such as Haiti remove them?

7. Devise a plan for clearing the streets of rubble in a suburb of Port-au-Prince, and then create a budget and timeline for completing the project, keeping in mind the logistical problems you will face.

8. As a global citizen you have a greater awareness of the hidden agendas that NGOs may have when they are delivering aid. What can you do with this knowledge?

9. Steven Sampson (2002) states: "the most suitable term for Western intervention in the Balkans would be benevolent colonialism." Research the reasons behind his statement, and determine whether his contempt is justified.

SUGGESTED READINGS

Apale, A., & Stam, V. (2011). *Generation NGO.* **Toronto: Between the Lines.**

This is a must-read book for anyone contemplating international aid as a career. It provides personal accounts of Canadian young people working in international development, dealing with issues such as inequality, abject poverty, stereotyping, and injustice.

Vachon, M., Bugingo, F., & Phillips, C. (2008). *Rebel without borders.* **Toronto: ECW Press.**

This is a sharply critical but fascinating examination of global humanitarian aid through the lens of the Doctors Without Borders organization, providing a behind-the-scenes look at the burgeoning business of aid.

Chapter 4

Population Growth: Is the World Over-Populated, and Should Governments Have the Right to Control Birthrates?

Key Terms: body politics, cultural imperialism, developed nations, developing nations, human rights, one-child policy, over-consumption, over-population, population theory

INTRODUCTION

"There is a well-documented correlation between poverty and high birthrates. In little countries and big countries, capitalist countries and communist countries, Catholic countries and Moslem countries, Western countries and Eastern countries ... exponential population growth slows down or stops when grinding poverty disappears. This is called demographic transition. ... Our job is to bring about a worldwide demographic transition ... by eliminating grinding poverty, making safe and effective birth control methods widely available, and extending real political power (executive, legislative, judicial, military ...) to women. If we fail, some other process, less under our control, will do it for us." Carl Sagan, quoted in Alter (2010).

The idea that the world is over-populated and headed for environmental collapse is deeply ingrained in the Western psyche, and is difficult to refute because of its fundamental logic: too many people using too few resources will result in hunger, poverty, environmental degradation, and political instability. But is this hypothesis accurate or only part of a much larger issue? Is population growth the harbinger of socio-economic, environmental, and political ills or merely a symptom of global injustice and inequality? Are population-control policies designed to curtail rapid population growth in developing countries or to ensure adequate resources are available for developed countries? And finally, is the movement to control birthrates another form of **cultural imperialism**?

Environmentalists have long argued that population pressures are the main reasons for climate change and destruction of the planetary biodiversity. Those who hold this view advocate strict control of birthrates in countries with rapid population expansion to protect limited natural resources. Yet others suggest that **over-population** is not the problem; rather, **over-consumption** in developed nations is depleting the world's resources, as well as preventing people in developing nations from accessing much-needed resources. Since 1950, the richest 20 per cent of the global population has doubled its consumption of energy, meat, forests, and metals, and quadrupled car ownership (Firth 2012: 5). Critics

FIGURE 4.1 LAVISH AMERICAN BUFFET

of imperialism, then, believe that population-control programs are designed to provide wealthy Western nations with uncontested access to the resources they demand (Tobin 2004). Some critics even suggest that the pervasiveness of the over-population notion legitimizes the authoritarian actions perpetuated by wealthy nations against developing nations and their people.

Body politics also plays a significant role in population policies – women's reproductive rights are pitted against a political agenda to lower populations in developing countries. The issue of population is further exacerbated by a demographic saturation of young people – there are more than three billion people under the age of 25 in the world today, many entering their reproductive years. These youth will keep the global population expanding into the next century (Weiss 2012). In fact, 78 million people are born every year, or more than 200,000 people a day despite falling fertility rates (People and Planet 2011).

The socio-economic, political, religious, and environmental issues related to population growth are explored in this chapter. Although the poor in developing nations are often blamed for the socio-economic and environmental ills of the world, this chapter will present a more critical analysis of the so-called population problem and challenge prevailing claims concerning over-population. Every attempt is made to present a balanced discussion of this extremely complex and emotional issue through competing perspectives. For our case study we will evaluate the one-child, one-couple policy adopted by China in an attempt to curtail birthrates and improve the economic future of the country. China's policy, now 30 years old, has succeeded in reducing the rate of population growth in China, but at what social cost? The expertise of ecologists, NGOs, family-planning experts, anthropologists, and global demographers are drawn upon in this chapter.

THE NATURE OF POPULATION CONTROL

By the year 2050, the global population is projected to reach 8.9 billion,[1] with most people residing in **developing nations**, especially those in Asia, Latin America, and Africa (UN Department of Economic and Social Affairs 2004: 4). This estimate is lower than the dire predictions of the 1970s, but even this population level presents serious challenges. On the other hand, **developed nations**, such as Japan and Western European countries, are experiencing a dramatic decline in fertility rates. Countries with falling birthrates face looming labour shortages, aging populations, and a loss of vitality and innovation. Thus a demographic divide has evolved, with poor countries experiencing high birthrates, increasing populations, and low life expectancies, while wealthy countries have low birthrates, declining populations, and extended life spans. Table 4.1 illustrates the demographic divide between Tanzania, a developing nation, and Spain, a developed nation (Haub 2012: n.p.).

Proponents of population control policies operate under three premises: first, that over-population in developing nations is the major cause of hunger, environmental degradation, economic stagnation, and political instability; second, that people must be persuaded or even forced into producing fewer children, but not necessarily as a means to improve their economic situation; and, third, that birth control should be given to women in developing nations regardless of health and safety concerns (Hartmann 1995: xix).

Critics of population-control policies counter that rapid population growth is not the root cause of underdevelopment, resource depletion, or environmental degradation; rather, high birthrates are the result of the slow pace of social reform in developing countries. Blaming the planet's ills on over-population is a way to absolve the affluent of any responsibility. Indeed, population-control policies are often substituted for other strategies that would make a socio-economic difference, such as land redistribution, economic

> "We now realise that the disasters that continue increasingly to affect the natural world have one element that connects them all — the unprecedented increase in the number of human beings on the planet." Sir David Attenborough, in the president's People and Planet address to the Royal Society of Arts and Commerce (People and Planet 2011).

TABLE 4.1 DEMOGRAPHIC DIVIDE BETWEEN TANZANIA AND SPAIN

	TANZANIA	SPAIN
Population (2012)	48 million	46 million
Projected Population (2050)	138 million	48 million
Lifetime Births per Woman	5.4	1.4
Annual Births	1.9 million	483,000
Percent of Population Below Age 15	45%	15%
Percent of Population Ages 65+	3%	17%
Percent of Population Ages 65+ (2050)	4%	33%
Life Expectancy at Birth	57 years	82 years
Infant Mortality Rate (per 1,000 live births)	51	3.2
Annual Number of Infant Deaths	98,000	1,600
Percent of Adults Ages 15–49 with HIV/AIDS	5.6%	0.4%

---

1 Estimates of population are highly variable, with UN projections ranging from 7.4 to 10.6 billion.

and social development, employment creation, and universal education and health care. These policies would reduce poverty, as well as economic, gender, and racial inequities, and ultimately result in fewer children per family (Hartmann 1995).

"When the affluent few regard the impoverished majority as simply a dark, faceless crowd overpopulating the earth, they deny poor people their humanity and diminish their own." (Hartmann 1995: xxi)

As far as claims that over-population is polluting the world are concerned, Rodriguez-Trias (1995) points out that it is militarism that destroys the landscape and pollutes the environment with toxins, and that wasteful production and consumption patterns, as well as corporate greed, are the real causes of environmental destruction and resource depletion. As an example, the United States produces a quarter of the world's carbon dioxide emissions – 5.43 tons as compared to 0.7 tons in most African countries (Population Connection 2009).

HISTORICAL CONTEXT

Historically, **population theories** have placed the blame for the planet's ills on the poor. This viewpoint became so entrenched in the seventeenth and eighteenth centuries that any attempt to provide relief for the poor was soundly criticized because it would encourage them to have more children. Rev. Thomas R. Malthus, known as the father of population theory, used the scientific principles of the Enlightenment to "prove" that population growth among the poor must be checked (Tobin 2004). Although accused of being classist, Malthusian theory set the stage for modern-day misconceptions regarding over-population.

In 1844, economist Friedrich Engels countered Malthusianism by pointing out that the productive capabilities of humanity could be unlimited, considering new technologies, scientific inventions, capital, and labour potential, and therefore population growth was not a problem (Tobin 2004). Marxist critics of Malthusianism argued that uneven distribution of resources and wealth, not over-population, caused poverty, and that the consumer class, not the poor, were destroying the forests, releasing pollutants into the atmosphere, and causing the extinction of animal species (Tobin 2004).

The consequences of unrestrained population growth, including resource depletion and diminished economic and social development, became a serious concern in the mid-twentieth century, when demographers suggested that if current trends continued, the global population would soon become ecologically unsustainable. Neo-Malthusians of the same period, such as Dr. Paul Ehrlich (1971), coined the phrase "population bomb," a concept that was instrumental in the development of current population policies. Demographers and biologists took up the mantle, exacerbating fears of food shortages, highlighting the perceived inadequacies of peasant farming, and pushing for foreign private investment in agribusinesses (see Chapter 10 for further discussion of agribusinesses and food security). Some Malthusians even predicted that deterioration of the climate would inevitably lead to Malthusian checks, including war, famine, and epidemics, and Zhang et al. (2011) contend that population collapses are inevitable when over-population and climatic deterioration occur at the same time. However, modern-day critics of neo-Malthusianism continue to argue that the upper classes, with their voracious consumer appetites, are the real cause of pollution emissions, natural resource consumption, and habitat disruption (Tobin 2004).

Nonetheless, neo-Malthusians continue to claim that over-population is the primary cause of war and political instability – the need to conquer new lands and compete for scarce resources. Fear that uncontrolled population growth could lead to international conflicts has influenced population-control programs. However, this theory ignores the foreign policies of wealthy countries like the United States, which have created political instability in areas such as the Middle East (see Chapter 13 for a discussion of global conflicts).

Today, many demographers and population experts take a more balanced perspective on global population issues. They recognize that depletion of resources is partly due to high birthrates in some developing countries, but they also understand that irresponsible demands from wealthy nations for resources is causing most of the depletion of resources and exacerbating social inequalities in developing countries (Wirth 1995: 78).

> "The gaping divide in material consumption between the fortunate and the unfortunate stands out starkly in their impacts on the natural world. ... The consumer society's exploitation of resources threatens to exhaust, poison, or unalterably disfigure forests, soils, water, and air." (Durning 1994: 42)

POPULATION PRESSURES

Most population pressures are also environmental pressures, including deforestation, water shortages, contamination of the air, land, and water, and loss of biodiversity. The question we should all be asking is this: If we reach the environmental limits of the planet, what other options does the human race have? Population experts Hinrichsen and Robey (2000) point out that expanding populations consume more energy and resources, drive more cars, build more houses, and eventually may use space beyond what the planet can provide (CWAC. net n.d.). According to entomologist Edward O. Wilson, 27,000 plant, animal, and insect species go extinct every year because of human encroachment on their habitats (People and Planet 2011). Research on the correlation between over-population and climate change suggests that if global warming and the ensuing environmental problems (e.g., stunted crops, droughts, water shortages, violent weather) continue, the carrying capacity of the land will shrink, increasing the very real danger of mass starvation and population collapse (Zhang et al. 2011). However, whether we can blame these realities on population growth in developing countries or over-consumption in developed countries remains unclear.

Water and food shortages are increasing in some developing countries; according to the UN Food and Agriculture Organization, one in seven people is chronically hungry. However, the problem is not food shortages, but access to land and reasonable income distribution (Hartmann 1995). Poorer people tend to be landless, so they cannot grow their own food and do not have the money to purchase food. The issue of water shortages is more difficult to address; the two largest consumers of water are large-scale irrigation systems for agriculture (70 per cent) and industry (20 per cent), while residential use accounts for only 10 per cent, even in cities with large populations (Web of Creation n.d.). By 2025, more than two and possibly as many as three billion people, particularly in sub-Saharan Africa, will not have ready access to clean water (People & Planet 2011).

> "Each person's 'environmental footprint' has on average grown to 22 hectares of the planet but the report estimates the 'biological carrying capacity' is somewhere between 15 and 16 hectares per person." United Nations' Global Environment Outlook-4 report, quoted in Wilkinson (2007: n.p.).

Numerous problems have contributed to water shortages, including climate change and inefficient agriculture. Increases in temperatures in mountainous regions due to global warming are reducing the amount of snow and ice for run-off during dry seasons. As a

"A country's ability to feed itself very much depends on three factors: availability of arable land, accessible water and population pressures. The more people there are, especially in poor countries with limited amounts of land and water, the fewer resources there are to meet basic needs. If basic needs cannot be met, development stalls and economies begin to unravel."
Dr. Nafis Sadik, Executive Director of the United Nations Fund for Population Activities (UNFPA), quoted in FAO (n.d.).

result, mountain glaciers, known as "reservoirs in the sky," are melting. Leaky irrigation equipment, agri-chemicals that end up in the rivers, and the need for continuous irrigation have dried up rivers, lakes, and underground water sources (Raulkari, Toledo, & Harvey n.d.). Unsafe drinking water is responsible for numerous diseases. Indeed, the World Health Organization (WHO) estimates that 1,000 people die every day in West Africa from drinking unsafe water (*PBS Newshour* 2012).

Global deforestation is an example of the convoluted nature of population and environmental degradation. In Haiti the hills have been stripped of their trees, and environmental degradation on the island has reached crisis proportions. Despite the prevailing belief that Haitians have denuded the hillsides for cooking fuel, this is only the most recent assault on the forests in Haiti. The most devastating deforestation took place in the early 1800s, when the newly independent nation had to sell its timber to pay off its debt to France. Since then the logging industry has grown to meet the constant cooking-fuel shortage in the country. Following the 2010 earthquake, foreign NGOs built temporary shelters on a fragile, protected mountainside, clearing all the trees to do so. All of these activities exacerbated the deforestation problem in Haiti, and by 2012 only two per cent of forest cover remained in the country (Laurent 2012).

"Our future hinges on whether we can strike an equitable balance between human numbers and consumption and the planet's capacity to support life.... Sustainable development."
(Wirth 1995: 78)

In Brazil, large-scale commercial farming, ranching, logging, mining, and highway construction have destroyed much of the Amazon forest. None of these activities are a direct result of population growth but are instead due to consumer demands for products, mainly in developed countries. Deforestation in the Philippines was blamed on landless people moving into the uplands, but closer analysis shows that dictator Ferdinand Marcos gave logging concessions to relatives and cronies (Hartmann 1995). As for the poor of the Philippines, they suffer from a shortage of fuel, so they cut down trees and have been pushed into marginal lands on the hills, which also results in deforestation. Nevertheless, their impact is minimal compared to that of the logging companies.

CHINA'S ONE-CHILD POLICY

In 1979, the Chinese government implemented the "one child, one couple" population-control policy. Deng Xiaoping, then-leader of the Chinese government, hoped that implementation of a **one-child policy** would relieve the population stress created by escalating birthrates and assist in his plan to transform the country into an industrial powerhouse (Nakra 2012). The political and scientific discourse that led up to this policy championed the ideology that over-population was "a serious threat to future living standards and the viability of economic reforms" (Bulte, Heerink, & Zhang 2011: 25). Marxist population theorists drew on Friedrich Engels' twofold concept of social production – production of subsistence and production of humans – and under a socialist system, both required controlled planning. The goal was to establish a stable population of 1.2 billion people by the year 2000. However, as anthropologist Ann Anagnost (1995: 27) points out, reducing fertility rates was not the only goal; improving the *quality* of Chinese people, through improved education, and increasing general knowledge in areas such as health care, child-rearing, law, and technology were also seen as vital to future prosperity in the country.

The State Family Planning Bureau controls the timing of marriage and childbearing, as well as the size of families in China (Bulte, Heerink, & Zhang 2011). Although one child is the rule, in rural China, farmers may be allowed to have a second child after five years if their first child is a girl. Ethnic minorities, such as Tibetans, are also allowed to have more than one child. In recent years, in families with a disabled first child, or where the parents are both from one-child families, a second child may be allowed. However, for most urban residents and government employees, the one-child policy is strictly enforced (Nakra 2012).

Administering this policy is where most of the controversy arises. Initially, officials relied on media propaganda and education; however, financial incentives for producing only one child, including paid pregnancy leave for three years, a salary increase, and preferential access to housing, schools, and health services, soon followed (Richards 1996). The policy is enforced through residential registration, certificates of birth approval, birth certification, and social ostracism, as well as economic sanctions, such as fines, confiscation of property, and loss of government jobs. In addition, parents who contravene the policy are required to pay for their child's education and health care (Bulte, Heerink, & Zhang 2011).

Critics have called the one-child policy a vehicle for **human rights** abuses that exacerbates the very real problem of female infant abandonment and infanticide in China (Batabyal & Beladi 2004). Birth quotas in every city and province have led to reports of forced abortions and sterilization of both men and women (Bulte, Heerink, & Zhang 2011). Indeed, some of the methods for enforcing the one-child policy appear draconian;

FIGURE 4.2 A CHINESE ONE–CHILD FAMILY

for example, in Hunan province officials have been accused of confiscating "illegal" babies from families that violated the policy, and putting these babies up for sale (*The Economist* 2011). These reports of parental or human rights abuses, whether substantiated or not, have resonated with many Westerners, specifically pro-life foundations and those with anti-Communist political agendas (Greenhalgh 2003a), but also with ordinary people who strongly object to any violation of human rights, including the right to have a family. However, the Chinese government contends that human-rights abuses, such as forced abortions, are the exception rather than the norm. They are quick to point out that the policy is working, and that 300 million births have been prevented.

"Li Aihai, happily married and the mother of a 2½-year-old girl, had a problem. She was four months pregnant with her second child. Sihui county family-planning officials ... told her what she already knew: She had gotten pregnant too soon. She hadn't waited until her daughter was four years old, as Chinese law required of rural couples. The officials assured her that, because her first child had been a girl, she would eventually be allowed a second child. But they were equally insistent that she would have to abort this one. It was January 2000." (Mosher 2006).

On the surface this policy has been successful; indeed, China now has one of the lowest fertility rates in the world (*The Economist* 2011). The most obvious benefit of this policy has been a significant improvement in the standard of living for many Chinese citizens no longer burdened with large families to support on meagre incomes. However, the success of this policy has also created far-reaching socio-economic consequences and presents some difficult challenges for China in the future. China's fertility rate is now 1.5 children per woman (Nakra 2012). This rate, which is 30 per cent lower than needed to ensure population stability in the future, has created a low dependency ratio, which means fewer economically active adults to dependent citizens (Eberstadt 2010). In China's case, the ratio stands at three working adults per non-working dependent. This low dependency ratio and the "greying" of China's population will soon have far-reaching implications – economists have predicted that one third of China's population will be over 60 by 2030 (Nakra 2012). Fewer young people will be available to care for their elderly parents and grandparents or pay income taxes that provide infrastructure such as health care. In the very near future Chinese officials will have to grapple with pension plans and health care for their aging society and to take over the roles that children used to assume.

A second major consequence of the one-child policy has been a sex-ratio imbalance. Johnson (1996: 79) suggests that the reason for this imbalance is cultural preference for male babies: "Girls occupy a structurally marginal place in a patrilineal kinship system." In rural areas, parents prefer sons to help on the farm or to migrate to cities with labour shortages to gain employment and send remittances back to their parents. Sons are also seen as care providers for parents in their old age. Thus, couples restricted to one child turn to ultrasound technology to determine sex. This has led to an increase in abortion of female fetuses, as well as female infanticide and abandonment (Bulte, Heerink, & Zhang 2011). The inability to find wives has caused socially disruptive behaviour among Chinese men, including kidnapping of women for wives. Indeed, human trafficking of girls, especially from Sichuan and Anhui provinces, and transporting them to prosperous coastal areas where they are sold as brides is a burgeoning business for rings of pedlars (Anagnost 1995).

One of the most dramatic social costs of the one-child policy is the creation of a black-listed population of children not registered in the national household registration system because their parents were not allowed to have another child. Their numbers are estimated to be in the millions, most of them girls from rural areas (Canada, Immigration and Refugee Board 2007). Many of these children are the result of a rural underground culture of escape; women hide their "illegal" pregnancies and even their child after birth. They may flee to other regions and become part of the "floating population" on the edge of cities (Greenhalgh 2003b). These unregistered children are denied the most basic of citizenship rights, including state health care and education, and suffer from social and economic marginalization. In adulthood, unregistered people may have difficulty gaining employment, enrolling in the army, or marrying.

The increased prosperity and economic freedom in China's cities has led to some children living lives of luxury that in some cases has created the "little emperor" syndrome. These lone children tend to be spoiled with material possessions, seldom receive punishment for bad behaviour, and expect everything to come easy. The increased egotism, selfishness, rude behaviour, and moral poverty among children of the one-child policy are causing concern about their ability to become productive citizens or future leaders (Clark 2008).

Acceptance of the one-child policy has been a long and difficult process with some serious social costs. However, by 2012, many young adults, having grown up in a commodified environment, now equate their ability to acquire goods to their country's low birthrate (Anagnost 1995). Consequently, many of them now consider small families preferable. For this reason, Zuo Xuejin of the Shanghai Academy of Social Sciences believes the policy is no longer necessary (*The Economist* 2013). Public scrutiny and rejection of the policy has increased in recent years, so the future of the one-child policy is no longer as certain.

THE ETHICS OF POPULATION CONTROL AND FAMILY PLANNING

The controversy surrounding China's one-child policy brings home this question: should governments be allowed to control birthrates? When China implemented its one-child policy the West applauded the move, hoping the possibility that China would take over the world by sheer numbers could now be laid to rest. But Western pundits ignored the human-rights abuses that such a policy might entail. Indeed, the International Planned Parenthood Foundation (IPPF) and the World Bank provided financial assistance to their Chinese counterparts to set the policy in motion and awarded full membership in the IPPF for their initiatives. Individuals and organizations such as the United Nations Population Fund (FPA) lauded the Chinese policy (Aird 1994). However, critics remind us that the human cost of the one-child policy cannot be ignored. On an individual level, being denied the right to have more than one child, despite economic means, is a human-rights tragedy.

Religion has always played a strong role in family dynamics. With regard to women's reproductive rights, some powerful religious forces and anti-choice movements have taken an active interest in population politics, although opinions vary considerably between religions and even within religious sects. Catholicism is widely criticized for its condemnation of contraception and abortion. In the 1968 *Humanae Vitae* encyclical, section 14 prohibited the use of birth control pills, artificial barriers, sterilization, and abortion (Tobin 2004). Indeed, the Vatican led a movement to delegitimize the 1994 Cairo conference on reproductive choice. Buddhism, on the other hand, promotes curbing excessive over-consumerism and over-population, considering both to be agents of Earth's destruction (Gross 1995: 167), while Hinduism considers the number of children to be a woman's matter (Iyer 2002). Islam permits family planning, although there is considerable debate and even contradiction among clerics regarding interpretation of scriptures. In Egypt, for example, couples are told they should not actively prevent conception, as it is Allah's will, although choosing to have only a few children is acceptable.

"I'm a Catholic, but women need access to contraceptives ... over and over again women have told me that all they want is to be able to put time between one child and another child. It's a universal thing to want to feed your children and to educate your children, and women know that the only way they can do that is not have so many." Philanthropist Melinda Gates, quoted in Moorhead (2012: n.p.).

According to James N. Gribble (2012), vice-president of International Programs at the Population Reference Bureau, the reproductive rights of women, especially in developing countries, must be addressed through family planning. Family planning is not the same as population control; rather, family planning means providing access to contraceptives and empowering women through education and employment to make their own choices. Ultimately, family planning increases the economic well-being of everyone, since parents of smaller families are better able to provide more educational opportunities and regular health care for their children. As Dr. Amarjit Singh, executive director of the National Population Stabilization Fund, states, "An educated girl is your best contraception" (Yardley 2010).

The 2012 London Summit on Family Planning centred on control of family size and spacing between births. More specifically, the objectives were to improve access to contraceptives and to empower women to make reproductive choices. The organizers at the summit claimed that doing so would reduce maternal deaths by 200 million and result in 110 million fewer unwanted pregnancies, 50 million fewer abortions, and 3 million fewer babies dying before age one (Tran 2012). Empowering women in developing countries is an urgent global issue, especially since neo-liberal policies have resulted in increasing gender inequality in countries such as India (Shah 2012).

"At 20, Francisca Kanyari already had two children and her husband wanted more. He had six other children by another wife, common in a country where polygamy is legal. He supported both households on one salary.

Kanyari believed she and her two boys would be better off if she stopped having babies. So every three months, she sneaked away from her thatch-roof hut in northern Kenya to visit a clinic and receive an injection of the hormonal contraceptive Depo-Provera.

'With Depo,' she said, 'no one sees it. And I'm free.'" (Weiss 2012: n.p.)

One of the major obstacles to empowering women is access to safe, effective contraceptives (Hartmann 1995). At the 1994 United Nations International Conference on Population, held in Cairo, Egypt, the voices of women from African nations were finally heard. These women protested international programs that focused on population control and birthrates rather than sustainable development. They also pointed out that Western contraceptives (e.g., banned Depo-Provera injections) were being dumped in their countries and threatened the health and well-being of African women.

Deeply rooted cultural practices and preference for male progeny represent another obstacle to population reduction. As in China, the cultural bias toward sons in India has resulted in abortion of female fetuses once the couple sees the ultrasound, thus creating a sex imbalance[2] (Yardley 2010). Marriages are often arranged at a young age, and starting a family immediately is still encouraged. Several policies have been put in place to curb population growth and address cultural practices, ranging from forced sterilizations in Andhra Pradesh state in the 1990s of women after their second child, to more benign campaigns to convince young couples to wait two years before starting a family. In Satara district in Maharashtra state, nurses visit each village and try to convince

---

2 The term "sex imbalance" is used here rather than "gender imbalance," which is commonly used in the literature, because gender is a cultural construct, while sex is a biological reality.

parents not to marry their daughters off until they have finished school. Young couples are offered the "honeymoon package," which consists of cash bonuses if they wait two years to have a child.

India's birthrate is currently 2.6 children per family, well below earlier birthrates, but still above the 2.1 ratio needed to stabilize the population. Even when the rate falls to 2.1, India's population will peak in 2060 at 1.7 billion people (Weiss 2012). To address this issue, on May 1, 2000, Maharashtra, the second most populous state in India, established a population-control policy whereby a third child born to a family would not receive benefits, such as reimbursement of medical expenses (Government of Maharashtra Public Health Department 2000).

As a model for future government-endorsed family planning, Thailand launched a successful government-supported family-planning program in 1971, following years of rapid population growth. The high-profile public-education campaign encouraged family planning and offered incentives such as loans that were linked to the use of contraceptives. Alternative income-generation projects were developed so that families no longer had to have large families working in the fields. None of the initiatives were coercive and, most important of all, were linked to women's rights, increased employment opportunities, better health care, and support from the Buddhist religion (Frazer 1996).

> "... the world can neither support everybody living an American lifestyle nor living as hunter-gatherers. The answer lies in between. ... those of us from the highly consumptive societies are going to have to find ways to do with less." Biologist Thomas Lovejoy, quoted in Tucker (2006).

CONCLUSION

Population growth is extremely difficult to model; however, many demographers suggest there is a significant probability that the global population will reach its peak between 2050 and 2075 at just under nine billion, and then decline by the end of the century (Lutz, Sanderson & Scherbov 2001). Although this sounds like good news, a population this size will still place enormous strain on the Earth's ecosystems. Yet, as has been pointed out numerous times in this discussion, large populations in developing countries are not the main source of socio-economic woes from a global perspective. There are many factors at work, not the least of which is rampant consumerism in wealthy developed nations. The footprint left by a multinational corporation or a coal-burning plant is much larger than that left by any group of people.

Ultimately, if the basic needs of people for food, shelter, clean water, health care, education, employment, and elder security are met, people will no longer feel the need to produce large families to ensure their social and economic well-being. Population numbers do not need to be addressed as much as socio-economic conditions and gender, as in countries such as India where birthrates are still high, to compensate for high mortality rates, the need for child labour, and to care for aging parents (Hartmann 1995).

China's one-child policy was designed to slow population growth but also to change people's attitudes about family size. From my own observations and discussions with young Chinese urbanites, it has succeeded, but this may not be due only to the one-child policy. Media have brought the world to China, making viewers more aware of the benefits of small families, and many Chinese couples are enjoying their new-found economic prosperity too much to jeopardize it with large families. However, there is also a great deal of opposition to such a drastic population policy, and growing evidence that the policy has created new and unforeseen consequences that threaten China's development plans as much as rapid population growth once did.

"We have the capability to tackle these great issues and carve out a sustainable future ... but we have to persuade ourselves of the seriousness of the threats we face, so that we act." Former news editor Fred Pearce, in interview with Jon Stewart (Alter 2010)

In answer to the opening questions, the world may not be over-populated, as claimed by population-control advocates; however, over-consumption is threatening our environment and biodiversity, and therefore also the ability of the Earth to sustain its current population. Despite this looming threat, the use of force or other coercive practices to control population growth is unjustified and predicated on cultural imperialistic agendas. As suggested by numerous advocates, people in developing countries need economic security and alternatives to large families; only then will birthrates fall and quality of life improve. Equally important to resource sustainability is the call for people in developed countries to critically assess their current conspicuous consumption practices.

QUESTIONS FOR CONSIDERATION AND CLASSROOM ACTIVITIES

1. Choose a country, such as Burkino Faso, and trace its food-production and environmental-sustainability policies. Are these policies making a difference?
2. Class debate: is the world over-populated or over-consumed?
3. Choose a developing country and investigate its birthrate. Does the government provide any incentives to lower the birthrates? How does the populace react to these measures, and are the measures successful? Investigate the reasons behind this country's birthrate.
4. What measures do you think would best serve to reduce unsustainable population growth and improve the lives of people in developing countries?
5. Many of the resources on the web are directed toward the dangers of rapid population growth. Critically evaluate the assertions in these websites and report on their accuracy.
6. Search out websites that present a balanced picture, and critically assess the real causes of resource depletion and environmental degradation.

SUGGESTED READINGS

Hartmann, B. (1995). *Reproductive rights of women and the global politics of population control.* Cambridge, MA: South End Press.

An insightful analysis of population politics and the effect that population policies may have on women. The author uses case studies to explain the historical and political origins of population-control policies.

Pearce, F. (2010). *The coming population crash: Our planet's surprising future.* Boston: Beacon Press.

Former news editor Fred Pearce presents a balanced, insightful discussion of population growth that ignores the doom-and-gloom rhetoric of many population theorists. Many of the views expressed in this chapter are discussed in greater detail in this book.

Part Two

CULTURE CHANGE AND
CHANGING IDENTITIES

In this second section of *Global Issues*, the inevitability of culture change and the ways in which culture change can affect identity are addressed. In Part Two, "Culture Change and Changing Identities," five diverse topics are considered: language loss and revitalization, the transnational flow of an ideal body image, legalization of same-sex marriages and changing family structure, the power of social media to exact change, and the changing identities of global nomads.

In Chapter 5, "Heritage Languages: Are they an endangered species?", the importance of saving endangered languages and the impact on personal and cultural identity when a language is lost are investigated. This chapter emphasizes the value of every language and presents several examples of both successful and unsuccessful revitalization projects. In Chapter 6, "Body Image: How does body image affect identity and status, and how has the transnational flow of Western ideals of beauty impacted other cultures?", we examine the impact of body image on identity, and changing political and economic conditions that can also change body ideals.

In Chapter 7, "Same-Sex Marriage: What are the socio-economic, religious, and political implications of same-sex marriage and changing family structure?", the interrelatedness of social norms, religious tenets, economic realities, and political influences are addressed through the struggle for equality. The importance of recognizing same-sex marriage and same-sex families for personal identity and national well-being are stressed. Chapter 8, "Social Media: What is its role in socio-political revolution?", is a timely investigation of the power of social media in causing and even directing culture change through political protest. Chapter 9, "Global Nomads: Do Third Culture Kids own a national identity?", may seem an unusual topic for a global issues book; however, as more and more people look to other countries for economic opportunities, children living in several nations during their formative years and who may call no nation their true home is rapidly becoming a global issue.

Part Two, then, speaks to the human condition and to humans as social beings in a continually changing world. The stage is also set for Part Three, where conflict is intertwined with cultural imperialism, human rights, and culture change.

Chapter 5

Heritage Languages: Are They an Endangered Species?

Key Terms: endangered languages, heritage languages, identity, language, language loss, language shift, linguicism, linguistic diversity, linguistics, revitalization, speech communities

---

INTRODUCTION

"Faced with ... losing half the world's languages within the next century, and of the distinct possibility of a world with only one language in a few hundred years hence, it is this generation which needs to make the decisions. ... We can sit back and do nothing and let things run their course. Or we can act, using as many means as possible to confront the situation and influence the outcome. Revitalization schemes can work. But time is running out. It is already too late for many languages, but we hold the future of many others in our hands." (Crystal 2000: 165–166).

If we were to choose one characteristic that separates humans from other animals, it would be complex language. **Language** involves communicating with sounds or gestures that are organized in meaningful ways, according to a set of rules. Humans transmit knowledge and share lived experiences with others through language. Language, then, provides a medium for expressing our ideas and concerns, beliefs and values, and is vital to our cultural integrity and identity. In other words, language is an essential cultural marker, one that defines who we are, where we come from, and how we view the world around us.

The modern scientific study of language is known as **linguistics**. The study of language is important in many disciplines, most notably anthropology, psychology, indigenous studies, and sociology, but also education, human geography, and literary studies. Linguistic anthropologists explore the ways humans use language to create, practise, and transmit culture, and the way members of a speech community use language to form social relationships. Linguistic psychologists or psycholinguists study the cognitive processes that influence and are influenced by language, and in particular, how the languages we speak shape the way we think, while sociolinguists study language variation and its relationship to social factors. The expertise of these specialists will be drawn upon in the following discussions.

Global **linguistic diversity** is seriously threatened today. Of the 6,000–7,000 languages still surviving in the early years of the twenty-first century, at least half of them are considered endangered, and 95 per cent of the global population speaks one of only 400 languages (Harrison 2008). Indeed, two billion people speak English as a first or second language, one billion Mandarin Chinese, while Spanish, Hindi, and Arabic each have one half billion speakers.

"Linguistic diversity is one of the most important parts of our human heritage." Linguistic anthropologist K. David Harrison, quoted in Munro (2012: n.p.).

Ostler (2001) estimates that a language is lost every two weeks, and some linguists predict that by the end of the twenty-first century, 90 per cent of human languages may be lost (Krauss 1992: 7). To counter this loss of languages, preservation and **revitalization** projects have taken on added urgency among language activists, including linguists, and the **speech communities** that are threatened. Indeed, applied linguists are dedicated to saving or at least recording as many **endangered languages** as possible. For example, linguistic anthropologist Anvita Abbi served as director of a documentation project called *Vanishing Voices of the Great Andamanese*. The Great Andamanese people of the Andaman Islands in the Indian Ocean speak a language that no one else in the world speaks, a language that may be one of the few surviving Palaeolithic languages (VOGA n.d.). As recently as the early eighteenth century, the Great Andamanese spoke ten dialects, but then the people adopted a Hindi dialect that gradually replaced Great Andamanese. Great Andamanese is now an endangered language with only seven speakers remaining, and even they tend to use a mixed language in everyday conversation. In attempts to restore this language, Abbi and her colleagues compiled a 5,000-word trilingual dictionary with translations in English and Hindi, a comprehensive grammar, and extensive video and audio recordings of narratives, songs, etc. Research during this documentation project confirmed that Great Andamanese is the fifth language family of India (Abbi 2009).[1] Abbi and her team also collected oral histories, photos of local habitats, and sociolinguistic sketches representing local beliefs and knowledge of the biodiversity of the islands.

In this chapter we will examine the global phenomenon of language loss and address the following questions: What do we lose when a language disappears? What processes cause languages to fade and then disappear? What are linguists doing to mitigate language loss? We will also investigate why some language revitalization projects are more successful than others by examining the Maori, Irish Gaelic, Hebrew, and Basque revitalization projects.

THE NATURE OF LANGUAGE LOSS AND REVITALIZATION

In the fifteenth century, there were approximately 15,000 extant languages, but wars and ethnic conflicts, genocide, government suppression of languages, and colonial expansion and assimilation agendas destroyed half of these languages over the next five centuries (Sampat 2002). **Language loss** continues today, at an alarming rate: of the 250 indigenous languages spoken in Australia, 90 per cent are nearing extinction; many South American languages disappeared following the Spanish conquest; in Africa, 200 languages are endangered; and more than half of the indigenous languages in Asia have fewer than 10,000 speakers (Sampat 2002). Today, linguists speculate that it is English, the dominant language of the global economy and the Internet, which is the greatest threat to other languages.

In Europe, language loss is very much a reality. Manx, once spoken on the Isle of Man, became extinct in 1974, when its last speaker died. However, the language's demise was overstated, and today Manx is undergoing a revival, partly because the language was well recorded. On a less positive note, Ubykh, a language spoken in the Caucasus region and that had the highest number of consonants ever recorded, disappeared when Turkish farmer Tevfik Esenç died in 1992 (Haspelmath 1993). One of the Celtic languages, Cornish, began

---

1 Genetic studies also confirmed this hypothesis. Besides the four recognized language families of India – Indo-Aryan, Dravidian, Tibeto-Burman, and Austro-Asiatic – all other Indian languages had been classified as "Other" until this discovery.

its decline at the end of the nineteenth century. Several attempts to renew the language failed until 1995 when a new version of United Cornish was developed, and an English-Cornish dictionary was created in 2000 (Binion & Shook 2007). Today, some schools have developed language programs and produced children's books, films, and other media to continue the revitalization of the Cornish language.

In Asia, globalization has posed a serious challenge to many languages (Goswami 2003). South Asia possesses the greatest linguistic diversity on that side of the world; however, many languages have become extinct. The Tibeto-Burman language, Pyu, once spoken in Myanmar, is one example of an extinct language, as is Rangkas, a Western Himalayan language that survived into the twentieth century before dying out (van Driem 2007). According to Rujaya Abhakorn, historian at Chiang Mai University in Thailand, people in Southeast Asia consider English their pathway to economic success; thus, their heritage languages are falling out of use (Goswami 2003: n.p.).

Language loss continues in Asia, particularly among language isolates, which are "languages that have not been demonstrated to belong to any other major language family or linguistic phylum" (van Driem 2007: 305). Great Andamanese, reviewed earlier, is a language isolate, as is the Vedda language in Sri Lanka. Ryklof van Goens recorded this language in 1675, after which most Veddas became assimilated into Tamil- and Sinhalese-speaking populations, through intermarriage, government acculturation policies, or by adopting one of those other languages. Whether this language is completely extinct is unknown.

> "Our language has been ripped from the world, stripped of shape, smell, color and form, cleansed of the grit and graffiti, the rumpus and commotion that make up real life." Goenawan Mohamad, founding editor of the Jakarta-based *Tempo* newsmagazine, quoted in Goswami (2003: n.p.).

In North and South America the situation remains dire for indigenous languages. Only two of the 20 native Alaskan languages, Central Alaskan Yupik and Siberian Yupik, are still taught to children, meaning that all of the others will disappear when the adult speakers pass away. Fifty of 300 Central American languages and 110 of 400 South American languages are considered moribund, or no longer sustainable (Krauss n.d.). Efforts to revitalize these languages are ongoing, with differing degrees of success. Indigenous peoples in Canada are divided into three groups: First Nations,[2] Inuit, and Métis. First Nations peoples speak languages that belong to ten different families. Linguists estimate that somewhere between 300 and 500 First Nations languages were spoken before Europeans arrived in North America. Two hundred of these languages remain, although First Nations children learn only 34 of them as first languages (Krauss 1998). Indigenous languages in Canada are fragile, the only exceptions being Cree and Ojibwa in the Algonquian language family and Inuktitut in the Aleut-Eskimo language family. Yet even these vibrant languages are in decline as youth turn to English.

A dominant language is unlikely to become extinct, regardless of the number of speakers; however, it can happen. For example, Icelandic has 250,000 speakers and although not considered in imminent danger, even this language is threatened by the increasing use of English. On the other hand, Breton, formerly with a million speakers, is now struggling to survive following decades of suppression from the French government (Krauss n.d.). Navajo, an indigenous language of the southwestern United States, was thriving in the 1960s, with 200,000 speakers, but began to decline when the United States Bureau of Indian Affairs imposed English as the first language. Even the primary languages of the world

---

2 First Nations is the term used in Canada for indigenous peoples other than the Inuit and Métis.

TABLE 5.1 SCALE FOR THREATENED LANGUAGES

Stage One	Spoken within national government and in higher education.
Stage Two	Spoken at the local government level, and used by media in the community.
Stage Three	Spoken in business arenas and by employees in less specialized work areas.
Stage Four	Language of instruction in elementary schools.
Stage Five	Language still spoken in the community.
Stage Six	Spoken between generations, e.g., grandparents and grandchildren.
Stage Seven	Adults of second generation speak the language; their children do not.
Stage Eight	Only a few elders speak the language.

"When I was in school, we were beaten for speaking our language. They wanted to make us ashamed ... I have 17- and 18-year-old kids coming to me crying because the elders of their tribes won't teach them their own language." Marie Smith Jones, a full-blooded Alaskan Eyak, quoted in Raymond (1998: n.p.)

are not safe from decline. According to Černý (2010), German and Italian could be reduced by 10 per cent in the next 50 years, and Russian will also lose speakers because of the independence of former Soviet republics. However, Spanish and Portuguese will continue to grow as their populations grow in Europe and Latin America. Although France's population has peaked, French is still prestigious, and the country remains an economic, cultural, and military powerhouse; its strength outside France, however, for example in Canada and former French colonies, is open to question. As for English, no language rules forever.

Anthropologist Joshua Fishman (1991: 88–91) identified eight stages through which a language passes on its way to extinction (see Table 5.1). Language activists, with the assistance of linguists, have developed strategies to protect or preserve languages in all of these stages.

WHAT WE LOSE WHEN A LANGUAGE DISAPPEARS

The loss of linguistic diversity is of great concern to linguists. Losing a language causes an erosion of cultural and environmental knowledge about local plant and animal life because "information about local ecosystems is so intricately woven into these languages that it cannot be replaced simply through translation" (Swarthmore News 2012: n.p.). Abandoning indigenous or what are often called **heritage languages** causes a loss of culture

"Take [language] away from the culture, and you take away its greetings, its curses, its praises, its laws, its literature, its songs, its riddles, its proverbs, its cures, its wisdom, its prayers. ... You are losing all those things that essentially are the way of life, the way of thought, the way of valuing, and the human reality." (Fishman 1996: 81).

and **identity**, and is symptomatic of the loss of cultural diversity. Many indigenous languages are oral, which means losing their vocabularies is a form of cultural impoverishment; communities are deprived of their history, artistic expression (e.g., songs, poems), cultural and environmental knowledge, and human experience. Speech communities, and indeed the world, lose the unique identity and worldview attached to a language when it disappears.

As mentioned earlier, when a language disappears, so does a great deal of cultural knowledge. In central Siberia, Ket is an endangered language with fewer than 200 speakers in the upper Yenisei Valley. A Russian-only linguistic policy during the Soviet era led to the demise of this unique language, which has one of the most complex grammars ever documented by linguists. Indeed, the language "is filled with living links to their ancestors, their past, and their traditions" (Solash 2010: n.p.). The impact of losing Ket is incalculable. Indeed, early studies suggest that Ket may be related to Navajo. If this theory proves accurate, then Ket substantiates the theory of early migration from Asia to North America and extends the prevailing estimates of the scale of these human migrations.

Linguistic research has also raised the question of a language's influence on the way speakers think and develop cognitive skills. In the 1930s and 1940s, American linguists Edward Sapir and Benjamin Lee Whorf suggested that speakers of different languages perceived the world differently. Although the strong form of the Sapir-Whorf Hypothesis was ultimately rejected, recent linguistic research suggests that the way we think influences the way we speak, and vice versa. For example, teaching someone new colour words may change their ability to identify colours (Boroditsky 2011). Therefore, losing languages means we are losing diverse and perhaps crucial ways of thinking and solving problems.

REASONS FOR LANGUAGE LOSS

Reasons for language loss are complex, resulting from internal and external factors that reduce a language's use until it disappears. At the most basic level, if fewer and fewer young people are learning their heritage language each generation, it becomes moribund and then dies. In fact, a measure of the health of a language is whether the children are being taught their language at home. The second internal issue is the notion foisted on members of a speech community, especially children in school, that their language is inferior (Haynes 2010). They are shamed into speaking the dominant language and rejecting their own language. Language activists draw attention to the social inequalities and human-rights abuses that are at the root of this treatment. Therefore, internal socio-political factors, such as seeking social acceptance and inclusion, conforming to the norms of mainstream society, and the necessity of communicating with peers, may lead to rejection of a heritage language and a shift to the dominant language.

External factors also contribute to language loss. Earthquakes, floods, and other natural disasters can destroy a small speech community, as can drought and other environmental disasters that force people to move away, likely into a larger community with a different, often dominant language (Černý 2010). For example, in Kuala Lumpur, Malaysia, migration patterns made the Sindhis a linguistic minority and resulted in their having to learn English (Khemlani-David 1991).

Mass media, heavily favouring English, presents an ideal picture of English-speaking life that may spur indigenous people, especially youth, to abandon their way of life and their heritage languages (Ostler 2001). This immersion in English media plays a major role in weakening indigenous languages. To counter this external factor, linguists encourage local media, such as television programming, to help heritage languages gain visibility and prestige. In some cases communities and language activists have used web-based technology to save endangered languages. For example, Siletz-Dee-ni, an indigenous language in a small community in Oregon, began to decline in the mid-1850s when several cultural groups, speaking different languages and dialects, were placed on the same reservation (Munro 2012). To communicate, they began to use a Chinook jargon that displaced Siletz-Dee-ni. Fortunately, the language has been immortalized in a "talking dictionary" using one of the last surviving speakers, Bud Lane III, as the narrator. This talking dictionary now contains 14,000 words, and with the language on the Internet, young people in the community are beginning to learn the language – they even text in Siletz-Dee-ni. Other communities with endangered languages are also embracing social media – YouTube, Facebook, and websites – as a vehicle for saving their languages. For example, Microsoft programs have been translated into Inuktitut for the Inuit.

Language suppression is one of the ways in which states overpower minority cultures. Indeed, language loss has become synonymous with government assimilation policies (Baloy 2011). An historical example is the Nazi German attempt to destroy the Slovene culture by demanding the surrender of all Slovene books, even prayer books (Lemkin 1944). In the United States, powerful political and social processes promote English to the detriment of other languages: "To be American, one must speak English" (Fillmore 2000: 207). Speaking English represents social acceptance, loyalty to the American ideal, and provides economic opportunity. This changing language ideology creates an imbalanced contact situation where one group dominates politically, militarily, economically, and/or religiously (Yamamoto, Brenzinger, & Villalón 2008: 61).

Since language is so important to culture, the indigenous peoples of Canada worry that the nineteenth-century colonialist government assimilation policies that forced First Nations children to enrol in residential schools where only English was spoken may become a reality in the twenty-first century for several reasons. Many people are moving to urban centres where they need to use English to advance in school or find employment. Wilson & Peters (2005) liken urban First Nations people with global nomads in that they live and work in the city, but try to maintain close ties with their home nation. To counter logistical problems, the revitalization programs that have been developed in rural areas are being brought into the city to help First Nations people retain their language and reinforce linguistic ties with their home (Baloy 2011). Revitalizing indigenous languages in Canada has proven difficult because many rural linguistic enclaves are surrounded by English- or French-speaking people. Nonetheless, indigenous language curricula, educational programs, a national policy on heritage languages, and a recent renewal of passion for their heritage language among some indigenous youth all offer hope.

People choose to speak one language over another for social, economic, and political factors; this causes language shift. **Language shift** refers to speakers turning away from their heritage language and adopting another language, either by force or voluntarily (Nettle & Romaine 2000). Giving up a heritage language eventually leads to its extinction. Class, status, ethnicity, and outside influences, such as media and education, affect language and influence language shifts. For example, in Mexico, Spanish is most closely identified with literacy and academia (Francis & Nieto Andrade 1996: 167) and ultimately with higher socio-economic class. In a colonization situation, the smaller culture invariably must accommodate the dominant culture, and this is when language shift will most likely take place. Although there are 68 officially recognized indigenous languages in Mexico, and 364 distinct dialects, only six per cent of the population speaks any one of them; all others speak Spanish (Mexicoinsider.com 2008).

Irish Gaelic, also known as Erse, is an Indo-European language with an ancient history that has suffered drastic decline due to language shift. The shift began in the seventeenth century when Ireland was conquered by British forces (Laukaitis 2010) and English became the language of power. Irish Gaelic continued its decline during the Great Famine

(1845–52), when poor economic conditions forced many to migrate to English-speaking countries in search of work. This led parents to encourage their children to learn English in the hopes of future employment. Irish soon became stigmatized as the language of the poor. The Gaelic League was formed in 1893 to address the persistent decline of Irish Gaelic. The League began promoting Gaelic in the context of national unity; however, by 1901 only 14 per cent of the population still spoke Irish Gaelic (McMahon 2008).

The goal of the Gaelic League was to de-Anglicize Ireland (Laukaitis 2010), and the political underpinnings of this campaign demonized England and uplifted Ireland to create a nationalistic consciousness. As the twentieth century progressed, nationalism grew, and the Legion was able to establish Irish in schools. Unfortunately, their efforts were doomed because of the status and prestige English had acquired. Parents, leaders, and Catholic priests all approved of and promoted English. Without the community's support, therefore,

MAP 5.1 GAELTACHT REGION OF IRELAND

Irish Gaelic could not flourish. Today, less than 10 per cent of Irish people are fluent in Gaelic (GaelicMatters.com 2011); however, immersion courses are being established that may improve the language's position in the future.

LANGUAGE PRESERVATION AND REVITALIZATION PROJECTS

Linguistic anthropologist Akira Yamamoto (1998) has identified nine factors that can help save a language, including the need for speakers to possess a strong sense of ethnic identity, bilingual educational programs in school, and environments where speaking a heritage language is encouraged by teachers, parents, and community leaders (Ottenheimer 2009). In this environment, the dominant culture must support linguistic diversity, or any attempts to rejuvenate and protect a heritage language are doomed. UNESCO has played a vital role in mobilizing worldwide efforts and attention to save endangered languages (Gallegos, Murray, & Evans 2010). In 2001 UNESCO adopted the Universal Declaration of Cultural Diversity, calling on a participatory and collaborative approach to the documentation, maintenance, and revitalization of languages.

National Geographic, along with linguists David Harrison and Gregory Anderson, has launched the *Enduring Voices* project, which to date has created eight talking dictionaries with 32,000 word entries and more than 24,000 audio recordings from native speakers. One of the best documented languages is Tuvan, spoken in Siberia and Mongolia, with over 7,000 dictionary entries, 3,000 audio files, and 49 images. Even the Matukar Panau community in Papua New Guinea, which has approximately 600 speakers, knew about the Internet and requested that their language be put on the web, despite not having electricity in their community. Harrison and his team helped them create a "talking dictionary" (Messieh 2012). Harrison believes that going global with a language sends a powerful message of pride throughout the speech community, and provides heritage languages with increased status and prestige in the global linguistic community. Speakers, especially the younger ones, learn that their language is as good as any other language, including English (Munro 2012).

"Endangered language communities are adopting digital technology to aid their survival and to make their voices heard around the world. This is a positive effect of globalization." David Harrison, quoted in Gray (2012).

When the Māori language, te reo Māori, was in danger of extinction more than 30 years ago, elders and other community members developed immersion programs called *Te Kohanga reo*, which means "language nests." Language nests are immersion programs that teach very young children their heritage language. Elders are teamed with children to form these nests (Reyhner 1999). These community-based immersion education programs were key to the te reo Māori language's survival, and according to Fishman's eight-stage classification system, te reo Māori is now in stage one, with 150,000 speakers (Gallegos, Murray, & Evans 2010). This was not always the case.

By the mid-1800s, as a means to acculturate the Māori people, the colonialist government established English as the dominant language in New Zealand and the language that would be used in British schools. Te reo Māori was banned in schools as early as 1905. The Māori accepted this move, seeing English as a means to economic opportunity. Urbanization in the Second World War also eroded the Māori culture and furthered the decline of the Māori language. Māori people, especially the youth, had grown ashamed of their language, believing it was lower-class and uncouth. By 1985, only 12 per cent of the Māori could speak te reo Māori (Gallegos, Murray, & Evans 2010).

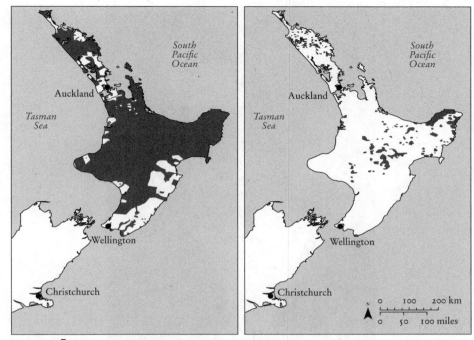

MAP 5.2 MĀORI TERRITORY IN 1860 AND 2000

In 1985, the Māori Language Board of Wellington filed a Treaty claim asking for te reo Māori to be declared an official language of Aotearoa, New Zealand. Their request was granted, and the Māori Language Act of 1987 established a Māori Language Commission to develop language policies and assist in the revitalization of the language. The Act placed te reo Māori on an even par with English, which went a long way toward improving the status of the language. The Māori people established hundreds of nursery schools, kindergartens, and day-care language nests using a curriculum consistent with Māori values. All subjects in the school were taught in te reo Māori, and the schools maintained close ties with families in the community. Today, the New Zealand government funds the language schools at the elementary and secondary levels (Gallegos, Murray, & Evans 2010).

Although the immersion programs have been a resounding success and the Māori children are thriving, all those involved recognize that in order for te reo Māori to flourish, the entire family and community must remain involved. To that end, Māori television programs have been established to strengthen the Māori voice. The language nest model has since been adopted around the world, including in Hawaii, where *Pūnana Leo* (language nest) immersion schools have been created.

Another amazing success story is that of Hebrew, a Semitic language belonging to the Afro-Asiatic language family. Though not spoken for 1,500 years,[3] except in liturgical rituals and scholarly pursuits, in the late nineteenth century scholar Eliezer Ben Yehudah led the

---

3 The number of years since Hebrew was last spoken varies widely, depending on the source.

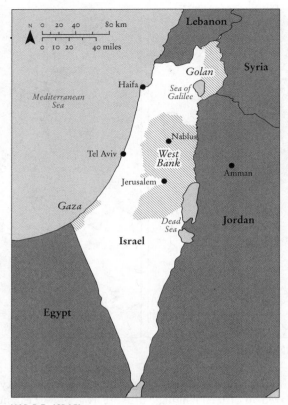

MAP 5.3 ISRAEL

revival of Hebrew (Krauss n.d.). Yehudah created 4,000 modern Hebrew words based on an-cient Hebrew roots. He wrote a dictionary for the language, beginning with carpentry terms for parents and kindergarten terms for children (Fishman 1996: 89). Some teachers learned the language and then passed it on to their students, who lived with them in the children's home on the kibbutz.[4] By 1916, 40 per cent of the adults and 75 per cent of the children used Hebrew as their first language, and in 1921 Hebrew became the official language of Israel (Nahir 1988: 289).

This revitalization project was a resounding success because the Hebrew language gave Jewish people a sense of unified identity (Krauss n.d.). However, the revival of Hebrew was not without controversy; some felt it was sacrilegious to use the sacred language in everyday life. Others point out that Modern Hebrew is not Classical Hebrew, but rather a hybrid language of both Semitic and Indo-European origin (Zuckermann & Walsh 2011). Despite the controversy and questions of true origin, Modern Hebrew remains the only successfully revived "clinically dead" language.

As has been the case with Israelis, struggles for autonomy and international rec-ognition are often struggles for linguistic survival. This is also true of the Basque people

---

4 In the Israeli kibbutzim, children do not live with their parents, but rather in an age-grade dormitory with caregivers/teachers.

who endured decades of political oppression and linguistic suppression of their language, Euskera. Euskera is an ancient language isolate. Though it was formerly used only in the domestic sphere and excluded from government, administration, and religious use, Euskera is thousands of years old (López-Goñi 2003).

During the rule of Franco (1936–75), Euskera was labelled vulgar, barbaric, uncouth, and animalistic, which shamed the Basque people. Only Castilian Spanish was allowed outside the home – Basque names could not even be placed on tombstones. This is a classic case of linguistic discrimination or **linguicism** – forbidding the use of a language and/or the intentional destruction of a language (Charny 1999: 9). In a backlash to this repression, the Basque people united around their language and it became a symbol of Basque identity (Krauss n.d.). Euskera provided the people with a platform from which to demand their rights to a cultural and linguistic identity (López-Goñi 2003: 671) as well as ideological and political freedom. After the end of the Franco regime, the Basque people therefore wanted to reinstate Euskera as a living language with national status.

The role of education in language survival should not be underestimated. *Ikastolas*, which are community-based schools, played a key role in revitalizing Euskera. Though Euskera was outlawed and the schools disappeared under Franco, they were revived in the 1960s. These semi-clandestine schools became a haven for Basque people, creating a cultural space that supported their language (Fishman 1996: 89). Parents enrolled their children in *ikastolas* because of the identity the children gained through the Basque language, and because they did not want their children to endure the Franco-era schooling they had experienced (López-Goñi 2003). Today, *ikastolas* are mixed infant schools set up in local villages. In some of these schools, children

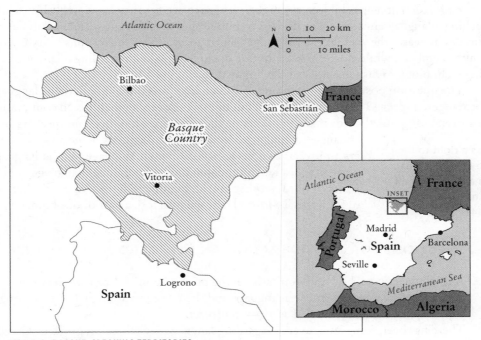

MAP 5.4 BASQUE-SPEAKING TERRITORIES

"To choose to use a language is an act of identity or belonging to a particular community. We believe the choice to be who one wishes to be is a human right." (Nettle & Romaine 2000: 174)

are taught in Euskera, while in others they are taught Euskera itself. The schools are run by parents, with assistance from young people, community members, and teachers. *Ikastolas* thus became a symbol of Basque nationality and a social microcosm, and the participation of community members in the education of their children helped revive Euskera and the Basque identity.

CONCLUSION

Fishman (1996: 82) calls language the mind, the soul, and the spirit of the people. Yet thousands of languages are in imminent danger of extinction. Language loss and the ensuing linguistic homogenization is a global process, fuelled by the increasing use of dominant languages in economic transactions, communications, and transportation, at the expense of heritage languages. This loss of linguistic diversity is a loss for us all, and one that all of us, as global citizens, should resist. The human species needs linguistic diversity as much as biological diversity because languages express identity, are repositories of history, and preserve millions of years of accumulated knowledge.

Globalization and homogenizing forces, including English-only education policies, are a serious challenge to linguists and to the communities where endangered languages are spoken. The revitalization of Irish Gaelic was not a success because the community felt English would be of more benefit for their children, whereas Euskara, te reo Māori, and Hebrew revitalization projects were successful because they symbolized group identity.

Protecting and revitalizing heritage languages requires community effort – parents, teachers, and leaders, as well as linguists, need to be involved in the process. Parents are vital in supporting and strengthening their children's heritage-language skills in the home. This reinforcement helps children retain their language even as they learn English at school. Teaching a language in schools or using it in public spaces such as government offices and churches increases the visibility and prestige of a language, and is the responsibility of community members, while the responsibility for documenting and recording a language, and using technology to disperse it, lies with linguists.

The question posed at the beginning of this chapter was this: "Are heritage languages an endangered species?" The answer is yes, but this does not mean that speech communities are surrendering quietly. For many speakers or those who wish to become speakers of an endangered language, working with linguists, educators, and others to preserve or revitalize their own language, or the languages of others, has taken on paramount importance. Language is like a window onto another world, another way of living, another way of thinking. To lose a language is to lose a part of our humanity.

"Every people has a right to their own language, to preserve it as a cultural resource and to transmit it to their children." (Nettle & Romaine 2000: 14)

QUESTIONS FOR CONSIDERATION AND CLASSROOM ACTIVITIES

1. As a global citizen, how can you assist in the preservation and/or revitalization of an endangered language? Choose a language and then design a strategy for protecting it. This activity is best completed as a group project.
2. There has been some controversy regarding language revitalization projects. Critics suggest that if there were only one world language, there would be more unity and

communication between nations, and commerce would flow more freely. How important do you think speaking a heritage language is? What would we lose and what would we gain if we had one world language?

3. Trace the linguistic journey of a dominant language. Now trace the linguistic journey of an isolate. How are they different, and how are they the same?

4. Create a map of the linguistic hotspots on a continent of your choosing. How many of these endangered languages are undergoing revival?

5. "Speak English!" seems to have become a crusade for some North Americans. How would you feel if people in your adoptive country treated you with disrespect because you had not learned their language yet? What impact would their insistence that you give up your native language and speak only their language have on your identity and well-being?

6. The Sapir-Whorf Hypothesis suggests that the way we think influences the way we speak, and vice versa. To delve into this theory in more detail, consider prejudiced or culturally insensitive language. If people make a concerted effort not to use insensitive language – language that will hurt people – will it make them more culturally sensitive? First, use yourself as the subject for your investigation, and then consider children. If a child grows up in a home where derogatory or prejudiced statements are never made against another group of people, will that child grow up to be less prejudiced? If a child constantly hears negative comments about people who are different, will they grow up bigoted? Use this topic for a class discussion once all of you have investigated it on your own.

SUGGESTED READINGS

Crystal, D. (2000). *Language death*. Cambridge UK: Cambridge University Press. http://dx.doi.org/10.1017/CBO9781139106856

David Crystal addresses the fundamental question, "Why is language death so important?" in a readable, concise analysis. He presents the crisis of endangered languages but also reviews the projects and programs being developed to preserve and revitalize endangered languages. One of the highlights of this book is the "personal" examination of languages that are dying and what this means to the communities.

Harrison, K.D. (2008). *When languages die: The extinction of the world's languages and the erosion of human knowledge*. Oxford: Oxford University Press.

K. David Harrison addresses what humans lose when a language is lost from a global perspective. Of particular relevance is the cultural and environmental knowledge that we lose. This book contains anecdotes and portraits of the last remaining speakers of some of these languages. Up-to-date, it is a fascinating read.

Chapter 6

Body Image: How Does Body Image Affect Identity and Status, and How Has the Transnational Flow of Western Ideals of Beauty Impacted Other Cultures?

Key Terms: body dissatisfaction, body image, body modification, body politics, cultural identity, cyberpunks, eating disorders, ethnicity, fatness, globalization, Modern Primitives, queer subculture, ritual, self-discrepancy theory, social comparison theory, symbolic capital

INTRODUCTION

"You can never be too rich or too thin." Wallis Simpson, Duchess of Windsor, quoted in Feminism and Women's Studies (2012).

The perfect body – what does this mean? Is it a size-two woman with an impossibly small waist and large breasts, or a woman whose neck has been artificially elongated with brass rings? Is it a man with bulging muscles and a flat stomach, or a man covered with intricate scarification? Every society has its own image of beauty, and in every society, men and women are, to a certain extent, defined by their body image. In North America, tall, blond, thin women continue to represent the body ideal. This narrow, "Barbie-doll" beauty standard is perpetuated by media – television, magazines, and the Internet glamorize thinness and equate it with perfection. Women are inundated with advertisements for Botox, cosmetic surgery, diets, exercise equipment, and "self-help" programs that feature ways to "improve" their appearance – what Nichter and Vuckovic (1994) call "body work."

Despite some rather convoluted psychological definitions, quite simply **body image** is the way we think our body looks, and how we think our body *should* look – a mental image of an ideal body that is culturally constructed (van Esterik 2001: 20) and learned from birth. In this chapter we will investigate the social, economic, and cultural influences that perpetuate an ideal body image. The transnational flow of people and ideas is spreading Western perceptions of beauty to other countries, resulting in many of the same body-image issues as seen in the West. Indeed, Western perceptions of the ideal body have resulted in global anxiety about personal appearance and body image. We will consider the consequences of this **globalization** of the West's body image, and the ensuing changes in identity, drawing on expertise within various fields of medicine, psychology, sociology, and anthropology.

Obsession with the ideal body has led many women and men to feel inadequate and dissatisfied with their bodies. **Body dissatisfaction** refers to "a negative self-evaluation of

71

one's own appearance and desire to be more physically attractive" (Cash & Pruzinsky 2002, quoted in Ferguson et al. 2011: 458). Language may also reflect body image. Nichter and Vuckovic (1994) commonly encountered the phrase "I'm so fat" during their ethnographic research on body image and dieting among adolescent North American girls. This "ritualized talk" signals unhappiness, a call for peer support, and apology for bad behaviour. The consequences of body image dissatisfaction and the risky behaviour that young people engage in to reach their image of the ideal body is of increasing concern. The psychological and physical problems that can result from body dissatisfaction will be addressed in this chapter, including the increase in eating disorders in many societies.

Not all cultural groups agree with the North American perception of beauty, however, especially the view that a thin woman's body is ideal. In some non-Western cultures, the body is considered a means for women to carry out social, economic, and reproductive roles. For a very different perspective on the ideal body, we will explore the concept of "fatness" as symbolic capital among the Tuareg of northern Niger and northern Mali. **Body politics** and power relations, including identity, ethnicity, class, gender, and sexuality have become important themes in the study of the human condition, from the quest for women's rights to self-expression and activism communicated through body modification. We will explore body modification practices as they are used to defy oppression and assert sexuality, identity, and political resistance in the queer, cyberpunk, and Modern Primitive subcultures.

THE NATURE OF BODY IMAGE

In *The Body Image Trap*, psychologist Marion Crook (1991) defines the perfect female body as tall, blond, and size 10 – an outdated image, considering that most twenty-first-century North American women preoccupied with thinness would be horrified to reach a size 10. According to the **self-discrepancy theory** (Higgins 1987), everyone has an image of their ideal self, and of an ideal self they believe others want them to be. If they cannot achieve this ideal (e.g., smaller than a size 10), they feel disappointment, leading to lower self-esteem.

The pursuit of thinness among women is a highly valued behaviour, especially in Western countries, and even though there are other places where thinness is preferred, anthropologist C. Counihan (1999) has never encountered a local culture where it is acceptable to starve oneself to become thin, and contends that the self-destructive relationship that many Western women have with their bodies differs from that of women in non-Western cultures.

Hesse-Biber (1996) likens the quest for thinness to a religious cult, with all the requisite characteristics – isolation, obsession, and excessive **ritual** (dieting, exercise, daily weigh-ins, and calorie counting). The media and entertainment industry provides icons to worship (e.g., Jennifer Aniston) and ceremonies, such as beauty pageants, to reaffirm the ideal. Diet clubs (e.g., Weight Watchers), sages (e.g., Dr. Atkins), and gurus (e.g., Oprah Winfrey) often take on a quasi-religious connotation. It is difficult to shed the attitude that the perfect body and weight are not important when shows such as *Entertainment Tonight* (CBS) feature at least one and sometimes several vignettes on a celebrity's rising or falling weight on every program. Consequently, weight loss and cosmetic surgery have become big business as women struggle to emulate the North American ideal body. Women with bodies outside the ideal often suffer from society's disapproval and become marginalized. They experience difficulty finding jobs and are considered lazy and lacking in self-discipline and will power (witness the TV show *The Biggest Loser*).

Ethnicity may also play a role in body image (Kawamura 2002). Western media tend to stereotype the features of minority groups, and seldom use them as role models to exemplify beauty. Discrimination based on physical characteristics can be harmful to self-esteem, leading young people to dislike the physical features they inherited. For example, Gillen and Lefkowitz (2011) found that Latino American women, like Euro-American individuals, compared their bodies to others and desired thinner bodies, believing that men preferred slim women.

According to the **social comparison theory** (Gillen & Lefkowitz 2011), body image (negative or positive) is shaped by the way others see us or the way we think they see us. Kaplan-Myrth (2000) discovered that even visually impaired individuals are self-conscious about their appearance, despite not being able to see their own image: they find their body image through the eyes of friends and family around them. The most powerful influence on body dissatisfaction, then, is peer pressure and criticism (Ferguson et al. 2011), although media images of idealized body types may contribute to a sense of inferiority. Peer influences can be active (a conversation with peers about the ideal body, or bullying because of appearance) or passive (the presence of competition). Indeed, the Ferguson et al. study found that body dissatisfaction increased in the presence of competitive females, especially if an attractive male was present. Therefore, from an evolutionary perspective, body dissatisfaction is one ramification of females competing for males. Other studies have found that individuals respond to media hype in different ways, although women who already suffer from body dissatisfaction are more influenced by media ideals of female beauty (Trampe, Stapel, & Siero 2007).

The ideal body image is culturally defined (Sault 1994). For example, Chinese foot binding involved bending the toes under the sole, and making a pointed front – arching the foot like a small hook (Ping 2000). This practice was popular in tenth-century China and for a thousand years afterward, but it eventually faded out when Mao Zedong and the Cultural Revolution transformed China's political and social environment. Most North Americans find foot binding cruel, yet this symbol of traditional Chinese femininity and beauty[1] is remarkably similar to the current Western practice of young women undergoing breast augmentation, or the historical practice of wearing a tightly cinched and physically damaging corset. In a similar example, the Kayan women of northern Thailand wear brass neck coils that reduce their clavicle and create an image of an elongated neck. This body modification gives women their **cultural identity** and sense of beauty (Mirante 2006). In Vietnam, the newly infused Westernized perception of an ideal height lies at the root of a dangerous fad – leg-lengthening surgeries (Cudd 2005). This new body image has even influenced employment opportunities; some companies have set height restrictions and will

> "Fat people are simultaneously invisible and derided for possessing several negative characteristics, thrust upon them by virtue of how they look on the outside." (Kenlie 2011).

> "We urban, Jewish, black, Asian and Latina girls began to realize slowly and painfully that if you didn't look like Barbie, you didn't fit in. Your status was diminished. You were less beautiful, less valuable, less worthy. If you didn't look like Barbie, companies would discontinue you. You simply couldn't compete" (Gilman 1998: 236).

---

1 Foot binding also served to isolate and control women since they were unable to walk very far from home.

FIGURE 6.1 MEDIA PORTRAYAL OF YOUNG, BEAUTIFUL, "PERFECT" WOMEN HAS LED MANY WOMEN TO FEEL INADEQUATE

not hire individuals who do not fit within this ideal height. Some Asian women are even resorting to cosmetic surgery to remove their epicanthic folds and create a double eyelid to meet Western standards of beauty.

Although body image dissatisfaction is more prevalent among women, this pattern is not restricted by age or gender – both males and females are concerned with their appearance and expend enormous time, energy, and money in achieving the perfect body. Hesse-Biber (1996), for example, found that men are also concerned about their weight. This body dissatisfaction has opened up a huge market for weight-loss programs, exercise equipment, health spas, and various men's products. The strategy appears to be working, because the rate of body dissatisfaction among men is increasing.

The first recorded weight-loss program took place in 1558, when Italian Luigi Coronaro ate sparingly to change his overall health. He became thin and energetic, and his writings on the value of "dieting" convinced others to try losing weight to improve their health (Crook 1991). The Western obsession with thinness began in the 1960s, in part due to media adulation of British fashion model Twiggy. Before this time, the ideal woman was full figured and healthy looking, signifying her ability to bear children. Then Twiggy appeared, and the desperate quest for thinness began. At about the same time, Barbie, the fashion doll, appeared on store shelves. This doll inspired young girls and women to strive for her impossible-to-emulate beauty standard – what Gilman (1998) calls the Barbie doll syndrome.

> "You're busted, Babs. You've been found guilty of inspiring fourth-grade girls to diet, of modeling an impossible beauty standard, of clinging to homogeneity in a diverse new world." (Edut 1998: 1)

Despite their symbolism, Barbie and Twiggy were merely physical manifestations of the fashionable emphasis on thinness, at a time when other equally significant socio-cultural transformations were taking place. During the 1960s, young women were being inundated with conflicting demands that created an identity crisis (Bruch 1978). New education and career opportunities conflicted with women's traditional roles as nurturers and homemakers, thereby creating confusion and a feeling of powerlessness (Gordon 2000) that eventually led to a rise in eating disorders.

EATING DISORDERS

Body image is about power. Brumberg (1989) found that fasting is one of the few forms of protest available to young women who may feel powerless in other aspects of their lives. Sociologist Hesse-Biber (1996) agrees, noting that refusing to eat offers a sense of empowerment – a way for women to gain control and autonomy over their lives. Fasting is also symptomatic of a concern for virtue, of feelings of being unlovable, and of a desire to improve self-esteem by losing weight (Mackenzie 1991). With the reduction in women's domestic roles as mothers and housewives and the splintering of kinship networks, women's social roles and status have changed, and attractiveness has become a measure and mechanism for success (Littlewood 2004).

North American children as young as seven are aware of whether eating a particular food will make them fat, and judge their self-worth according to their body size. This all-consuming desire to achieve a perfect body has led to serious psychological, socio-cultural, economic, and health consequences in the West and, increasingly, in other parts of the world. **Eating disorders** are symptomatic of cultural expectations and revolve around identity issues and body image (Gordon 2000). Anorexia nervosa, the avoidance of food to the point of starvation, and bulimia, binge eating followed by self-induced vomiting, are two of the most common eating disorders (Holmberg 1998). So prevalent have these eating disorders become, that "pro-ana" sites on the Internet provide tips for losing weight and encourage young people to be as thin as possible.

FIGURE 6.2 THIS EXTENSIVE COLLECTION OF BARBIE DOLLS SYMBOLIZES NOT ONLY AN IMPOSSIBLE-TO-ACHIEVE STANDARD OF BEAUTY BUT ALSO OUR OBSESSION WITH HER TYPE OF BEAUTY

Eating disorders are shaped by social and cultural phenomena (Pike & Borovoy 2004), meaning they arise because of unique cultural experiences stemming not from a fear of fatness, but from a fear of loss of control (Lee 2001). Risk factors for developing eating disorders include being female or an adolescent, experiencing rapidly changing social conditions, and living in Western countries. Changing gender roles and beauty ideals have impacted women in Japan, for example, where the incidence of eating disorders and an obsession with thinness has been

> "When I'm out of control of my eating and my weight, I'm out of control of my life!" (Mackenzie 1991: 408)

"Anorexia nervosa (and other eating disorders) is not really about losing weight, eating or not, exercising like a maniac or not, it is about self-esteem, it is about how you feel about yourself." Judy, a recovering anorexic (Sargent n.d.).

increasing throughout the twentieth century (Pike & Borovoy 2004). Japanese women have been exposed to Western ideals of beauty, while also having to deal with Japanese cultural values and changing gender role expectations and social pressures in Japanese culture and society.

The "Thin Commandments"

If you aren't thin, you're ugly.
Being thin is way more important than being healthy.
You must do anything to make yourself look thinner.
Thou shall not eat without feeling guilty.
Thou shall not eat fattening foods without punishing yourself accordingly.
Thou shall always count calories.
The scale is everything.
Losing = Life, Gaining = Death
You must become thin.
Being thin and perfect are signs of true determination (*Anorexia 10* 2006).

In Florence, Italy, Florentines view the body as a source of pleasure and a reflection of family. Both men and women love food and love to eat and nurture their bodies. Though they enjoy eating, Florentines also believe in control – gluttony destroys the pleasure of eating and leads to obesity. Thus, Florentines believe in "enjoying food greatly but consuming it moderately" (Counihan 1999: 182). Unlike North Americans, who may feel guilty after a day of overeating and resort to strenuous exercise and dieting, Florentines do not. A plump body signifies health and fertility, while a thin body may mean illness or emotional upset. Despite their healthy relationship with food and their bodies, Western influence is seeping into Italian consciousness. Florentine women are being bombarded with North American images of thin women, which are affecting the way young Florentine women view themselves. Counihan (1999) also found that eating disorders in Italy were on the upswing by the 1990s.

"We now have damning evidence from Fiji of the impact of Western ideals of beauty where, in a three-year period after the introduction of TV (mainly US programmes), 15 per cent of the teenage girls developed bulimia. The penetration of Western images coupled with an economic onslaught, had destabilised Fijian girls' sense of beauty, infecting them with a virus more lethal than the measles Britain exported to the colonies 100 years ago." (Orbach 2001: 1)

In many Asian countries, plumpness was once a sign of prosperity, good health, and beauty. Recent studies have shown that this is no longer the case; the North American quest for thinness has reached these societies too (Kawamura 2002). In Latino cultures, Western ideals of thinness have led to a dramatic increase in eating disorders – girls in private schools in Brazil, for example, have adopted Western body ideals, leading to abuse of laxatives and diuretics (Altabe & O'Garo 2002). It appears the more acculturated a group becomes to North American values, the more body dissatisfaction they experience. Even in relatively isolated regions, Western influences are being felt. In Samoa, feeding the body to make it plump is a sign of social success. However, as Brewis (1999) discovered, those Samoans living in an urban setting in Auckland, New Zealand, and thus more exposed to Western ideals, possessed slimmer body ideals than those still living in Samoa.

THE CONCEPT OF "FATNESS"

Although this discussion has focused on North American body image and the spread of this ideal to other cultures, the pressures to conform to a certain body image are not the sole domain of Westerners. Southeastern Nigerians consider curvaceous women the ideal. They see a plump woman as healthy, her family as prosperous, and her sexuality as alluring (Simmons 1998). To that end, young women undergo an age-old rite of passage when they are isolated in a fattening room, fed forcefully to gain weight, and instructed in the ways of a proper wife and mother. The age when girls enter the fattening room varies, from as young as seven to just before marriage. The general guideline is the bigger the better, although today most families can afford to support their daughters in the fattening room for only a few months rather than the traditional two years.

In the northern regions of Niger and northern Mali, female **fatness** is also valued; however, changing political and economic conditions and patterns of settlement have affected this idealized body image. The Tuareg are a socially stratified Muslim people living in the Sahara. In former times, adolescent females of noble families underwent fattening rituals in their mothers' tents before marriage; however, conflicts and droughts have reduced the prosperity in these regions, leading to a decline in the fattening ritual.

Anthropologist Susan J. Rasmussen[2] (2010) explored the changing meanings of female fatness and the ambivalence that some Tuareg now feel toward body fat. Rasmussen compared two communities, one a nomadic group practising pastoral transhumance, the other, agropastoralists settled on an oasis. Rasmussen analyzed the cultural, medical, and psychosocial meanings of body image and body politics, and how attitudes have changed over time.

Contemporary Tuareg noble women still feel pressure to gain weight in order to earn prestige and identity, to appear healthy and fertile, and to maintain a separation from women of lower status. This is particularly true of the nomadic community. Fatness is symbolic of aristocratic status and a sign of social strength (Bourdieu 1977). "Soft" fat, from eating milk and meat, symbolizes purity, happiness, and abundance, while hard muscles are associated with physical labour and having to eat grains. In the more sedentary oasis community, attitudes toward female fatness are more ambivalent; some still value fatness, while others feel it interferes with the physical labour necessary for farming. Tuareg women in the oasis gardening community work hard to become an economic asset to their husbands. This presents what Rasmussen (2010) calls a double-bind dilemma for the women: refrain from heavy work and gain weight, but risk their husbands acquiring more wives to do the work; work hard and risk becoming too thin, infertile, and unattractive to their husbands, who will then take younger wives.

The conjugal and reproductive roles of women are very important in Tuareg society. Traditionally, a woman's role in the matrilineal nomadic pastoral community was as a

---

2 All information on the Tuareg is taken from Rasmussen (2010) unless otherwise noted.

FIGURE 6.3 AMONG THE TUAREG, BODY FAT IS HIGHLY VALUED

mother and educator of Tuareg children, while in the oasis community, where matriliny is weakening, men have become the educators, and emphasis is now placed on women's fertility. Fear of hunger also accounts for the value placed on bodily fat; however, Rasmussen cautions that the fat aesthetic holds many other meanings, especially since status from fatness applies only to noble women. Female fatness also signifies a man's role as a productive husband, father, and son-in-law to his affines. Therefore, the condition of a woman's body represents a man's economic success or failure.

"Fatness envelops and comforts women, fortresslike, in 'layers' of protection, from several dangers: literal hunger; diminution of prestige and self-respect of noble, mother and wife and, also, violence and hunger." (Rasmussen 2010: 632)

Thus, cultural, social, and economic processes encourage attitudes and meanings assigned to fatness. In both communities, fatness is a sign of mastery of cultural and political-economic challenges, and represents **symbolic capital**. Fatness is considered a sign of free choice, independence, and prestigious social and gender status. Among the nomadic herders, fatness represents prosperity and freedom from heavy physical labour. The Tuareg believe that not eating enough decreases sexual appetite; therefore, a woman eating well and growing fat increases her sexuality and fertility. In the oasis, on the other hand, women would prefer to be fat, but physical labour prevents them from gaining weight. As well, many members of this community now disdain fat because it impedes the physical labour necessary for oasis gardening and cereal processing. Despite this ambivalence toward female fatness and labour, psychologically the ideal body image still remains that of a fat woman.

BODY MODIFICATION

Body modification is the alteration of body parts in a non-medical way, most typically through tattooing, piercing, and cutting, but can also involve scarification, branding, and implants. Although some body modifications (e.g., tattoos and piercings) have gained acceptance in mainstream society, many of the practices still remain neo-tribal – the domain of indigenous cultures. Among the Rashaayda Bedouin of eastern Sudan, tattooing is used to communicate identity and symbolize relations with others. Rashiidy women tattoo their bodies in three places: the forearms, the lower half of the face, and the upper legs and thighs (Young 1994). Arm tattoos are merely decorative, while face and leg tattoos are private symbols reserved for the eyes of their loved ones. An unmarried girl may have her thigh tattooed with a man's camel brand to announce her love for him. Only the women's husbands will ever see the tattoos because their faces are covered with veils and their legs with long skirts.

> "Amidst an almost universal feeling of powerlessness to 'change the world,' individuals are changing what they do have power over: their own bodies." (Vale & Juno 1989: n.p.)

According to sociologist Victoria Pitts (2003: 21), body modification is still considered outside normal behaviour and a social problem, thereby encouraging the development of body-modification subcultures. Indeed, body modification performed with others may create a sense of community, empowering the performers and fostering feelings of self-assertion. Body modification, then, provides a means for coping with stress and a way of expressing resistance to mainstream society for those who are or feel they are marginalized.

For female body modifiers, modification is a way to reclaim their bodies, often in response to sexual abuse or violence, and a way of contesting patriarchy. This body modification also challenges androcentric, racist, and classist concepts of beauty and body image. Thus, body modification should be viewed as a feminist, cultural, and political act (Klesse 2007: 277) that gives voice to the marginalized.

This holds true in **queer subculture**, where body modification expresses and symbolizes resistance to oppression and marginalization in modern society. The most prominent forms of body modification among queers are piercing, branding, cutting, tattooing, stretching, various forms of surgery, and body alterations for BDSM[3] and fetish play. Body modification articulates queer identity and is an expression of rebellion or disobedience (Klesse 2007). This transgression is often sexual among queers, exceeding the boundaries of permissible or imaginable behaviour in the eyes of mainstream society (Jenks 2003). Body modification, then, contests heteronormativity – behaviour norms that place people in a society's "normal" gender identities (e.g., men and women). By provoking shock with their distinctive tattoos, scars, and brandings, queer body modifiers emphasize the symbolism of the body (Pitts 2000) and challenge mainstream concepts of beauty.

Modern Primitives are a small countercultural movement that originated in the 1970s and 1980s in the United States and continues to grow in popularity (Klesse 2007). These white, middle-class individuals adopted neo-tribal rituals and practices, such as the traditional Sun Dance of Plains First Nations, which involves hanging from piercings in the chest muscles and requires displays

> "All sensual experience functions to free us from 'normal' social restraints, to awaken our deadened bodies to life." Vale & Juno (1989), quoted by Bonetti (n.d.) in a review of *Modern Primitives* (1989).

---

3 Bondage and Discipline, Dominance and Submission, Sadism and Masochism.

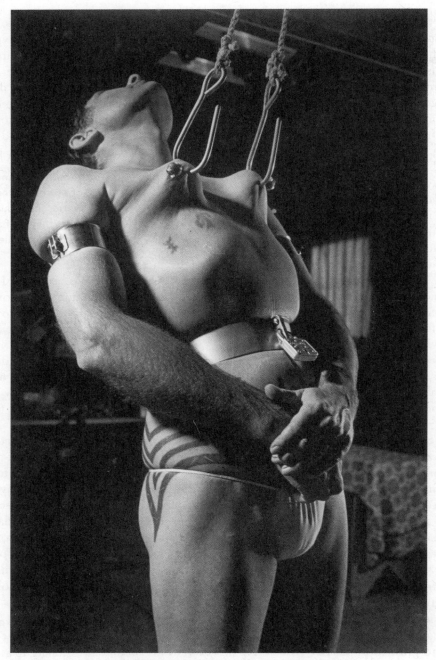

FIGURE 6.4 MODERN PRIMITIVES EMULATE TRIBAL BODY-MODIFICATION RITUALS

of stoicism and bravery. These rituals signify "spiritual enhancement, sexual liberation and embodied cultural dissidence" (Klesse 2007: 279). Modern Primitives attempt to "rescue the body and self from the problems of the world" (Pitts 2003: 3). Therefore, this group is using body modification to stretch cultural boundaries of what is appropriate to display in public.

There are also socio-economic implications from this movement, since modern "primitive-ness" has become trendy, with some members of mainstream society, especially youth, becoming consumers of Modern Primitives' lifestyle and ritual.

Cyberpunks, a high-tech counterculture, use implants and technological invasion of the body (e.g., prosthetics) to create hybrid humans or "cyborgian bodies" (Pitts 2003: 152). Like the Modern Primitives, cyberpunks have cyber-communities of body modifiers and ezines to maintain communication. Cyberculture and its dystopian view of the near future are growing in popularity, especially among curious youth who feel disenfranchised from society. Although body modification is an important component of cyberpunk counterculture, science-fiction literature featuring dystopian futures, where machines rule and human life has been devalued, is also a hallmark of this counterculture.

"The magnetic implant is not the most sophisticated or rich sensation, it was just the easiest to implement with our available technology." Unidentified cyberpunk following implant of a small magnet in his thumb (Cyberpunkreview.com 2006)

These three examples of body modifiers – queer, Modern Primitive, and cyberpunk – use the body as a place of resistance and empowerment. The body, then, becomes a site of social, political, and cultural contestation for marginalized people (Pitts 2003).

CONCLUSION

The ideal body, body image, body modification – these are all concepts that symbolize the quest for identity and acceptance. Human identity and sense of belonging are revealed through body image; men and women are willing to endure all sorts of inconvenience and discomfort to attain the ideal body in order to earn the status and approval of their society. Thus, body image, and by association the ideal body, are cultural constructs.

Over the last half-century, Westerners, particularly women, have developed a distorted sense of the ideal body that has created emotional and physical problems. Eating disorders have increased dramatically since the 1960s, especially in North America and Western Europe. Young people the world over are adopting the Western ideal of beauty and developing similar body-image problems and eating disorders. However, culture is dynamic, and even the obsession with thinness may be shifting; for example, Israeli authorities have banned thin models from the runway in the hopes of reducing the exposure of young girls to extreme thinness (*The Talk* 2012).

A continuing theme in this chapter has been the influence of culture and the social relations within a culture on body image. As is obvious, North American society stresses thinness as the ideal body. In other cultures, health and childbearing capabilities are the ideal. Among the Tuareg, fatness is a symbol of beauty, prosperity, and high status, and represents a woman's value as a mother and educator – fatness, not thinness, becomes symbolic capital.

Body modification is often used to signify resistance to the status quo. Countercultural movements such as the Modern Primitives use body modification as a medium for expressing their discontent and to create a sense of belonging with other body modifiers. Body image, the different forms of body modification, and the many meanings of "the ideal body" are complex issues embedded in body politics and power relations. Ultimately, this chapter reflects culture change at work, impacting personal and cultural identity through the transnational flow of ideas, values, and perceptions, and internally changing political, economic, and social systems.

QUESTIONS FOR CONSIDERATION AND CLASSROOM ACTIVITIES

1. The transnational flow of the Western ideal of beauty to other parts of the world is affecting young women's sense of well-being. Choose a country and investigate the influence of Western body ideals on people's perceptions of beauty and how they have responded to these changes.
2. How prevalent are eating disorders in your network of friends and family? Identify the symptoms and behaviours of someone with an eating disorder.
3. Class debate: How thin is too thin? Should models be forced to maintain a healthy weight? Should employers have the right to fire employees (e.g., cocktail waitresses, flight attendants), if they gain weight?
4. Conduct an in-depth study of a counterculture that uses body modification. What are the underlying reasons for their rejection of so-called mainstream behaviour?
5. Debate question: Eating disorders appear to be on the increase in developed countries. What are the likely mechanisms for this phenomenon? While these disorders are rising in prevalence around the world, is it possible that their incidence could be levelling off or even declining in the West, and why?
6. Is the knowledge that the ideal body is a cultural construct with global implications and little basis in reality of any help to you as you form your own body image?

SUGGESTED READINGS

Edut, O. (Ed.). (1998). *Adios, Barbie: Young women write about body image and identity*. Seattle: Seal Press.

A delightful collection of cross-cultural essays that consider the social impact of the Barbie doll. The young women featured in this book show little interest in resembling a Barbie doll, yet they address many of the body-image concerns and issues faced by women in our global society.

Nasser, M., Katzman, M.A., & Gordon, R.A. (Eds.). (2001). *Eating disorders and cultures in transition*. New York: Routledge.

An exploration of the cross-cultural factors in eating disorders in South America, Asia, Africa, and Eastern Europe. This book examines culture change and its impact on emotional issues.

Chapter 7

Same-Sex Marriage: What Are the Socio-Economic, Religious, and Political Implications of Same-Sex Marriage and Changing Family Structure?

Key Terms: cultural imperialism, culture change, family, feminist/queer critics, lesbian and gay assimilationists, gender identity, marriage, same-sex marriage, social conservatives

---

INTRODUCTION

"Being denied a marriage licence suggests that Mike and I do not love each other, and that our hopes, our dreams, our life together do not exist. Mike and I, while supposedly equal citizens of this great country, are deemed non-persons, because we are gay." Affidavit from Michael Leshner, quoted in Egale Canada (2011).

On June 28, 2005, the Canadian parliament passed Bill C-38, and Canada became the fourth country in the world to legalize same-sex marriages. The Bill changed the definition of marriage to a union between two people rather than between a man and a woman. The long battle leading up to this historic vote was both disturbing and divisive. The struggle for same-sex marriage rights came to a head in 2003, when Ontario's Court of Appeal ruled that the current Canadian definition of marriage was unconstitutional. This opened the door for gays and lesbians to legally marry and signalled a Western shift in acceptance of same-sex marriage.

The politicization of marriage is not a new phenomenon; indeed, societal rules and restrictions have been a part of marriage systems for a very long time. In the West, state authorities have increasingly weighed in on issues of family and private life (Baskerville 2006). Changes in family structure, such as the rise of single-parent families, have increased the political influence on what used to be a private matter, and now the cacophony surrounding the legalization of gay and lesbian marriages has pushed the debate into the larger political sphere. Religious opposition, although political in nature as well, has also been vocal in its objection to same-sex marriage on moral grounds.

Same-sex marriage is the marriage of two people who are of the same biological sex. The contested issues surrounding same-sex marriage are complex. First, religious and social conservatives morally object to homosexuality as a lifestyle. Second, there is strong opposition from many walks of life to changing the "traditional" definition of **marriage** as between a man and a woman. Third,

"This is about the Charter of Rights. We are a nation of minorities. And in a nation of minorities, it is important that you don't cherry-pick rights. A right is a right and that is what this vote tonight is all about." Former Canadian prime minister Paul Martin (Whittington & Gordon 2005).

feminists reject marriage of any kind, including same-sex marriage, for perpetuating a patriarchal and oppressive system on heterosexual women as well as gays and lesbians. Those opposed to same-sex marriages and the redefinition of marriage fear that marriage is being threatened, and that ultimately family structure and society will break down.

Although the academic study of homosexuality and same-sex marriage has been somewhat limited until recently, when the debate regarding same-sex marriage heated up and legislation, such as former president Bush's constitutional amendment to ban gay marriages, was enacted, the American Anthropological Association (AAA) felt compelled to issue a strongly worded statement:

> The results of more than a century of anthropological research on households, kinship relationships, and families, across cultures and through time, provide no support whatsoever for the view that either civilization or viable social orders depend on marriage as an exclusively heterosexual institution. Rather, anthropological research supports the conclusion that a vast array of family types, including families built upon same-sex partnerships, can contribute to stable and humane societies. The Executive Board of the American Anthropological Association strongly opposes a constitutional amendment limiting marriage to heterosexual couples. (AAA 2004: n.p.)

As anthropologists point out, same-sex marriages, especially for economic reasons, have been accepted in other cultures without dire consequences, and that marriage is practised in a variety of ways around the world. Marriage is a dynamic institution that has changed considerably over time, and to cite any one form of marriage as "traditional" is misleading. In this chapter we will consider what marriage means, and the way marriage has been culturally constructed to meet the needs of various groups of people, including gays and lesbians. The socio-economic, religious, and political implications of legalizing same-sex marriages will be explored, including the following question: Will same-sex marriage, as it gains legal and social acceptance, transform both the queer and traditional meanings of marriage? Marriage, regardless of its form, creates a family; we will also examine the impact of same-sex marriages on the concept of family.

The question often arises whether marriage is a religious or a social institution. Anthropologists respond that it is both, and much more. Long before institutionalized religions (e.g., Christianity, Islam, Judaism), people were joining together in what even the most limited definition would consider a marriage. They were doing so for many reasons – to regulate sexual behaviour and create families, of course, but even more significant were the economic benefits of marriage. The roles that marriage plays in society, now and then, will be discussed through the lens of same-sex marriage and from social conservative, critical feminist/queer, and gay and lesbian assimilationalist schools of thought. In this chapter, sociological, political, legal, psychological, and anthropological approaches are drawn upon.

THE NATURE OF MARRIAGE AND SAME-SEX MARRIAGE

Marriage is a universal pattern of human behaviour, although many forms of marriage are practised. Marriage means different things to different people and is shaped by economic, ecological, historical, and demographic factors (Stone 2004). Haviland, Fedorak, & Lee (2009: 189) define marriage as "a relationship between one or more men (male or female) and one or more women (female or male) who are recognized by the group as having a continuing claim to the right of sexual access to each other." This rather convoluted definition recognizes that, globally, there are many forms of marriage, including same-sex marriage. It is also important to recognize that marriage is a cultural construct designed to meet the needs of a group of people, unlike mating, which is a biological behaviour. Consequently, developing an inclusive definition of marriage remains a challenge; to date a definition that represents global marriage practices has not been produced.

ROLES OF MARRIAGE

An important role of marriage is to establish families in which to create and raise children; marriage confers legitimacy or birthright status on children produced in the union (Stone 2004). Today, children born outside marriage in Western societies are far more recognized than in the past, and issues of child legitimacy are not as important, legally or socially. However, in the eyes of **social conservatives**, same-sex marriage foregoes establishing real families and the creation of children, and they fear that legalizing same-sex marriage may influence the next generation of children to redefine marriage to exclude childrearing (Baskerville 2006).

Parentage has also changed with advances in technology, such as surrogacy. Indeed, Stone (2004) identifies three types of "mothers": birth, genetic, and legal. With the advent of DNA testing, fatherhood and paternity have become more certain, which is an important consideration in traditional societies. Despite these changes, marriage still acknowledges the relationship between a set of parents and their children (Baskerville 2006): "Kinship laws still establish married men's paternity through marriage, not through their biological relationship with children. ... By this means, women are equated with nature and their relationship to children is biological, whereas men's relationship to children is established politically through the law of marriage" (Josephson 2005, quoted in Baskerville 2006: 65). Therefore, legal systems around the world recognize fathers through marriage, not sperm.

For same-sex married couples, marriage confers social and legal benefits that may assist in parenting. In Green's (2010) study of same-sex married couples, the respondents felt that being legally married in the eyes of the law and society provided a stronger sense of stability and socio-legal support that enabled them to parent with more confidence. Family formation and parenting, then, are viewed as part of their marital relationship, which is consistent with the attitudes of heterosexual married couples. Marriage, socially and symbolically, legitimizes same-sex couples and family, thereby maintaining the **lesbian and gay assimilationist** stance that supports same-sex marriage for the benefits and rights that same-sex married couples would enjoy if legally married – inheritance, health benefits, taxation, and childcare (Walters 2001).

A second significant role of marriage is to constrain or provide guidelines for sexual behaviour. According to some social conservatives, marriage exists to "civilize" men, to control their sexual behaviour (Baskerville 2006), and to channel sexual desire into reproduction within marriage. However, social conservatives do not believe that marriage will "tame" the libido of homosexuals because sexual desire in traditional marriage is channelled into reproduction, whereas same-sex marriage has no such goal (Green 2010). Indeed, the same-sex married couples Green interviewed deviated from so-called marital norms when it came to fidelity. Secure in their marriages and committed to their partners and children, many felt that if they chose to, seeking sexual partners outside their marriage was acceptable.

Marriage creates the most basic of economic units, the household. From the household flows a great deal of economic activity, such as tilling the land and raising livestock in traditional societies, and, in more recent times, earning wages and establishing businesses. The third role of marriage, then, is to define the roles and responsibilities or division of labour for each spouse. Women have traditionally cared for the children and household, while men hunted, worked the land, or earned a wage to support the family. In this way each spouse complemented the other in economic duties. This is no longer the reality in most modern societies, despite the social-conservative view that marriage creates division-of-labour guidelines. When both men and women work outside the home, division of labour is often dictated by choice – personal preferences and abilities, rather than gender. This more egalitarian system is a product of today's wage economy and the economic independence of women. Green (2010) found that this is also the case among same-sex married couples, who divide housework and other family responsibilities according to preference, skills, and abilities.

Westerners consider marriage a joining of two people, but in most cultures marriage is the joining of two families to create an economic and political support network. In North American society, marriage brings respectability that also creates social networks. Gays and lesbians in Green's (2010) study reported their relationships gained legitimacy when they married; family, friends, and coworkers paid them more social respect, and they now enjoyed the same support and standing that heterosexual couples enjoyed.

In sum, marriage, both heterosexual and homosexual, curtails and regulates human sexuality, defines gender roles, and provides a stable environment for procreating and raising children. Marriage also creates social, economic, and political networks between families, creating an expanded kinship network, and commands increased status and respect.

SAME-SEX MARRIAGE IN TRADITIONAL SOCIETIES

Same-sex relationships and marriage have a long history and wide geographical distribution (Lahey & Alderson 2004). In the southern Fujian province of China during the Yuan and Ming dynasties (1264–1644), men married male youths in elaborate ceremonies (McGough 2004). When the marriage came to an end, the older man in the relationship paid a brideprice to acquire a wife for the young man. In a similar vein, Japanese Samurai warriors entered battle with their apprentice warrior-lovers at their side. A formal exchange of written and spoken vows legitimized the relationship, which was based on romantic love and loyalty. Besides the sexual aspects of these relationships, the samurai provided "social backing, emotional support, and a model of manliness for the apprentice" (Eskridge 1996:3). The apprentice, in turn, was expected to become a good student of samurai manhood. In medieval Europe, same-sex relationships were recognized, even celebrated, in several societies. Records of ancient Rome and Greece show evidence of homosexual unions. In the Classical period, Greek men (*erastes*) and youths (*eromenoi*) entered into same-sex marriages. These marriages required the father of the youth to give his consent to the union (Pickett 2002).

North American aboriginal groups, such as the Ojibwa, Lakota, Yuma, and Winnebago, also recognized and accepted unions between Two-Spirit individuals (Williams 1986). Two-Spirits are androgynous males or females who take on the roles, dress, and behaviour of the opposite sex. They gain social prestige for their spiritual and intellectual qualities, and they often possess shamanic or special ceremonial powers, such as burial and mourning rituals (Bonvillain 1998). Two-Spirit marriages have also been recorded in the West Indies, and among the Aztec, Maya, and Inca civilizations (Eskridge 1996).

Same-sex marriages among the Mohave of the southwestern United States were institutionalized and socially accepted. A young man at the age of 10 participated in a ritual dance where he was proclaimed a Two-Spirit (*alyha*) and given a female name. According to Williams (1986), the Two-Spirit marriage closely emulated "regular" marriage in that it divided duties based on gender – the man took on the roles of a male and the Two-Spirit took on the roles of a woman. In some groups, such as the Lakota and Zapotec, the Two-Spirit was likely a second or third wife, while the husband had a female wife to produce children. The main reason for Two-Spirit marriages appears to be economic – Two-Spirits could take on the roles of both a man and a woman, and in the process enhance the social status of a group. By the late nineteenth and early twentieth centuries, Two-Spirits almost disappeared after Europeans settled in North America. They refused to accept the existence of more than two genders, declaring homosexuality a violation of natural and divine laws (Bonvillain 1998).

More than 30 documented cultural groups in four regions of sub-Saharan Africa practised woman–woman marriage in the twentieth century. In northern Nigeria, the Yoruba, Yagba, Akoko, Nuper, and Gana-Gana commonly practised woman–woman marriage (Herskovits 1937). Sometimes a barren woman married a young girl who then mated with the barren woman's husband to produce children. In other cases, a wealthy older woman (female husband) married a young woman. The young woman mated with a man to produce children for the female husband. Traditional marriage rituals, including offering a brideprice to the father of the girl, were practised in these marriages. Herskovits (1937) suggests that sexual activity between the women also occurred, although other researchers have refuted this claim. During the colonial era, attempts to eradicate woman–woman marriage were largely successful, although among the Kuria clan of Tanzania, woman–woman marriage is on the increase today, especially among women of independent means (Chacha 2004).

The Azande of Sudan practiced one of the most extensively documented types of same-sex relationship (Evans-Pritchard 1974). Military men took "boy-wives" as their marriage partners. The parents of a boy paid a brideprice, and brideservice was performed. This marriage was both sexual and economic, in that the boy performed household and sexual duties. Some men had both female wives and boy-wives – they took the boy-wives into war with them to take care of the camp, while the female wife remained at home and cared for the children. This type of marriage was legally and culturally sanctioned by the Azande. As with the woman–woman marriage, colonialist forces, under the guise of cultural imperialism and economic domination, stamped out the practice of boy-wives.

SAME-SEX MARRIAGE IN MODERN SOCIETIES[1]

Canada is not the only modern state to recognize same-sex marriages. In 1989, Denmark became the first country to offer same-sex couples rights on a par with heterosexual couples, although they could not marry in a church. In 1996, Norway, Sweden, and Iceland passed

---

1 It should be noted that the laws regarding same-sex marriages are continually changing.

similar legislation, followed by Finland in 2002. The Netherlands granted full civil marriage rights, including the right to adopt, to gay couples in 2001, becoming the first country to do so. Belgium followed suit in 2003. On July 2, 2005, Spain legalized same-sex marriages and the right of same-sex couples to adopt, becoming the third country to legalize same-sex marriages (Robinson 2012).

Other European countries have enacted legislation that grants gay and lesbian couples certain rights: Germany allows same-sex couples to register for life partnerships; in May 2013, President François Hollande signed a law authorizing marriage and adoption by same-sex couples in France (Roberts 2013); Luxembourg recognizes civil partnerships (Demian 2005); and Britain passed the Marriage Bill in 2013, legalizing same-sex marriage (BBC News 2013). In other parts of the world, New Zealand has passed a law recognizing civil unions between same-sex couples, and with the exception of South Australia and Victoria, Australia recognizes same-sex partnerships. However, former prime minister John Howard amended the marriage laws in 2004 to ban same-sex marriages and same-sex couples from adopting.

In the United States, the struggle for same-sex marriage rights and equality is reminiscent of the anti-miscegenation laws that prohibited African Americans from state-sanctioned marriage until the early nineteenth century, and prohibited Whites from marrying non-Whites until 1967 (Green 2010: 402). Legislation in the United States defines marriage as between a man and a woman, and many states have banned same-sex marriages. However, several Supreme Courts have struck down these bans for violating equal-protection rights for gays and lesbians (Gullo 2012), most recently in California. Vermont has granted same-sex couples the same legal status as civil marriages, and on May 17, 2004, Massachusetts gave same-sex couples the right to civil marriage (Burns 2005). New Hampshire, Iowa, Connecticut, and the District of Columbia also grant same-sex marriage licences (Green 2010). More recently, New York has begun to recognize same-sex marriages (Layng 2009), and Maryland passed a law legitimizing same-sex marriage in February 2012 (Cathcart 2012). In May 2012, President Obama stated on national television that he now believed same-sex couples should be able to legally marry. This ground-breaking endorsement sent reverberations through American society and gave hope and validation to gay and lesbian couples everywhere. Indeed, in the 2012 presidential election, voters in Maine, Washington, and Maryland affirmed the rights of same-sex couples to marry and rejected an amendment to Minnesota's Constitution that defined marriage as between a man and a woman only (White 2012). Public-opinion polls in the early months of 2013 showed that a slim majority of Americans feel that same-sex marriage should be allowed (AngusReidPublicOpinion 2013).

Around the world, the struggle for equal rights is exemplified in gays and lesbians seeking the right to legally marry. Argentina was the first Latin American country to legalize same-sex marriage in July 2010 (SinaEnglish 2010). Gay rights have strong support in Argentina, although there is also a strong anti-gay sentiment in this predominantly Catholic country. Despite heavy lobbying by the Catholic Church, the bill passed, spurring activists in other countries, such as Chile and Paraguay, to lobby for similar rights. Mexico City legalized gay marriages and has gone so far as to

"Commitment ceremonies, weddings, and other ritual occasions that seek to celebrate lesbian and gay relationships are in many ways very diverse. ... But what they all attempt is to situate a relationship within a broader community context, to proclaim the authenticity of the relationship in a public manner." Anthropologist Ellen Lewin, quoted in Wood & Lewin (2006: 139).

FIGURE 7.1 TWO WOMEN CELEBRATE THEIR MARRIAGE

designate the city as a tourist destination for gay marriages (CNNWorld 2009). Indeed, some tourist enclaves in Mexico, such as Lake Chapala, have become a haven for gay and lesbian people seeking more freedom and acceptance than they can enjoy in the United States.

In most African countries, however, same-sex marriage is taboo; gay men and women face discrimination, violence, and jail time, and homosexual acts remain illegal in countries such as Kenya (Look 2012). In Nigeria, Senate President David Mark rejected same-sex marriage, stating, "It is offensive to our culture and tradition" (Awom & Ukaibe 2011). The taboo has resulted in gay and lesbian Nigerians living in "fake" marriages because to be respected in Nigeria, one must be married. So strong are the anti-gay sentiments in Nigeria that an anti–same-sex bill was passed on May 30, 2013, to criminalize same-sex marriage (*Vanguard* 2013).

Uganda enacted a ban on same-sex marriage in 2005, and an anti-homosexuality law was reintroduced in the legislature on February 7, 2012. This bill criminalizes homosexual acts in Uganda and entrenches the stigma against those with HIV. This stigma was further exacerbated by evangelical aid programs that promoted abstinence-only in Uganda (Smith 2012). The bill created international attention and condemnation that increased when Ugandan gay-rights activist David Kato was beaten to death on January 26, 2011 (Gettleman 2011). Given that the United Nations Development Programme (UNDP) 1994 Human Development Report defines human security as free from fear (personal safety) and free from want (equity and social justice), this bill became both a human-rights and a global issue. For many Africans, religion, both Christianity and Islam, is at the root of their

"Marriage is a union of spirits and the spirit is not male or female." A Shaiva priest's view of same-sex marriage, quoted in *Vanita* (2010: n.p.).

rejection of same-sex marriage. For example, many Senegalese blame homosexuality on the West, given the movements to protect gay rights, and this has served to further entrench homophobia in Africa. In South Africa, same-sex unions have been legalized – the only African country to do so – but a social stigma is still deeply attached to homosexuality even in that country.

In Asia, attempts to legalize same-sex marriage in Taiwan, China, the Philippines, and Cambodia have so far been stymied by opponents in the legislature, although some politicians and even monarchs support legislation that legalizes same-sex marriage. In India, love marriages (*gandharva vivaha*), including same-sex marriages, were accepted, even celebrated, before the colonial period when British missionaries attacked Indian sexual mores (Vanita 2010). Since then, India has become more homophobic. Despite this setback, female couples are marrying in temples, often without the blessing of their families. Legally, the Indian courts have upheld same-sex couples' right to live together, and even among religious leaders, opinions vary from absolute rejection to acceptance.

In China, there have been small achievements. In 1997, the law that outlawed sodomy was repealed, and in 2001 homosexuality was no longer classified as a mental illness (Li 2010). To date, four unsuccessful attempts to amend the marriage laws have been proposed. Discrimination continues as most gays and lesbians must keep their sexual orientation a secret; societal and familial pressures usually force them into a straight marriage. The consequences of this systemic discrimination include rising rates of HIV/AIDS infection, psychological trauma, increasing suicide attempts, and a plethora of unhappy "straight" marriages that end in divorce.

THE DEBATE OVER SAME-SEX MARRIAGE

The debate swirling around same-sex marriage is based on few facts and a great deal of speculation on the part of both critics and activists as they contemplate social and cultural consequences of legally and socially sanctioned same-sex marriage. To many, the continued quest to legalize same-sex marriages in the Western world is seen as a threat to the foundations of civilization – the honourable institution of marriage, the biological need to reproduce, and the social condition of parenting (Weeks, Heaphy, & Donovan 2001). It is important to note that this debate is a manifestation of the difficulty with defining the place of homosexuals in Western societies and the power and influence of religious objections. Indeed, churches with large denominations, such as the Roman Catholic Church (including the newly installed Pope Francis) and the Southern Baptist Church, strongly disapprove of homosexuality.

Social conservatives believe that same-sex marriage will erode gender-role differentiation and nuclear families, increase infidelity, and decrease family stability. In other words, legalizing same-sex marriage would jeopardize modern society. The religious right views same-sex marriages as a violation of the teachings of a supernatural being (e.g., God), and believes that allowing same-sex marriage sanctifies deviant and immoral acts that go against religious teachings. If same-sex marriages were legalized, this would bestow societal approval on a way of life long maligned. The harshest criticism suggests that legalizing same-sex marriages opens the door to other forms of "deviant" marriage, such as polygyny, incestuous marriages, and marriage with animals. Obviously the latter two objections are based on fear and ignorance, while polygyny, when a man takes more than one wife at the same time, has been a successful form of marriage in many cultures outside Western countries.

Feminist/queer critics, although opposed to same-sex marriage, see the impact quite differently than social conservatives do. For feminist and queer critics, if gays and lesbians marry, they will be bolstering the traditional social order of gender inequality, sexism, and patriarchy (Green 2010). They are afraid that marriage will "colonize" gays and lesbians, reducing unique queer culture to a mirror of heterosexual marriage, thereby creating a form of homonormativity (Duggan 2002: 176). Their criticism of same-sex marriage is directly linked to their long-held criticisms of the institution of marriage as a source of women's oppression and disempowerment. From the perspective of feminist/queer critics, then, same-sex marriage is a sell-out (Baird & Rosenbaum 1997: 11).

Gay and lesbian assimilationists, on the other hand, support same-sex marriage and believe that legalizing such unions will strengthen same-sex families, afford them social respectability, and ultimately promote monogamy. Assimilationists make the case that this is a human-rights issue, and that same-sex families deserve equal rights with their straight peers (Queers United 2008).

Green (2010) attempted to determine whether same-sex married couples would prove or disprove the positions of these schools of thought. He conducted in-depth interviews with 30 legally married same-sex couples in Toronto. These interviews suggest that marriage for same-sex couples provided social legitimacy, reaffirmed commitment to spouse and family, facilitated parenting, and created a social support network of family, friends and co-workers, just as it did for heterosexual couples. Psychologists Heather Macintosh, Elke D. Reissing, and Heather Andruff (2010) corroborated these findings when they examined the effects of legalizing same-sex marriage on gay and lesbian couples in Canada. They found that the couples interviewed recognized that legalizing same-sex marriage affected their relationships, as well as their legal status and social standing. Overall these couples expressed greater satisfaction and less insecurity about their relationships. Like other couples, they face challenges, but the respondents felt overwhelmingly that legalizing their marriage was a positive move. These findings support the stance of assimilationists and, to some degree, the feminist/queer critics who fear same-sex marriage will "tame" homosexuals. On the other hand, Green also found that same-sex married couples are not as tied to traditional norms, such as monogamy and gendered division of labour, as heterosexual couples are, although it is important to point out that we are referring to idealistic norms of monogamy and gendered division of labour in traditional heterosexual marriages, not reality. These findings support the fears of social conservatives, even if the deviations from marital norms are not that different from those found in heterosexual marriages.

This conformity versus nonconformity among same-sex couples is not surprising, given that gays and lesbians are socialized in two worlds – that of heterosexual tradition which valorizes marriage and kinship, and that of queer tradition which promotes sexual freedom and non-traditional gender roles. Green's (2010) study, then, suggests that same-sex marriage both supports and subverts "traditional" marriage norms.

Those who support the right of same-sex couples to marry reject religious dogma influencing legal institutions

"[I]t is not at all clear that, say, same-sex marriages will present a fundamental challenge to the institution of marriage or that gay parents will construct truly new ways of raising children. ... These are, as we social scientists like to say, empirical questions." (Walters 2001: 353)

such as marriage, and feel that granting same-sex couples the right to marry is a matter of equality. They also suggest that being able to make long-term commitments in a marriage encourages stability and monogamy. Proponents also believe that banning same-sex marriages is a form of discrimination against an identifiable group that has been marginalized for too long.

SAME-SEX MARRIAGES AND THE FAMILY

Social conservatives worry that **family** structure is jeopardized by same-sex unions, and that a traditional nuclear family is the best environment in which to raise healthy, moral children, which in turn leads to a moral society (Josephson 2005). Is this true? How do we define family? Is it a nuclear unit composed of a mother (female), father (male), and 2.2 children? Or is it a young, unmarried woman with a newborn baby and a 10-year-old basset hound? Is it a middle-aged Chinese man with his wife, their daughter, his wife's parents and her brothers and sisters, spouses, and children? Is it a Masai woman with four children, married to a polygynous husband who has three other wives and many children? Or is it two Canadian men raising their three children from previous heterosexual relationships? As with marriage, a family can mean different things to different people.

Social-conservative concerns about the disintegration of family are somewhat justified. The traditional institution of family is in a constant state of flux, sometimes known as a "crisis of the family." What this means is that nuclear families, the preferred form of family in the West, are being challenged, and the definition of family now encompasses alternative family structures – what Weeks, Heaphy, and Donovan (2001: 9) call "families of choice." Indeed, in some areas of the United States, single-parent families outnumber nuclear families. Blended families, the result of adults with children from previous marriages getting married, have also become common. The fastest growing demographic in Canada is the common-law family, which now has legal recognition, and in the United States some couples living together are now signing "commitment contracts." These and other forms of family illustrate the ability of the so-called family institution to adapt and change its structure to meet the needs of a changing society. This expansion of the concept of family has caused a great deal of concern and confusion among people with a firmly entrenched idea of what should comprise a family. On the other hand, these changes have freed families, including same-sex families, from narrow interpretations of what a family means.

Opponents of same-sex marriages express concerns about the well-being of children in same-sex families. They raise the issues of gender identity and sexual orientation – will children raised in a same-sex family grow up homosexual? Questions concerning the "fitness" of gay and lesbian parents have also been broached, yet studies by Flaks et al. (1989) found that lesbian mothers seemed more concerned with good mothering than did heterosexual mothers, and proponents of legalizing same-sex marriages argue that same-sex couples can and do provide the same nurturing atmosphere as heterosexual couples.

Research into the development of **gender identity** in Western states has found that children living in same-sex marriages experience little confusion about their feelings of identity, and they appear happy and comfortable with their gender. Behavioural studies found no difference in toy preference, favourite television shows and characters, activities, interests, and choice of future career among children regardless of whether their mothers were lesbian or heterosexual. Most children identified themselves as heterosexual, and no evidence of an increase in the numbers of gay and lesbian children from same-sex families has

FIGURE 7.2   A SAME-SEX FAMILY ENJOYING A DAY PLAYING TENNIS

been found. Peer relationships also appear normal among children of same-sex parents; they develop close friendships with same-sex peers as do children from heterosexual homes.

CONCLUSION

Culture change is an inevitable part of human society. Technology is the most obvious change, but our beliefs and patterns of behaviour also change, albeit more slowly. The process of expanding the definition of marriage is an example of culture change at work. It is also an example of the most difficult and, some would say, most painful type of culture change, where people slowly alter their ideas of what is right and wrong. Has marriage changed? Despite the protestations of traditionalists, marriage has changed considerably, even within the last century (Sullivan 2004).

To remain culturally relativistic while examining such a sensitive subject as same-sex marriage is extremely difficult. Marriage speaks to the heart of our societies. It is more than a civil, social, political, or religious union; it is central to our sense of well-being and identity. This is why the debate over same-sex marriage elicits such a passionate response, both from those who oppose any change in the definition of marriage, and from those who seek greater recognition of their identity through the right to marry. In Western countries, heterosexual relationships are predicated on love and commitment, as are same-sex marriages. Gay and lesbian couples simply want the same rights and respect as heterosexual couples. However, to suggest that the struggle for same-sex equality is a new and Western concept is erroneous. Same-sex relationships and marriages are a historical fact, and are found in virtually all nations of the world, albeit at different stages of recognition and acceptance.

Will legally recognized same-sex marriages ever become a full reality in our global society? Perhaps, since it has already happened in Canada and several European countries, and none of the disastrous predictions of social conservatives have come to pass. As people become more aware of different ways of life, through the efforts of activists and global citizens, they also become more accepting. The gay rights movement has been gaining strength and becoming a powerful political voice since the 1960s. Gays and lesbians are no longer willing to remain marginalized on the edge of society.

Yet homosexuality and same-sex marriages are far from universally accepted. Moral and religious issues still factor heavily in the debate, despite the recognition of civil rights, and likely will for some time to come. Even if we step outside the civil and religious arguments, many of which are valid, there is still the matter of deep-seated sentiments attached to marriage that tend to be fairly rigid and difficult to change. As Sullivan (2004: xxx) expresses it: "In this culture war, profound and powerful arguments about human equality and integrity have clashed with deep convictions about an ancient institution."

Marriage is an evolving system; indeed, it always has been. Today, many countries are undergoing a transformation in marriage, family, and kinship that is predicated on choice as well as biology. The legalization and acceptance of same-sex marriage as a legitimate form of marriage are merely the most recent steps in this evolution.

QUESTIONS FOR CONSIDERATION AND CLASSROOM ACTIVITIES

1. Why do you think there is always a battle between liberal and conservative forces in society? Does this conflict promote healthy dialogue or does it divide society? How have the opposing views stymied and advanced the rights of gays and lesbians? Examine these questions within the context of a developed and a developing nation.
2. In your opinion, what constitutes a family? How does your definition fit with the diverse family structures of the twenty-first century in your country? Develop an inclusive definition of family. Does your definition offer the possibility of same-sex families?
3. Politicians and religious leaders worry about the family unit and society. Do you think allowing gays and lesbians to marry will result in the breakdown of family and society? Why or why not? Now research the reality in Canada or a European country where same-sex marriage is legal. What impact has legalization had on family structure and societal norms?
4. Culture change is an inevitable part of human society; changing one system of culture often has an impact on the other systems of a culture. Identify some of the changes in economic, social, political, and religious institutions when same-sex marriage is legitimatized.
5. Do you believe same-sex marriages should be legalized in your country? Globally? Give reasons for your answer.
6. Many of the examples of same-sex liaisons and marriages in this chapter come from Africa, yet today Africans suffer extreme censorship and punishment for homosexuality. Why do you think this is so? Choose a country and research the struggle for gay and lesbian rights.

7. As a global citizen, what steps can you take to assist same-sex couples in gaining recognition and acceptance?

SUGGESTED READINGS

Knauft, B. (2005). *The Gebusi: Lives transformed in a rainforest world.* Toronto: McGraw-Hill.

A forthright and clearly written ethnography that does not shy away from issues of homosexuality.

Sullivan, A. (Ed.). (2004). *Same-sex marriage: Pro and con.* New York: Vintage Books.

A comprehensive reader that presents solid arguments for and against same-sex marriages from an anthropological perspective.

Chapter 8

Social Media: What Is Its Role in Socio-Political Revolution?

Key Terms: civic media, flashmobs, globalization, netizens, participatory media, participatory politics, smart mobs, social media, social networking

---

INTRODUCTION

"This revolution started online. This revolution started on Facebook. Everything was done by the people [for] the people, and that's the power of the Internet." Wael Ghonim, Egyptian protest leader, in interview on CNN (Cohen 2011: n.p.).

A remarkable and unprecedented showing of people power took place in Cairo, Egypt, on January 25, 2011. Hundreds of thousands of Egyptians, from all walks of life and political spectrums, joined together to demand a change in government and a chance for a better life. **Social media** platforms, in particular Facebook and Twitter, have been credited with spearheading these political protests and facilitating their success. Wael Ghonim, an Egyptian activist and Google marketing manager, became a symbol of these protests when he created an anti-Mubarak Facebook page that emboldened Egyptians to take to the streets to demand that President Hosni Mubarak step down. The spectacular events in Egypt have raised some important questions regarding the role of social media and the Internet in the mobilization of contemporary socio-political reform.

According to Wu and Mao (2011: 2), the twenty-first century has become the age of "accelerated globalization and digitization." Social media is a product of this new digital age and has become a technological forum that has contributed to the **globalization** of communication systems. Although complex and amorphous, social media are web-based channels of communication that permit social interaction between members, and often create a sense of shared community among users. Unlike any era before, social media allows ordinary citizens to enter public discourse and exact influence over the values and opinions of others, and the events and policies that affect their lives.

"It should be clear by now that the interactions and uses by which people make meaning, act, or build societies is as inextricably linked to software, networks, computers, devices, and infrastructures as we insist it is to kinship or social organization." (Kelty 2010.)

The debate regarding the power of the Internet began long before Facebook or Twitter existed, and long before the Egyptian and Tunisian protests. However, the spectacular events in Egypt and earlier in Tunisia have raised some new questions regarding the role of social media and the Internet in mobilizing contemporary socio-political reform. Studies have shown that the more access to information, including the Internet, that people

"If Facebook were a country it would be the third largest, behind only China and India." (Grossman 2010: n.p.)

have, the greater their participation in the political landscape (Etling, Faris, & Palfrey 2010). Facebook, as an example, has evolved from a platform for interaction between friends to a communication tool now used to solve socio-political problems and to explore ways of improving the world. Indeed, the late Michael Hauben coined the term **netizens** to represent a new form of citizenship emerging from widespread use of the Internet and social media (Hauben 2011b: 19–20). Hauben considered netizens crucial for building a more democratic human society.

"Welcome to the 21st century. You are a netizen (net citizen), and you exist as a citizen of the world thanks to the global connectivity that the Net gives you. You consider everyone as your compatriot. You physically live in one country but you are in contact with much of the world via the global computer network. Virtually you live next door to every other single netizen in the world. Geographical separation is replaced by existence in the same virtual space." Michael Hauben, quoted in *The Amateur Computerist* (2011: 2)

The increasing use of social media in "people movements" may have far-reaching implications that are only beginning to be addressed in social and behavioural academia. Mobile communications expert Howard Rheingold (2003) suggests that, with the advent of the Internet, people were able to act together in what he calls **smart mobs** that facilitate the organization and coordination of group action. An early example of a smart mob was the *No Mas FARC* protest, where a young Colombian activist mobilized 13 million people to denounce the FARC guerrilla army[1] (Etling, Faris, & Palfrey 2010), and more recently smart mobs have been used to report election fraud (Rheingold 2008).

In this chapter we will consider several questions, beginning with whether social media has the power to topple governments or if it is only one factor in a much broader context. In other words, is social media as powerful as suggested by political activists, or is it simply an effective communication tool? Television has been a powerful enculturative force for 50 years; is social media now assuming the place of television by influencing and shaping its users' perceptions, or is it merely a reflection of ongoing social change? Given recent events, have social media platforms empowered people to bring about socio-political change, and have they changed the way people react to socio-political repression?

Alarms have been raised about the negative aspects of uncontrolled communications networks, so what are some of the inherent dangers and limitations of social media? Is the role of broadcast media or mass media, such as Al Jazeera or CNN News, changing in light of social media's success, or are they mutually beneficial types of media? Since studies of media and technology are, by necessity, both inter- and multidisciplinary, and can be found in sociology, anthropology, human geography, culture studies, communications and media studies, philosophy, and economics, to name but a few, this discussion will draw upon the expertise of several of these disciplines.

THE NATURE OF SOCIAL MEDIA

In 2013, approximately two billion people from all walks of life belonged to social networks. Social media can motivate and mobilize participants, organize actions such as protests, recruit

---

1 The FARC guerrilla army in Colombia is accused of financing its political and military battle against the government with kidnappings, extortion, and drug trafficking (In Sight 2011).

new participants to a cause, give voice to the marginalized, disseminate critical information, capture broadcast media's attention, and captivate worldwide audiences. A key factor with social media, then, is its participatory nature. Gathering local and international support, social media has exerted political influence on governments, circumvented media censorship, and created global awareness of important issues such as human rights. Social media is most commonly used by youth, who are also the largest demographic in developing countries and the most likely to demand change. Thus, the socio-political impact of social media is enormous. Astute politicians and leaders are beginning to realize this; for example, President Barack Obama used social networks to reach millions of people during his 2008 election campaign. His social-media–savvy team built on this relationship for the 2012 presidential campaign. They understood that the real power of social media lies in creating political dialogue among users through portals such as Facebook and Twitter (Rutledge 2013).

> "Humans [have] been empowered with the ability to engage and understand social networks in a profoundly different way to ever before." (Shah 2009: n.p.)

Historically, Arab Spring activists were not the first to use Internet technology to revolutionize their society. In 1991, Russia's leader, Boris Yeltsin, foiled a coup d'état using the fledgling Soviet Union email system known as RelCom (Zaks 2011). The coup plotters shut down newspapers, radio, and television, but they knew nothing of the forerunner to the Internet, hidden in the Kurchatov Institute. RelCom fed its news, via email, to a pre-Internet global forum known as UseNet, sending tens of thousands of emails to the Russian people appealing for their support, in a move remarkably similar to the Facebook and Twitter movement in the Middle East.

Social media provides an opportunity for social and behavioural scientists to study media as a communicative practice, a cultural product, a social activity, and an historical development. For example, computer scientists Choudhary et al. (2012) analyzed discourse on Twitter related to the Egyptian revolution. They discovered that most sentiments or memes[2] expressed in tweets were negative and lacked cohesion. They also determined that most tweets were re-postings to broadcast news, such as CNN News, to keep users inside and outside Egypt informed. In this case, social media was being used as a communicative tool and a recorder of historical events as they unfolded. Indeed, YouTube videos of the protests, Twitter tweets, and Facebook postings provided an "unfiltered history of events from a multitude of perspectives" (Choudhary et al. 2012: 74).

According to Hutton & Fosdick (2011: 564), the dominant force in social media is **social networking**, which has become a global movement. Anthropologist Robin Dunbar believes that today's societies are so mobile that social networking is extremely important for maintaining relationships and creating large networks of associates that are forever expanding (Shah 2009: n.p.). Dunbar's prophetic words also recognized the potential for social media to create **flashmobs** and the herd effect that can transform into coordinated social action, as was seen in Moscow in 1991 and Egypt in 2011.

Social networking to exert political pressure gained momentum at the beginning of the twenty-first century. A chain of text messages encouraged a million Filipinos to occupy a highway and demand President Joseph Estrada's resignation in 2001. This was the first time that social media had played a role in forcing a leader from power (Shirky 2011).

---

2 Ideas or symbols.

MAP 8.1 WORLDWIDE SOCIAL NETWORKS

Facebook
V Kontakte
Odnaklassniki
Drouglem
Hyves
Zing
Mixi
Orkut
Ozone
Unknown

In a different kind of movement, Chinese citizens were informed via text messaging of a dangerous flu raging in Guangzhou in 2003. This action forced the Chinese government to acknowledge the problem (Suárez 2011). When the *Boston Globe*'s 2002 exposé of sexual abuse in the Catholic Church went viral, the public took action, instigating lawsuits and demanding court action. Social media ensured the scandal would no longer be covered up (Shirky 2011).

THE VALUE OF SOCIAL MEDIA

One of the most significant benefits of social media is the ability of people to evade media censorship, so common in authoritarian regimes and within tightly controlled media systems. Social media, through its anonymity, provides netizens with opportunities to enter political discourse and to criticize governments and their policies. Social media and networking is also a way for new voices to enter the debate, with less fear of reprisal and more opportunities to learn about an issue and offer their opinions.

Social media has the ability to upload almost instant global news. Tyrants have little ammunition against this speed and outreach, making cover-ups more difficult. Citizen journalists can take control of information and its diffusion, becoming the producers of media rather than only consumers (Etling, Faris, & Palfrey 2010). Social platforms such as Twitter also kill propaganda and enable mainstream journalists to verify the truth. For example, when the military cracked down on Bahrain protesters, people on the scene tweeted that live ammunition was being used and posted photos of people with gunshot wounds at the hospital (Else 2012), countering the government's claims. When schools collapsed in Sechuan, China, during the 2008 earthquake, netizens used social media to share information and documentation of collusion between construction companies and the local government (Shirky 2011). Thus, corruption and attempts to hide the truth can become public knowledge through social media.

Social media also provides an ongoing commentary on daily life and the events that matter to people and continue to do so long after conventional media lose interest in a particular story, such as happened when major North American broadcast media lost interest in the Egyptian revolution. Thus, the shared awareness that social media generates serves to keep interested individuals more informed.

The symbolic value of social media, especially Facebook, is also significant. Facebook symbolizes a new political voice and the freedom to express this voice. Awareness of this new "people power" is evident everywhere in Cairo, from graffiti on the walls of buildings, to memorabilia and t-shirts emblazoned with the Facebook logo. As the voice of the people, social media provides previously invisible or marginalized groups with a means to protest ill-treatment. An Iranian female student who suffered horrendous brutality during the post-election crackdown by Iranian authorities used social media to recount her suffering (Tomlin 2011a). She spoke about her experiences and encouraged other women to follow her example. A 28-minute segment of her testimony was broadcast on YouTube, where she gathered worldwide attention and support. Hadi Ghaemi, executive director of New York-based International Campaign for Human Rights in Iran, sees social media as a vital communication tool in this regard. Social media opened up discussions on abuse, and even fuelled a campaign to persuade the United Nations to hold President Mahmood Ahmadinejad accountable for human rights abuses in Iran. In an impressive display of

participatory media, 160,000 Twitter users turned their profile photos green as a sign of solidarity during post-election protests in Iran (Zuckerman 2011). Social media, then, is not only produced and consumed; it is action-oriented and a forum for socio-cultural change.

Social media is also being used to challenge attitudes about the treatment of women. Rape has traditionally been silenced in the Middle East and the victim stigmatized or blamed. Using social media to inform viewers of what has happened is changing deeply entrenched attitudes about women and sexual abuse. In Egypt women are using social media to hold authorities accountable for atrocities during the revolution, and to challenge attitudes that keep women silent if they have been sexually harassed.[3] YouTube postings by women such as Salwa-Al-Housiny Gouda, who was arrested, tortured, and subjected to "virginity" tests by police during the revolution, have brought sexual-harassment problems in Egypt to the world's attention (Tomlin 2011b). Partly because of social media, on December 27, 2011, an Egyptian court ruled that virginity tests on women in military custody are illegal (Afify 2011). The fact that these images went "viral" on social networking sites likely provided the political pressure that led to this court's findings. Harassmap, a social media site that enables women to report sexual harassment in Egypt by sending text messages, has brought the problem into the mainstream media spotlight. One of the goals of this project is to end victim-blaming by shifting the responsibility onto the perpetrator (Tomlin 2011b).

In Mexico, where violence between drug cartels has claimed innocent victims, Twitter is used to report gun battles and road blockades[4] (Cave 2011). Victims' names and how they died, as well as photographs and videos of the dead, are posted to alert the public. Thus, social media has played a valuable role in denouncing violence in Mexico and has become one of the loudest voices where traditional media has been largely silenced or compromised by corruption. On the other hand, the drug cartels are using their own websites to threaten anyone posting information (Shoichet 2011).

Saudi women have harnessed social media in their campaign for the right to drive (Zuckerman 2011). Najla Hariri, a woman living in Jeddah, Saudi Arabia, drove her children to school, and then tweeted about her experience. She received a flood of support in the Gulf nations via Twitter. A week later a computer security consultant, Marial Al-Sharif, drove her car, with her brother, son, and a Saudi women's rights activist along for the ride. She recorded the drive and posted it on YouTube. Saudi authorities arrested Al-Sharif and she was charged with violating public order. Her arrest garnered global attention and the support of Amnesty International. More protests by Saudi women followed, and a Facebook group was formed, rallying for a protest on June 17, 2011. The small-scale protest[5] was muted and went off with little incident. It did, however, gain a great deal of attention from Western politicians who tweeted their support, and viewers launched participatory responses. Social media gave their campaign momentum and advertised their struggle to a global audience. This is an example of **civic media**, where communities create and share actionable information using media (Zuckerman 2011).

---

3 The degree of sexual harassment of women in Egypt is astonishing. Most women, including me when I was living in Egypt, seldom pass a day without experiencing some form of sexual harassment from Egyptian men in the streets. Authorities are of little help; indeed, police on the streets are among the most common perpetrators of sexual harassment.

4 The vast majority of violent deaths in Mexico are among drug cartel members, not the general public, despite North American broadcast media sensationalism.

5 Only those with licences from other countries could participate.

Egypt's protests have been called a "Facebook revolution" that opened the way for other groups to utilize social media in their socio-political campaigns. Facebook became the primary tool of public outreach and citizen journalism, while Twitter was most often used to send information to mainstream journalists (Gaworecki 2011). Facebook was also used in Egypt to organize security in the streets after thousands of prisoners broke loose from the prisons during the revolution. On every street, including my own in the suburb of Maadi, Egyptians used Facebook to organize neighbourhood watches to protect people from looters and violence after the state police disappeared from the streets.

FIGURE 8.1 NAJLA HARIRI DEFIED A BAN ON WOMEN DRIVING IN SAUDI ARABIA AND THEN ANNOUNCED HER DEFIANCE USING SOCIAL MEDIA

Ahmed Mahir, one of the founders of the April 6 Youth protests in the Egyptian revolution, was instrumental in showing Egyptians that social networks could be powerful political organizational tools (Ackerman 2011). One revolutionary youth described Facebook as a "space of liberty" – a place to freely exchange information and ideas (Gaworecki 2011). The stories of police abuse galvanized the protesters, culminating in the photos of Khalid Said that went viral on the Internet. Facebook, with its capability to allow users to share videos of police brutality, express political anger, and announce protests on its dissident pages, helped build the momentum and set the stage for the "it was now or never" action in Egypt. This is why Tufekci (2011) believes that social media, or what she calls media ecology, is a game changer and a potent tool for socio-political change as it alters collective action dynamics.

"There's a current fascination with the idea popular movements can be created using virtual tools. While there's good reason to suspect that the role of Facebook has been overstated in the Arab Spring, there's also good reason to believe that the role was real and significant, especially as it came to documentation." (Zuckerman 2011: n.p.).

Other organizations have also realized the power of social media. In 2011, for example, Russian bloggers instigated a Facebook rally, wherein thousands of protestors took to the streets to protest elections they claimed were fraudulent. Social media circumvented the state-controlled media, which did not air the protests. According to journalist Sergei Packhomenko, "Nothing like this has ever happened before. This all started with a few posts on Facebook and [blogging platform] LiveJournal" (*Borneo Post* 2011: n.p.).

"Citizens or public audiences of today are no longer mere audiences, but part of the media revolution that is shaping the world today." Joyce Barnathan, President of the International Center for Journalism, quoted in Garcia (2011: n.p.).

CRITICISMS OF SOCIAL MEDIA

Peterson (2011) calls social media a vehicle for social change. Yet some media experts dismiss the power of social media. Journalist Malcolm Gladwell suggests that social media is not successful at "providing the discipline, strategy, hierarchy, and strong social bonds that

"People protested and brought down governments before Facebook was invented. They did it before the Internet came along." Malcolm Gladwell, quoted in Ingram (2011: n.p.)

successful movements require" (Gladwell 2010: n.p.), even though a great deal of organization and planning among protest leaders has taken place through social media. Ramesh Srinivasan, a professor of information studies, counters Gladwell, suggesting that using social media facilitated the organization of Middle Eastern revolutions, although people in charge of organizing the masses created and sustained the revolution. This, too, took place over social media (Srinivasan 2011).

Statistical analysis of social media's role in the Egyptian revolution by Kathleen Carley of Carnegie Millon University found that social media did not *cause* the revolution; rather, social influences (e.g., poverty) created an environment ripe for protest and revolution. Social media was merely one vehicle for people to express their anger and organize their protests. On the other hand, Philip Howard of the University of Washington found a strong historical link between social media and the Egyptian revolution: new media, whether the printing press in earlier revolutions or the Internet in the Middle East, is often involved in revolution (Reardon 2012). Indeed, there are some interesting parallels between autocratic regimes trying to restrict Internet freedom today and attempts by the Catholic Church in the fifteenth century and beyond to censor book publishing and limit the use of the printing press (Harry Ransom Center 2007).

One novel way of examining the power of social media is to ask how Hosni Mubarak in Egypt and Zinc Ben Ali in Tunisia held onto power for so long. What are the mechanisms that maintain authoritarian regimes? According to Tufekci (2011), the answer lies in a "collective action problem," or a society-level collective problem, where the cooperation of many people is required to solve a problem but where there are serious repercussions and disincentives for any one individual to participate, and the means for organizing dissent is quickly stifled through torture and lengthy prison sentences. Dissent is repressed through censorship and isolation – key mechanisms for a regime to survive. Twenty years ago the Jordanian bread revolution, fuelled by high unemployment and increased costs for bread and oil, created a popular uprising that barely registered on the global media radar (Dahdal 2011). Why? The protestors lacked an effective communication tool that could sidestep the heavily censored Jordanian media, and they lacked social media and its power to mobilize protestors and to advertise their protests in the international community, yet they were still successful. Therefore, social media does not ensure revolutionary success. This, more than any other argument, places in doubt the overall power of social media in revolution. For example, the 2010 Red Shirt uprising that took place in Thailand floundered when the Thai government cracked down on protesters in downtown Bangkok, killing dozens (Shirky 2011), despite the use of social media.

Rheingold (2003) warns that authoritarian regimes can also use social media to control citizens or discredit opposition, as the Iranian regime did in 2009. Leaders of authoritarian regimes can use the Internet to spy on dissidents or may use social media to control ideas. The popularity of social media in revolution can also backfire – some authoritarian regimes such as China have blocked Facebook and Twitter (Evangelista 2011). Other regimes have resorted to filters, surveillance, and cyberattacks to stop activists from using the Internet (Etling, Faris, & Palfrey 2010).

The reliability of social media is also open to question: Could Facebook be used to spread false information? Could Twitter become a gossip column? Does social media provide a complete picture of the situation? In the case of Egypt, many of the leaders of the Muslim Brotherhood were thrown in jail shortly before the protests. Tweeters complained that their leaders were invisible, without investigating why. Social media may be used for nefarious deeds as well. In 2007, text messages incited attacks against minorities in Kenya (Etling, Faris, & Palfrey 2010). In December 2011, images of a young Egyptian female protestor being beaten, stripped of her *hijab* and *abaya*, and then dragged through the streets by soldiers roused worldwide horror. However, the legitimacy of these images has been called into question by some Egyptians. Adel Abdul Sadek, head of the Arab Center for Cyberspace Research, warns that images or videos may be fabricated to promote particular ideas or motivate a particular response.[6] He also points out that this particular video only showed the girl being stripped, not the soldier who covered her up and protected her, therefore making the "story" biased and incomplete (Suleiman 2011).

THE EGYPTIAN REVOLUTION[7]

What caused the Egyptian revolution? Analysts have identified complex socio-cultural, religious, economic, and political factors that led to an inevitable explosion of anger: decades of government corruption and dictatorship; grinding poverty; high unemployment, especially among youth; police brutality; and an arrogant wealthy elite. All of these factors were catalysts for the Egyptian revolution and the earlier Tunisian revolution. Social media served as the mobilizing force, the tool through which activists called the people to rise up and demand change. Estimates vary from three to six million Facebook users in Egypt, many of whom used these platforms to organize the protests and share information and videos of the demonstrations in Tahrir Square. Their images captivated audiences around the world.

When the Egyptian government shut down the Internet in an attempt to stem the flow of information, engineers from Twitter and Google developed a "Speak-to-Tweet" service, a way to send voice messages through designated numbers that were automatically translated into type and sent on as tweets (Suarez 2011). Twitter provided police locations, meeting places for protestors, and updates on media coverage, all within seconds. Twitter was also used to rally new recruits to the protest and broadcast the goals of the protestors to the world at large. Thus, Twitter became the "eyes, ears, and voice of the day to day life of the protest" (Watkins 2011: 1).

> "Sometimes decades pass and nothing happens, and then sometimes weeks pass and decades happen." Vladimir Lenin, quoted in Sreberny (2011: n.p.)

Although the Egyptian uprising may have appeared spontaneous to outsiders, an unprecedented political alliance of disparate factions, including the secular leftists and Muslim Brotherhood, had quietly been working toward the overthrow of the Mubarak regime long before 2011 (Hauben 2011a). The *Kifaya* movement (*kifaya* meaning change)

---

6 Adel Abdul Sadek's comments should not be construed as confirming that this incident did not happen. The video in question was taken by a Reuters photographer and then distributed over both social media and broadcast media.

7 Not everyone agrees that a true political revolution took place in Egypt. The military rulers that took power were former henchmen of Mubarak, and they applied the same brutal tactics for suppressing opposition. Nevertheless, a mental/intellectual revolution is indisputable – Egyptians had never risen against their dictators *en masse*; thus the events of January and February 2011 changed the victim mentality and the apathy formerly so common in Egypt.

emerged in 2004–05, bringing together Islamists, communists, liberals, and secular-leftists in a common goal – the ouster of Mubarak. Activists in the *Kifaya* movement used the blogosphere to create a new political language free from terms of secularization or fundamentalism. An alliance between Egypt's workforce and online netizens spread information and encouraged online discourse. These blogs were used to report police abuse, while videos were used to incite the people to action. Indeed, by 2008, blogs had become the surrogate news media, easily and quickly circumventing Egypt's censorship laws (Mahmood 2011). These early movements heralded the organizing potential of social media. Anthropologist Charles Hirschkind (2011) believes that these online discussions coalesced diverse political ideas into a common political goal that finally erupted on January 25, 2011, the Day of Anger. On that day, protestors used social media to gather information, support, and news, and to send videos and photos across the network. In turn, mainstream media, particularly opposition newspapers, relied on bloggers for stories that journalists could not write without facing prosecution.

"This is a revolution in the making sparked by youth who are determined to alter the dominant paradigm of politics and power that precludes the central idea which undergrids democracy — citizenship under a social contract." (Hovesepian 2011).

Egyptians made use of a wide range of media during the revolution, ranging from email and mobile phones, to leaflets and other print media. Mahir Marc Lynch, director of the Institute for Middle East Studies, warns that although social media such as Twitter and Facebook played a significant role in the Tunisian revolution, the full impact was not felt until their images made it onto broadcast media. Broadcast news, particularly opposition media in Egypt, and later international television, relied on Twitter and other social media to receive instant news. In Egypt, the Day of Anger protest in Tahrir Square was coordinated via Facebook and Twitter, using the hashtag #jan25 to post news as it happened. Mainstream media then re-broadcast the images worldwide. Al Jazeera, the international television news network based in Qatar, played a pivotal role in getting the message out.[8] Nevertheless, when expediency is paramount, as during a natural disaster or the early moments of a revolution (Zuckerman 2011), social media has proven far more effective than broadcast media. However, as seen in the Egyptian revolution, broadcast media and social media can work together to provide different but effective news.

Imagery has always been a powerful tool and weapon in campaigns against injustice. Images of Khaled Said, who was beaten to death by security police when they arrested him at a cybercafé in Cairo, became an icon of the revolution when his brother posted postmortem pictures on Facebook (*Technology Review* 2011). A Facebook group called "We are all Khaled Said" addressed police corruption and brutality and is considered instrumental in organizing Egyptian protesters (Martin 2011). Some of the most profound images coming from Tahrir Square depicted the bonding of Egyptians from disparate walks of life in a common cause, from protecting each other during prayers, to cleaning up the trash in the square. Thousands of Egyptian protesters took on the responsibility of streaming photos and updates, and tweeting to the world. These protestors became the producers of news, giving new meaning to the term **participatory politics** (Watkins 2011).

In June 2013, on the eve of the first anniversary of President Mohamed Morsi's election, Egyptians took to the streets again, this time to demand Morsi's removal from office.

---

8 For people living in Egypt at the time of the protests, myself included, Al Jazeera International was a vital link to what was happening in downtown Cairo.

FIGURE 8.2 EGYPTIAN MAN USING CELL PHONE TO TWEET NEWS FROM TAHRIR SQUARE IN CAIRO DURING THE EARLY DAYS OF THE JANUARY 2011 REVOLUTION

According to media and communications expert Adel Iskandar (2013: n.p.), the movement known as *Tamarod* (rebellion) used social media to "disseminate their messages and document their experiences and efforts. This digitisation of Egypt's protest movement far exceeds that which existed ahead of the eighteen days of protest in January 2011." Thus, social media is increasingly being used to engage, mobilize, and document civil protest and participatory politics.

CONCLUSION

In the early 1990s, Michael Hauben recognized that the Internet would bring about "new social consciousness and identity" (*The Amateur Computerist* 2011). His prophetic words ring true in light of recent events. Facebook and Twitter have become major conduits for news, information, and commentary, uniting grassroots movements for socio-political change (Evangelista 2011). Freedom on the Internet to express an opinion has had a significant impact on political and cultural processes. Indeed, Laura Miller (1995) calls the Internet a rich soup of world cultures.

In this chapter, social media has been considered a communication tool rather than a catalyst. The value of social media such as Facebook lies in its ability to provide "a space where silence and fear are broken and trust can be built, where social networks can turn political, and where home and Diaspora can come together" (Sreberny 2011: n.p.). Social media has the power to influence and shape viewers' perceptions, beliefs, and behaviours while also empowering people by giving them a forum in which to participate in political action (Suárez 2011).

Would the Tunisian and Egyptian revolutions have happened without social media? Perhaps, but social media brought these revolutionary movements to the attention of the world, and this may have had a great deal to do with their success in the sense that "the world was watching." Postill (2011) believes that online activism is part of a broader twenty-first-century cultural revolution and a global shift in power and knowledge. Ultimately, these revolutions were about people power; social media was merely one of the tools that facilitated, albeit in a significant way, their success. Social media did not bring down the Egyptian government; people did, and this is especially true of the 2013 revolt. Social media is not the reason why revolutions occur, but it has changed the very nature of social activism in ways that media experts, political pundits, and academics have only begun to analyze.

"If you want to liberate a society, just give them the Internet." Wael Ghonim, quoted on NPR's Internet: Road to Democracy … or elsewhere? (2011)

The power of social media and social networking is not always predictable, but there is little doubt that it is transforming how people communicate, become informed, and advocate. The Egyptian activist leaders are quite vocal in their estimation of the power of social media: without it, their revolution would not have succeeded. Having personally witnessed and experienced the dramatic flow of instantaneous information and the incredible organizational feats during the revolution, I tend to agree. What social media gave the Egyptian people, then, was a new sense of empowerment, never before enjoyed. Our world has changed; the public now has the power, and the private elite will never again be able to coerce, force, or bully without the world knowing.

QUESTIONS FOR CONSIDERATION AND CLASSROOM ACTIVITIES

1. In this chapter, social media is classified as a communication tool, not a catalyst for change. Do you agree with this assessment? Why or why not? How much influence does social media have on your world view and your knowledge of political situations around the world? Are you involved in any activism platforms? Explain.
2. Smart mobs are defined as people using the Internet to act together to facilitate cooperation and group action. Find three or more examples of smarts mobs and their activism.
3. Are you a netizen? Why or why not? Would you characterize netizens as the new global citizens? Explain the future roles you see for netizens.
4. Create a chart of media used for communications. Identify the type of media best suited for activism, promotion, propaganda, news, education, etc.
5. Research project: How has social media been used in indigenous activism, anti-globalization protests, and local level activism?
6. Social media has been used to circumvent censorship in many parts of the world. Provide three examples of current socio-political action using social media, and research the efficacy of these actions.
7. Marginalized women are using social media to tell their stories. What other marginalized groups are using social media to demand change?

8. In your opinion, is the role of social media exaggerated? What future roles do you see for social media?

SUGGESTED READINGS

Campbell, D.G. (2011). *Egypt unshackled: Using social media to @#:) the system.* Llandeilo, UK: Cambria Books.

This timely book describes how social media can reshape history by using the riveting "tweeting history" of the last days of the Egyptian revolution. A must-read book.

Katz, J.E. (Ed.). (2008). *Handbook of mobile communication studies.* E-book. Cambridge, MA: The MIT Press.

This book contains expert analysis of the impact of social media on everyday life and culture, from around the world.

Chapter 9

Global Nomads: Do Third Culture Kids Own a National Identity?

Key Terms: biculturalism, cultural marginality, culture, culture shock, ethnoscapes, global citizens, globalization, global nomads, identity, nationalism, reverse culture shock, subculture, Third Culture Kids (TCKs), transcultural/transnational identity, transcultural literacy

---

INTRODUCTION

"While they had spent much of the last twelve years in front of the television, I had gone on safaris, visited African plains and tropical forests, eaten exotic foods and fruits, toured French chateaux and cathedrals, and ridden Eurorail to Paris." Third Culture Kid, quoted in Eakin (1998: 12).

Nolan (1990: 2) defines **culture** as "a pattern of meaning, a way of defining the world." Each of us has a sense of the way things ought to be – this sense is deeply ingrained and learned from birth. Our ideals, values, and beliefs generate acceptable behaviour in our cultural environment; however, when we move to another cultural milieu, we leave behind our familiar world and enter one that operates under a different set of rules and expectations. In this new environment, we are no longer able to predict the behaviour of other people, and we no longer feel secure until we "learn" the new culture.

This conceptualization of culture corresponds well with the reality of global nomads, since "culture" takes on new meanings for people who live in a foreign country and who do not own "roots" or a defined homeland. **Global nomads**, also known as expatriates/expats, are people who leave their passport or natal country and move to another country for economic, political, or experiential reasons. In 2010, approximately 200 million people lived abroad (Just Landed 2009),[1] some as permanent residents, others as temporary sojourners. Global nomads are mainly missionaries, military personnel, professional or business people (e.g., oil executives, educators, foreign service diplomats), and their families.

The transnational flow of people and knowledge is a process of **globalization**. These movements of people – what Appadurai (1991) calls **ethnoscapes**, have created a diaspora of people in virtually every country and have produced transcultural and transnational identities (Kearney 1995). For global nomads, then, "home" becomes fluid, a constantly changing place existing in multiple locations, while the concept of "culture" may become

---

1 Only estimates are available, since most countries do not keep records on people who have moved out of a country. In 2009, 2.8 million Canadians lived abroad (CBC News 2009).

deterritorialized (King 1991). This fluidity may challenge the creation of any sense of **nationalism**, which Smith (2001: 6) defines as "a sentiment or consciousness of belonging to a nation."

One of the most interesting phenomena to arise from global nomadism is **Third Culture Kids (TCKs)**. A Third Culture Kid is "a person who has spent a significant part of his or her developmental years outside their parents' culture. The third culture kid builds relationships to all the cultures, while not having full ownership in any," including their passport culture (Pollock & Van Reken 2001: 19). Indeed, sociologist Ted Ward called TCKs the "prototype citizens of a future," when global nomads will be [are] the norm rather than the exception (Van Reken & Bethel 2007). Understanding the world through the eyes of a TCK is important, since most TCKs return to their passport country for university and perhaps employment, where they have a great deal of international knowledge and skills to offer their community. Indeed, educator Kay Brananman Eakin (1998: 7) claims that "a multi-cultural society prepares them [TCKs] well to be citizens of an increasingly interdependent world," in other words, **global citizens**, and "uniquely suited for life in today's increasingly global society" (Bowman 2012: 1).

In the 1990s, a research project on TCKs sought to uncover the positive contributions that TCKs make to their home communities, workplace, and society in general (Useem 1993). This study focused on adult TCKs living in the United States. Some of the questions asked in this study included the following: What happens to TCKs when they grow up? What skills, worldviews, and opinions do they bring from a third-culture childhood? How are they affected by having spent some or all of their child/teen years abroad? More recently, sociologist David C. Pollock and Ruth Van Reken's pivotal book, *Third Culture Kids: The Experience of Growing Up Among Worlds* (2009), has become a major source of information on TCKs. Both of these sources are drawn upon in the following discussion.

In this chapter we will explore the experience of global nomads, in particular Third Culture Kids. We will examine the impact on TCKs' **identity** and worldview of spending their formative years in a foreign environment as well as their experiences with repatriating to their passport country, while also considering whether the formation of a national identity is jeopardized in TCKs. Personal narratives from Adult Third Culture Kids (ATCKs) and TCKs are found throughout this chapter. We will draw on the expertise and insights of psychologists, theologians, educators, anthropologists, and sociologists as we explore twenty-first-century global nomads.

THE NATURE OF GLOBAL NOMADS AND THIRD CULTURE KIDS

Although immigrants moving from developing countries to developed countries have been a major focus of immigrant studies, there is also a need to study global nomads and TCKs who move from developed states to other countries, including developing nations. Researchers have identified numerous benefits from global nomadism. The most commonly reported advantage of living abroad is an expanded worldview that develops from living in another culture and associating with people from the host culture as well as other foreign sojourners. Global nomads learn to be flexible, appreciative of difference, and more open-minded. They also learn to adapt and compromise, and they acquire cultural knowledge and skills from each culture they live in. Yet living abroad also brings challenges;

frequent moves cause difficulties adjusting to a new cultural environment and sadness at losing friends and a lifestyle they enjoyed. Global nomadism also affects kinship and family structure in the passport country, with long separations from loved ones, which can be very difficult, especially for children missing their grandparents and other members of their extended family.

Ward, Bochner, & Furnham (2001: 51) identify culture learning as the "process whereby sojourners acquire culturally relevant social knowledge and skills in order to survive and thrive in their new society." This is a significant accomplishment for global nomads, although it would be naive to suggest that people who move to a new country assume a new cultural identity. However, over time, global nomads, including TCKs, may take on some of the characteristics of an adopted culture. Ultimately, global nomads may develop multiple identities – their expat identity, their home culture identity, and even their professional or student identity. A form of **biculturalism** can develop, where they identify with and become a part of more than one culture. At times, this comes about through developing a rapport with members of the host community, at other times simply from immersion in the host culture to the point that some of their attitudes and perspectives are adopted. One example is modest dress. Some people, including myself, can find it difficult to adjust to the revealing, casual clothing that North American women wear after years of living in a Muslim country where even women who choose not to wear a *gallabiayya*[2] and *hijab*[3] dress conservatively.

Anthropologist/sociologist Dr. Ruth Hill Useem conducted a pioneering study of Americans living and working in India in 1957 (Useem 1993). These Americans were foreign service officers, businesspeople, missionaries, aid workers, educators, and media reps. Useem found that despite the heterogeneity of the American expats, they had enough commonalities to form a distinct **subculture** or third culture, different from their home culture and the host culture. During this research, Useem first applied the term Third Culture Kids to refer to children who accompany their parents abroad. Although Useem was referring to American TCKs, a growing body of evidence suggests that young people of other nationalities share the same characteristics and face similar challenges.

"I have a continuing love affair with Third Culture Kids (TCKs). They are all my children because they carry my name. They are the most interesting people because their rich inner lives belie their often bland, dull, and sometimes wary, presentation of themselves to others." Useem (1993: 2)

Global nomads, because of their cross-cultural experiences, tend to understand issues from multiple perspectives and recognize that people of diverse backgrounds have different values and beliefs (Langford 1998). Global nomads, then, have a greater appreciation for cultural diversity. Even those who attempt to hide in an "expat bubble" are affected by the culture of the host country. Conversely, global nomads have difficulty developing a "local" view, preferring an international perspective. As a result, they may never fully reintegrate into their passport country and may become impatient with the culture-bound attitudes of their peers.

Culture shock is a common problem that global nomads experience. They learn various coping strategies to deal with the feelings of disorientation, hostility, and loneliness, one of the most common responses being the creation of private spaces (e.g., the home) or

---

2 Full-length, loose garment.
3 Head covering/scarf (see Chapter 1).

boundaries (e.g., social interaction) (Fechter 2008). Forming close-knit communities, most likely at the private international schools their children attend, is also a common coping strategy, especially for mothers. Here, members of the community support each other and assist in familiarizing new expats with the community and creating social networks that alleviate loneliness and depression. At the international school where I taught, students freely interacted with each other during class time, regardless of ethnicity. However, like their parents who gravitated to other expats with lived experiences similar to their own, during breaks my students tended to associate with "their group," which was often based on country of origin or ethnicity. Despite these coping strategies, most global nomads, including TCKs, suffer bouts of culture shock.

WHO ARE THIRD CULTURE KIDS?

As mentioned earlier, the term Third Culture Kids (TCKs) was first coined by Useem in the 1960s (Ridout 2010). Third Culture Kids may be Korean children growing up in Cairo, Egypt, Canadian children living in Rio de Janeiro, Brazil, or American children in Moscow, Russia. Regardless of where they live or where they come from, these youths blend elements from all the cultures they experience to create a third culture that influences their values, beliefs, and worldview (Pollock & Van Reken 2001). This process has important implications for who they will become in the future, since children have yet to firmly establish their sense of personal or cultural identity. Indeed, their international life experiences will create a unique sense of identity that can have a dramatic impact on their lives and the lives of those around them when they return "home" and may preclude the development of a national identity.

> "The Third Culture Kid is always 'standing in the doorway,' on a threshold between two or more cultures in which s/he never has 'full ownership.'" Ridout (2010:5).

There are several types of TCKs, each with their own experiences: military kids, missionary kids, embassy kids, business kids, and kids whose parents work in education, NGOs, media, etc. The children of missionary parents, or missionary kids (MKs), are what Keuss and Willett (2009) call "the sacredly mobile" in that they are not united by experiences, but by the lack of a definable home. Experiences for MKs may not be the same as other TCKs: they may not live in as affluent circumstances; they may not be posted in thriving urban areas; and they may not attend private international schools. In fact, many MKs spend their childhood away from their passport country and away from their parents, instead living at boarding schools.

> "My MKness has completely shaped my life, my calling, my career, my major, my dreams, my identity, my taste in women, my nomadic behavior, my humor, my compassion, who my friends are, and so much more." A missionary kid, quoted in Keuss & Willett (2009: 14)

Despite their different backgrounds, TCKs share common characteristics, to the extent that Pollock and Van Reken (2009) agree with Useem's (1993) assessment that global nomads, including TCKs, form a distinct subculture. TCKs tend to possess strong self-esteem, advanced social skills, and adaptability, moving from one country to another with seeming ease. Generally speaking, they feel comfortable with foreigners or "cultural otherness," are fluent in several languages, and are aware, from an insider's perspective, of other cultures. This is known as **transcultural literacy,** a phenomenon that Heyward (2002: 10) defines as "the understandings, competencies, attitudes, language proficiencies, participation and identities necessary for successful cross-cultural engagement." Those possessing transcultural literacy can "read" a new culture and quickly learn and adapt to new symbols of everyday life.

TCKs enjoy significant benefits from growing up in a foreign culture, in particular, cross-cultural experiences that enrich their lives and create a multidimensional worldview (Gould 2002). As a result, TCKs tend to view themselves as global citizens rather than identifying with members of their own ethnic group or even passport country, which again calls into question the ability to hold a national identity. The degree to which this holds true varies, depending on whether they attend weekend language schools, and whether they associate with other students of their ethnicity, visit their home country regularly, and maintain close family ties. When TCKs become adults, they tend to raise their children to appreciate the cultural diversity with which they are familiar, rather than stressing a national or ethnic identity (Cottrell & Useem 1993b).

FIGURE 9.1 A GRADUATING CLASS FROM CAIRO AMERICAN COLLEGE AT THE PYRAMIDS. THE MAJORITY OF THE STUDENTS AT THIS SCHOOL ARE THIRD CULTURE KIDS

In the Useem study (1993), Anne Baker Cottrell also found that international experience made TCKs more understanding and aware of other people and cultures than most Americans. TCKs in the study tend to seek international occupations, hold a strong desire to visit and live abroad, and enjoy meeting foreigners. Because of their experiences, they tend to relate to cultural diversity. On the other hand, their extensive cross-cultural knowledge and skills present a challenge since most TCKs in the study felt they did not have ample opportunities in America to use such knowledge and skill sets.

Pollock and Van Reken (2009) identify five major stages in the cycle of mobility (and separation) experienced by TCKs: 1) involvement: the TCK belongs to a community and feels secure; 2) leaving: the TCK learns s/he is going to leave, and begins loosening interpersonal ties, emotionally separating from friends, and anticipates grief but tries to deny being sad; 3) transition: moving and all that entails, arriving in a new community, and feeling a sense of instability; 4) entering the new community: beginning the process of adapting, overcoming feelings of instability, insecurity, and culture shock; and 5) reinvolvement: becoming a member of the new community. This cycle may occur several times in a TCK's pre-adult life and may prevent a TCK from developing close relationships for fear of the grief that accompanies separation. TCKs may view relationships as short-term even when they return to their home country, and they continue to suffer unresolved grief and sadness over those they left behind. On a more positive note, the Internet and social media allow TCKs (as well as other global nomads) to maintain relationships with family and friends in their passport country, as well as those

"Growing up as a TCK has been a gift and has significantly shaped my life and work. As I interact with world leaders one day and with those living in refugee camps the next, I continually draw upon my experience of living among different cultures." Scott Gration, Maj. Gen. USAF (RET), President Obama's Special Envoy to Sudan, quoted in Amazon.com reviews of Pollock and Van Reken's *Third Culture Kids: The Experience of Growing Up Among Worlds* (2001)

"When I first came to Egypt, ten years ago, I faced some challenges dealing with local students. In a Canadian school, where mostly Egyptian students attend, I was mocked by my appearance. In addition, Egypt was the first foreign country that I have lived, so it was extremely difficult to communicate with other people in the school. As I got exposed to various other students from different countries, when I moved to CAC, I became more familiar with the different cultures and ideas. I realized that when I visited my home country, Korea, after several years. I could not look at things the way I looked at them before I came to Egypt. It was somewhat uncomfortable to interact the way I used to, before I was exposed to the variety of cultures." Sohyun Kim, an international student at Cairo American College they leave behind when moving from one country to another. This instant communication helps alleviate some of the grief and sense of loss from periodic relocation.

TCKs exhibit a strong cosmopolitanism, which means being comfortable in more than one cultural setting and owning multiple perspectives on complex issues, such as human rights (Vertovec & Cohen 2002). They are also more interested in international news and aware of what is happening, especially in countries where they have lived. TCKs of all types desire to associate with peers who have an understanding of the world, and are able to embrace change. Useem (1993) found that most TCKs tend to be high achievers, earning university degrees at a much higher rate than those in their home population. Their choice of program is often influenced by their international experience, choosing disciplines such as anthropology, international relations, and foreign languages, and choosing careers in international teaching, international relations, and international business.

"Spending time with people who are Third Culture Kids is always fun. My friends who are third culture kids would often tell me of stories in places that sound amazing. We would hear about what the schools were like, and how different the culture was compared to the culture [in Egypt]. Conversations with my friends were always so interesting because they always had the most unique view on what we were talking about. Each person would always have unique sayings that they had picked up from other cultures that they would often use on a daily basis. As much as I love knowing people who come from such a diverse background, it's sad knowing that one of my friends may end up leaving at the end of the year because of the company that their parents work for. Social networking has made it a lot easier nowadays to keep in touch with my friends who have traveled across the globe." Yasmin Shawky, an Egyptian student at the international school, Cairo American College

RETURNING "HOME"

Although TCKs enjoy intrinsic benefits in the form of enriched cultural experiences from living abroad, as well as extrinsic benefits such as receiving a superior education and offers from the most prestigious universities because of the quality of their education and international experience, they also face substantial challenges. According to Hill (1986: 332), "psychological adjustment [can] be stressful and the individual [is] at risk from naiveté, inadequate acculturation to Western values, and competitive materialism." Indeed, TCKs may feel like strangers in a strange land.

Many TCKs complain of rootlessness (Useem 1993). Even TCKs who are still overseas may feel this way, becoming restless after several years in the same country and wanting to "move on" to new experiences. This rootlessness can affect their university education and careers: TCKs tend to change colleges and programs several times, or leave college to travel, which puts them out of synch with other students their age.

TCKs also feel out of touch on a personal level: they feel alienated from their peers in their passport country, stand out because they have not caught up on local pop culture, such as movie stars, sports, and jokes, and experience **cultural marginality** (Van Reken & Bethel 2007). TCKs also tend to be dismayed by their peers' lack of worldliness, the racist perspective of some, and the lack of interest in the outside world of others (Kebshull & Pozo-Humphries n.d.). They may become frustrated when their peers show no interest in their travels and lived experiences (Eakin 1998), and they also face increased pressure to become sexually active and get involved with drugs and alcohol. Consequently, they may reject their home culture and their parochial peers and avoid forming meaningful friendships. Cottrell and Useem (1993a: n.p.) found that only 1 in 10 participants in their study felt "completely attuned to everyday life in the U.S." Rather, TCKs tend to feel more comfortable with foreigners, exchange students, and non-English speaking minorities because "they've been there." Their sense of home comes from relationships, not locations – the here and now of their lives. Indeed, many TCKs do not have a strong sense of home or feel that their host country is more home than their passport country.

TCKs may experience reverse culture shock when they return to their passport country. Pollock and Van Reken (2009) call this "re-entry stress." This stress may initially manifest in the form of anger toward their parents for taking them away from their friends. **Reverse culture shock** is the "temporal psychological difficulties returnees experience in the initial stage of the adjustment process at home after having lived abroad for some time" (Uehara 1986: 420). According to Useem (1993), many never adjust, but only adapt. For example, Bikos et al. (2009) found that MKs returning to North America were surprised by the excess consumerism and conspicuous consumption of North American culture and they marvelled at the size of cars and homes. Unlike other TCKs, MKs also had to deal with the label of "missionary kid" and

"I love and enjoy being a third culture kid. I have lived in such countries as the United States, Japan, Thailand, Malaysia and Egypt. I have been exposed to so many exotic cultures and it has changed my life in ways of how I looked at the world. Living in Egypt, I had the chance to live in history with the demonstrations going on. When I was a kid, I kept on wishing that I would move to the States, but now that I look back at my life, I don't want to trade any other life than the life I had. I did miss my friends every time I moved, and it was always hard to make new friends again, but over the countless times I have moved, I think I got used to it. It became part of my life. And I believe now that it is easier to make new friends.

I am also a Christian and I don't believe there was any trouble in keeping my faith in Egypt, with almost everyone being a Muslim. With all the Muslims surrounding me, and hearing the mosque calls every day, it has made me stronger in my faith and made me more assertive to my beliefs.

I did not struggle that much coming back to the States because my family and I went back to my father's home in Hawaii every year. So there wasn't that much of a culture shock. But it's always funny when people ask me where I'm from and so I say, Cairo, Egypt. Then they will say something like, 'Oh then do you know how to speak hieroglyphics?' or something like, 'Do you live in the pyramids?'" Johnathan Shimabuku, an international student formerly at Cairo American College.

the stereotypes and assumptions attached to that label. TCKs from military families tend to have the fewest problems re-entering the United States because of highly Americanized bases overseas, and because they tend to spend shorter periods (five or fewer years) abroad. They also appear to be the least critical of the United States (e.g., foreign policy, military ventures), and least interested in international involvement (Useem 1993). TCKs whose parents are international educators, executives, or embassy personnel are the most eager to live abroad again, and have the strongest desire to maintain an international dimension in their lives. Recognizing the seriousness of the adjustment problems faced by TCKs when re-entering their passport country, many international schools now organize transition programs to help students return to their home country, especially when entering university (Eakin 1998).

Obviously, most of the problems and challenges that TCKs encounter are related to a search for their own identity and a sense of belonging. According to psychologist Erik Erikson (1970), searching for identity is a major goal for any adolescent. For TCKs this becomes even more of a puzzle, given the diversity of cultures they have experienced:

"Although looking like an insider, an MK [or TCK] feels completely on the outside as he or she is lost in the slang or idioms, has acquired different tastes in food, struggles to maintain foreign customs, and is unfamiliar with the pop culture." (Klemens & Bikos 2009).

what identity should they adopt – that of their "home" country, the country they currently live in, or the country they enjoyed living in the most? Ultimately being a global nomad causes TCKs to question their belonging and their identity: "they feel at home everywhere and nowhere" (Cottrell 1999: n.p.).

CONCLUSION

Living abroad is a rewarding personal experience, tapping into an individual's resourcefulness, adaptability, and sense of self. Those who undertake a foreign posting, of whatever sort, gain an enhanced cross-cultural perspective, multidimensional worldview, and ability to adapt to changing situations. They also face numerous challenges, ranging from culture shock to always having to say good-bye. When expats are repatriated to their passport country they may have difficulty adjusting to excessive consumerism, provincial attitudes, community homogeneity, and a lower standard of living, while also grieving for the friends and lifestyle they left behind. Cultural immersion suggests losing oneself in another cultural environment. However, this is unrealistic; even after enculturation a foreigner remains part of the "Other." Comparing culture shock to a rite of passage seems apt; it is a period of personal growth and learning and reflects on a person's ability to adapt and accept new and unfamiliar ways of living.

Third Culture Kids experience difficulties on a greater scale than other global nomads because of living outside their passport country during their formative years. The most profound of the challenges is their lack of connection with their passport country and their peers within that country. They feel inadequate and cannot relate to the local pop culture, and they continue to value international issues more than local ones. Nonetheless, the benefits of living abroad far outweigh the challenges. TCKs are a hidden resource – they are cross-culturally savvy, and can add diversity and an international worldview to their participation in educational programs as well as when they enter the professional world. Young people who have lived overseas, even if only for a few years, will never see the world or their country of origin in the same way again, and are poised to take on a future role as cultural bridges and cultural brokers for their generation.

The opening question, do Third Culture Kids own a national identity, is difficult to definitively answer. At first glance, the answer is no. If nationalism is a sentiment or feeling of belonging to a nation, then TCKs may have difficulty owning a national identity. However, as time passes, some TCKs do become nationalistic, and, of course, each TCK is a unique individual with different responses (Useem 1993). Still, most Third Culture Kids struggle with identity and confused loyalties; they are not of one culture or of another, nor do they necessarily want to be – they are international rather than national – they are the "Other." Thus, Third Culture Kids are always "standing in the doorway."

QUESTIONS FOR CONSIDERATION AND CLASSROOM ACTIVITIES

1. If you moved to another country temporarily, would you try to hold on to your cultural practices and values or would you adopt (assimilate to) your new country's culture? Do you think it is possible to completely give up a natal culture and immerse oneself in a new culture? Why or why not?

2. Imagine yourself in a strange place, with no friends or family, unable to speak the language, unfamiliar foods in the stores ... you get the picture. How would you cope with this new life? Draft an action plan for dealing with culture shock in your adopted country, including the coping strategies that you would employ.

3. Investigate biculturalism. What advantages can you identify from having a bicultural perspective? What disadvantages?

4. Conduct an ethnographic interview with someone who has moved to your school from a different country. What problems did they encounter when they first arrived? How did they solve these problems? What elements of their culture are they maintaining, and what (if any) elements of their host country are they adopting?

5. Locate a TCK in your community and conduct an ethnographic interview. Organize your questions around challenges of living in a new country, benefits of an international lifestyle, and attitudes when they return home.

6. Class debate: are globalization processes and the transnational flow of people threatening national identity?

7. Living abroad obviously creates global citizenship, but are there ways in which monocultural young people can also develop global awareness and citizenship?

SUGGESTED READINGS

Pollock, D.C., & Van Reken, R.E. (2009). *Third culture kids: The experience of growing up among worlds*. London: Nicholas Brealey & Intercultural Press.

This easy-to-read book explores the world of children who have grown up in cultures other than their passport country. The challenges they have faced and the amazing benefits of an international upbringing illustrate the realities of contemporary global nomads. A must-read book for anyone who has lived overseas or is contemplating a move abroad.

Useem, R.H. (n.d.). *TCK World: The official home of TCKs*. http://www.tckworld. com/

This site provides a plethora of information on TCKs. Highly recommended for anyone who has lived in foreign cultures or for readers interested in learning about the experiences of TCKs and global nomads.

Part Three

ECONOMIC, POLITICAL, AND SOCIAL CONFLICT

In this final section of *Global Issues* we will explore three interwoven themes: economic challenges, the political nature of humans, and the social consequences of political and economic conflict. The continuing themes of culture change and changing identities, and cultural imperialism and human rights, are also evident in Part Three, "Economic, Political, and Social Conflict."

In Chapter 10, "Food Security: What are the economic and political determinants of food security and the global implications of world hunger?", the reasons behind world hunger are examined from a critical perspective that may give pause to current stances concerning poverty and food security. The role of cultural imperialism and political domination in the proliferation of world hunger is emphasized.

In Chapter 11, "Ethnic Conflicts: What are the underlying reasons and the consequences of these conflicts?", and Chapter 12, "Human Migration: What are the socio-economic and political implications of the transnational flow of people?", the impact of internal and external political forces on the safety and social and economic well-being of people is addressed. Cultural imperialism and its role in challenging human rights are also explored in these chapters.

In many ways, Chapter 13, "Global Conflict: Is the world safer because of military intervention, and what are the consequences of militarism?", is the thematic culmination of this book. Throughout *Global Issues* we have investigated conflict in its myriad forms: economic, social, religious, and, of course, political. In this closing chapter, global conflict and militarism are investigated, as is political domination. In particular, the impact of the Western leader of cultural imperialism, the United States, on regions and peoples of the world is explored.

Ultimately, *Global Issues* is not about politics, economics, or social organization; rather, it is about people, and how people around the world have been impacted through economic realities, political manipulation, and social and religious forces.

Chapter 10

Food Security: What Are the Economic and Political Determinants of Food Security and the Global Implications of World Hunger?

Key Terms: agribusiness, agriculture for development, contract farming, cultural imperialism, dependency theory, food security, food sovereignty, human rights, industrial agriculture, modernization theory, multifunctional approach, small-scale/subsistence farming

---

INTRODUCTION

"Food security exists when all people, at all times, have physical and economic access to sufficient, safe, and nutritious food that meets their dietary needs and food preferences for an active and healthy life." (Food and Agriculture Organization [FAO] 1996).

Despite the United Nations Millennium Development Goals' pledge to halve world hunger by 2015, and despite the fact that more food is produced today than ever before, in the early twenty-first century more than a billion people are living in poverty and hunger. To answer the question of "why" should be fairly straightforward; however, world hunger is mired in complex political and economic factors that have little to do with humanitarian crises and everything to do with power and wealth. To further complicate the issue, proposed solutions to world hunger appear contradictory, and are often designed to fulfill economic and political agendas, rather than the needs of hungry people.

"Nothing is more degrading than hunger, especially when man made." Ban Ki Moon, United Nations Secretary General quoted in World Food Council (n.d.).

Thirty-nine countries have been identified as hunger hotspots, with "widespread persistence and prevalence of food insecurity" (Mihalache-O'Keef & Li 2011: 72). Twenty-five of these hotspots are in Africa, 11 in Asia and the Near East, two in Latin America, and one in Europe (FAO 2006: 2). Sixty-five per cent of the world's hungry live in China, Bangladesh, the Democratic Republic of Congo, Indonesia, Pakistan, India, and Ethiopia (FAO 2008: 12).

Food security refers to having reliable access to sources of nutritious food, as the opening quotation in this chapter exemplifies. Food security is also a universal **human right** according to the United Nations' 1948 Universal Declaration of Human Rights, and in 1985, the United Nations created the Commission on Economic, Social and Cultural Rights, which promotes the rights of everyone to food security (González 2010). The World Bank calls hunger "the world's most serious health problem and a key indicator of social development" (Jenkins, Scanlon, & Peterson 2007: 826), as it affects health and well-being, educational achievement, gender equity, and social status. Growing evidence also suggests that food security is imperative for maintaining world peace (e.g., Bryant & Kappaz 2005).

Most food producers around the world have been **small-scale** or **subsistence farmers** with less than two acres of land per farm. These farmers produce most of the staple crops for both urban and rural populations. In Latin America, for example, 17 million small farms produce 51 per cent of the maize, 77 per cent of the beans, and 61 per cent of the potatoes consumed domestically. In Africa, 33 million small, mostly female-run, farms produce the basic foodstuffs without using fertilizers, and in Asia, 200 million subsistence farmers produce most of the rice. Small-scale farms have been so integral to food security that the International Planning Committee of Food Sovereignty claims that small farms "feed the world and cool the planet" (McMichael & Schneider 2011: 134). To demonstrate the value of small-scale farming, in this chapter we will briefly consider the success of organic agroecology in Cuba.

In many regions of the world, small-scale, sustainable agriculture has been replaced by intensive agriculture or agribusiness. The term **agribusiness** was first coined in the 1950s by agricultural economists John Herbert Davis and Ray A. Goldberg (Harvard Business School n.d.). Agribusinesses involve an interdependence among producers, manufacturers, and processing and distribution industries. They practise **industrial agriculture**, which is a "system of chemically intensive food production developed in the decades after World War II," with large "single-crop farms and animal production facilities (Union of Concerned Scientists 2012). Agribusinesses are market-driven and export-oriented enterprises with the goal of generating profits for foreign investors.

Proponents suggest that agribusinesses reduce the number of labourers needed, enabling some farmers to work off the farm, have a higher level of productivity, produce better-quality food and a greater variety of products with improved nutrition, use advanced technologies and research, such as genetically engineered foods, and increase the mobility of people. However, as will be seen below, not everyone agrees that these benefits ever materialize, and in some cases the supposed benefits are actually negative consequences.

The economic and humanitarian consequences of exporting food rather than feeding local communities is a key component of this chapter. We will explore the humanitarian implications of world hunger and visit a city in Brazil where people, in partnership with the civic and national governments, solved their own food-security problems. The environmental risks that arise from unchecked industrial agriculture are also addressed.

In this chapter, then, the political and economic reasons for world hunger and evolving food security issues are the main focus. Yet food security remains a contentious issue, with conflicting evidence and contradictory theoretical predictions (Mihalache-O'Keef & Li 2011). We will consider two opposing schools of thought that argue for the best way to ensure food security: market-based agribusiness and food sovereignty, and the modernization and dependency theories. The policies and practices of the World Bank and United Nations Food and Agriculture Organization (FAO) are often blamed for exacerbating poverty and hunger, and for declines in food security around the world; we will investigate the truth of these accusations.

The expertise and insights of several disciplines, including political economy, environmental science, food sciences, and international development studies are drawn upon. In

1977, world hunger experts Frances Moore Lappe and Joseph Collins (1977) published an article, "Why Can't People Feed Themselves?", which examined world hunger within a historical context. This question informs our examination of food security. Indeed, placing food security within a historical context not only explains what has happened in the past, but also provides a chilling image of what is happening today.

"What astonished us, however, is that there are not more people in the world who are hungry — considering the weight of the centuries of effort by the few to undermine the capacity of the majority to feed themselves." (Lappe & Collins 1977: n.p.)

Although every attempt is made to remain objective while addressing this contested topic, this chapter remains a critical analysis of how economic globalization, foreign investment, and industrial agribusinesses have endangered food security for hundreds of millions of people in developing nations. Helena Norberg-Hodge and colleagues (2013) ask the following question: "Is it logical to believe that destroying local economies will improve their [small-scale farmers'] lives?" The following discussion addresses this question on several fronts.

THE NATURE OF FOOD SECURITY AND WORLD HUNGER

The roots of twenty-first-century world hunger lie within the colonial era[1] when economic policies were set in place that changed agriculture on a global scale. Traditional agricultural production and distribution systems were based on mutual obligations (e.g., food sharing) and biodiversified production (mixed cropping). These practices, which fulfilled at least minimal needs for everyone in the community, were disrupted by colonial policies that undermined the ability of subsistence farmers to feed themselves and those around them – what Lappe & Collins (1977) call "scarcity-creating mechanisms." To rationalize their policies, colonial administrators in Asia, Africa, and Latin America dismissed small-scale agriculture as primitive and inefficient, which is a classic case of **cultural imperialism** at work. Indeed, colonial powers may have believed they were acting in the best interests of the people by setting them on the path to modernization and prosperity (Lappe & Collins 1977).

"A.J. Voelker, British agriculture scientist in India in the 1890s, counters the idea that small-scale farming was inefficient: 'Nowhere would one find better instances of keeping land scrupulously clean from weeds, of ingenuity in device of water-raising appliances, of knowledge of soils and their capabilities, as well as of the exact time to sow and reap, as one would find in Indian agriculture. It is wonderful too, how much is known of rotation, the system of "mixed crops" and of fallowing.... I, at least, have never seen a more perfect picture of cultivation.'" (Radha 1976: 26)

Colonial governments considered "the colonies" to be mere "agricultural establishments" that supplied Europeans with produce and wealth (McMichael & Schneider 2011: 130). To that end, diversified small-scale farms growing staple foods such as yams and rice were transformed into single cash crops (e.g., sugar, cocoa, tobacco), forcing farmers to neglect growing food crops to feed their families and their community. For example, rice used to be a staple crop in the Gambia, but during colonial rule the best land was converted to peanut crops for European markets and rice had to be imported to ward off famine (Lappe & Collins 1977). In another example, at the time of the American Civil War, the

---

1 The colonial era began in the mid-1500s with European expansion into Africa, and continues in some regions even today.

"Our West India colonies, for example, cannot be regarded as countries. The West Indies are the place where England finds it convenient to carry on the production of sugar, coffee and a few other tropical commodities." English economist John Stuart Mill, quoted in Lappe & Collins (1977: n.p.).

French converted the Mekong Delta in Vietnam to rice production for export. Large landowners grew rich, while landless Vietnamese went hungry (Owens 1976). This dramatic change in global agriculture is a primary reason for world hunger, then and today.

The most fertile land was expropriated by colonial governments to sell or lease to foreign landowners, who then established plantations to grow crops for export. For example, in 1870 the Dutch declared all uncultivated land in Java to be the property of the colonial government, and then leased the land to plantation owners. In a dozen countries in eastern and southern Africa, land was expropriated and the people were driven onto small reserves. Destitute conditions on these reserves forced hundreds of thousands of Africans to become cheap labour for the plantations (Lappe & Collins 1977).

In some colonial governments, such as the Dutch East Indies, small-scale farming was suppressed because the farmers were too efficient and competitive for European settlers and foreign agriculture. Indeed, foreign-owned plantation land might sit idle for years, just to prevent peasants from growing crops in the region. A modern-day example is in Guatemala, where Del Monte owns 57,000 acres of land but plants only 9,000; the rest of the land remains empty, except for a few grazing cattle (Lappe & Collins 1977).

"Whole families used to work on the land. We grew almost everything we needed. Now imported wheat is destroying our market. It's just not worth going to the trouble of producing food anymore, and the village is being emptied of people." Dolmar Tsering, a farmer in northern India, quoted in Norberg-Hodge, Merrifield, & Gorelick (2013).

Colonial policies also created a dependency on imported food among formerly self-sufficient farmers. Imported-food prices were kept artificially low to entice the people to buy food rather than grow it, eventually creating a dependency on imported food and a vulnerability to price fluctuations and supply. Cheap food flooding a region destroyed local markets, impoverishing farmers – a process that continues today with agricultural subsidies in developed nations and the dumping of cheap produce on the world markets, making it impossible for small farmers to grow their produce at a competitive rate.

The question arises, then, why the subsistence farmers complied. In essence, colonial powers physically and economically forced the farmers to grow cash crops. As incredible as it may seem today, guns and whips played a part in forcing farmers to grow cash crops (Rodney 1972, quoted in Lappe & Collins 1977: n.p.). More common than physical force was economic force through taxation. The colonial administrators levied taxes on livestock, land, homes, and even people, forcing the farmers to grow cash crops in order to pay the taxes. Some farmers worked on the plantations to earn enough money to pay their taxes.

CONTEMPORARY FOOD-SECURITY ISSUES

The historical processes that drove small-scale farmers off their land and initiated the decline in food security continue today with increasing speed and with growing implications for food security. Although the United Nations Food and Agriculture Organization (FAO) has developed a definition of food security that appears to address the needs of everyone (see the quotation that opens this chapter), Pottier (1999) suggests this is merely symbolic rhetoric: the FAO is using the definition as camouflage for policies and practices that have never taken the needs or preferences of the hungry poor into account. Indeed, González (2010) accuses the FAO of suffering from cultural ethnocentrism. As well as the FAO, other global institutions, such as the International Monetary Fund (IMF), World Trade Organization (WTO), and the World Bank, make decisions regarding food production, the allocation of economic and natural resources, and global trade without consulting the local people. In essence, these powerful institutions have silenced the voices of local producers. Indeed, these institutions remain unaccountable to any electorate (Weisbrot 2002). National governments also tend to yield to pressures from economic and political power-houses, such as Cargill and Archer Daniels Midland, who control 70 to 80 per cent of the world's grain trade (Norberg-Hodge, Merrifield, & Gorelick 2013).

> "One agribusiness, Phillip Morris, gets 10 cents out of every American food dollar — more than earned by all US farmers combined." (Norberg-Hodge, Merrifield, & Gorelick 2013).

In 2006, food prices began to rise worldwide, precipitating a dramatic increase in hunger and malnutrition in the global South,[2] especially among the most vulnerable, i.e., women and children. This rise in the cost of staple food, or agflation, is expected to continue, especially as climate change reduces available land for agriculture. Poverty-stricken people cannot afford to purchase high-priced imported food, but as you have seen, imported food dependency has been an on-going process since the colonial era, and many farmers no longer have the land or resources to grow their own food. As food prices continue to rise, more and more people will slide below the poverty line and no longer be able to afford imported food. Ironically, even the poorest countries grow enough food to feed their population, but governments have been lured into exporting much of the domestic produce, leaving their own people to go hungry (McMichael & Schneider 2011).

The rise in food prices has encouraged transnational corporations and private investors to purchase or lease even more agricultural land than in the colonial era, especially in sub-Saharan Africa. Indeed, Kugelman and Levenstein (2012) estimate that nearly 230 million hectares of farmland (the size of Western Europe) have been sold or leased to large corporations from the United States, China, and the United Kingdom since 2001. The consequences of these land grabs are only now being realized.

FIGURE 10.1 A MALNOURISHED CHILD FROM BURKINO FASO

Foreign investors promote export agriculture (cash crops) for the wealth it generates, while also promoting the purchase of seeds, chemical fertilizers, and pesticides in developing countries to generate profits for chemical industries (Horrigan, Lawrence, & Walker 2002). In Kenya, for example, domestic production of traditional crops, such as sorghum and millet, have declined, while tea, green beans, and vegetable exports have risen significantly. Ninety per cent of these exports end up in Europe. With the export earnings,

---

2 Also known as developing nations.

"The premise that export agriculture is an economic necessity is perhaps the most questionable assumption of the contemporary world from a social welfare, food rights and environmental sustainability perspective." (McMichael & Schneider 2011: 129).

the Kenyan government purchases wheat and rice to sell to the people. This trend has made Kenyans vulnerable to price fluctuations on the world market, and they have less access to local food reserves (McMichael & Schneider 2011).

Biotech or cash crops increase expenditures, creating a heavy debt load that eventually forces small-scale farmers to sell their land to the foreign agribusinesses-in-waiting. As in colonial times, agribusinesses and multinational corporations buy the land, reducing subsistence activities in the region and forcing migration to the cities. Consequently, the large shantytowns growing up around cities in developing countries are a product of land grabs and "de-peasantisation" promoted by the World Bank and similar organizations (McMichael & Schneider 2011).

AGRICULTURE FOR DEVELOPMENT VS. FOOD SOVEREIGNTY

The central focus of the World Bank's **agriculture for development** initiative is to invest in agriculture in order to increase production and productivity and bring subsistence farmers into the market economy (McMichael & Schneider 2011: 129). According to the **modernization theory**, foreign investment, international trade, and international aid provide access to foreign capital, technology, and knowledge that increases economic growth and income in all sectors of a developing nation, including among the poorest. Modernization also opens markets for products and offers cheap raw materials that increase productivity, create higher wages, and eventually lead to higher caloric intake, thereby alleviating hunger (Mihalache-O'Keef & Li 2011). Proponents of modernization tout high yields, chemical-industry profits, foreign sales, and so on as benefits of industrializing agriculture.

Although this market-driven policy suggests that transnational food corporations (agribusinesses) can feed the world, these enterprises mainly export food and other resources from developing nations to developed nations. This process, known as "enclave development," is where resources, such as minerals, water, and agricultural products, are taken out of the country without benefitting the local economy or the local population (Hirschman 1958: 110). As an example, in Somalia, 75 per cent of the earnings from banana exports leave the country (Samatar 1993: 25), and in Nigeria, oil revenues have had no effect on per capita GDP (Sala-i-Martin & Subramanian 2003). If anyone benefits economically in the developing country, it is the elite class, not the poor.

Contract farming as an alternative to agribusinesses is growing in popularity. Contract farming offers farmers agricultural advice, mechanization, seeds, fertilizers, and easy credit, but also "guaranteed and profitable markets for produce" (FAO 2001). In Northern India, 400 farmers are growing hybrid tomatoes that will be processed into paste. These farmers are producing higher yields and earning 50 per cent more from the company sponsoring their contract than they would on the open market. Contract farming also enjoys more "political acceptability," since many governments will no longer host foreign-owned plantations and are even shutting them down and redistributing the land to local farmers. In response to this changing atmosphere, multinational corporations in Central America are beginning to contract with individual banana growers, rather than establish plantations (FAO 2001).

Although contract farming appears more equitable, critics point out that this system is still a debt generator for small farmers and does little for development in the region. Farmers face the uncertainty of using new technology and growing new crops. Some of the less scrupulous sponsors may levy extra fees on the farmers, but most of all, the debt that may be incurred from production problems, poor technical advice, poor markets, and other costs can jeopardize the farmers' livelihood. Small farmers still face the problem of growing food for their families and the local market – contract farming does not solve this disruption of the local food supply (FAO 2001).

McMichael and Schneider (2011) argue that by disrupting the local food supply, agriculture for development has worsened food insecurity in regions that used to be self-reliant, supporting the **dependency theory**, which suggests that foreign direct investment (FDI) from multinational corporations tends to distort a national economy, widens the gap between the rich and poor, and removes much-needed food from developing countries. Ultimately, FDI contributes to "lower economic growth and worse quality of life, including lower food supply, higher infant mortality, higher inequality, higher pollution, and reduced access to clean water, doctors, and education" (Mihalache-O'Keef & Li 2011: 75).

Food sovereignty promotes the right for everyone to have access to safe, nutritious, and culturally appropriate food in sufficient quantity and quality to provide health and dignity (Altieri & Funes-Monzote 2012: 5). The food-sovereignty perspective supports domestic markets and small-scale biodiverse crops, and urges a refocus on social and ecologically sustainable agriculture. In other words, it advocates reinforcement of the agricultural practices that have worked for millennia, and encourage development of local markets with reliable agricultural aid,[3] thereby ensuring food security for people living in the region (McMichael & Schneider 2011). Despite colonial contentions that industrial agriculture is the most efficient system of farming, small-scale farms tend to be more productive (higher yields, lower losses to weeds, insects, and disease) than large monocultural[4] "factories in the field" (McMichael & Schneider 2011: 133–34). In fact, subsistence farmers use water, light, and nutrients more efficiently and display extraordinary resilience after disasters. When Hurricane Ike struck Cuba in 2008, small-scale farms suffered fewer losses and recovered productivity far more quickly than the large monocultural farms (Altieri & Funes-Monzote 2012).

Advocates of food sovereignty promote an integrated food approach that takes into consideration nutritional, environmental, and social needs of subsistence farmers, values farmer knowledge, protects natural and agricultural biodiversity, and promotes common resource-management systems. Conservation of agricultural land is promoted to produce food that fulfills the culinary preferences of the people. This is known as the **multifunctional approach,** which reduces poverty among subsistence farmers, improves social/gender equality, and has a stabilizing effect on rural people/cultures, lessens environmental degradation, and helps mitigate or adapt to climate change (McMichael & Schneider 2011: 132).

Food sovereigntists also advocate an end to subsidies to northern farmers for overproduction, shifting these subsidies to small-scale farmers in developing countries, as well

---

3 Ten countries that have 70 per cent of the world's hungry receive only 20 per cent of the global agricultural aid (McMichael & Schneider 2011: 121).

4 i.e., one-crop farms.

as subsidies for environmental stewardship. Thus, food sovereignty takes into consideration the needs of poor consumers and subsistence farmers, strengthens local and regional food systems, prioritizes local farmers' political and cultural rights, and provides access to resources such as seeds, land, and water (McMichael & Schneider 2011: 132–33).

CUBA AGROECOLOGY

When the Soviet Union collapsed in the 1990s, Cuba found itself in a food-production quandary, left stranded without fertilizers, pesticides, machinery and parts, or petrol (Altieri & Funes-Monzote 2012). In an unprecedented turnaround, Cuba reoriented itself to ecological and sustainable agriculture that has become a global model for food sovereignty. The success of Cuba's food system is partly due to a reliance on farm cooperatives, as well as to urban agriculture, organic farming methods, local markets, and strong grassroots organizations that support the farmers.

FIGURE 10.2 A SMALL ORGANIC FARM PRACTISCING AGROECOLOGY IN CUBA

As a first step, use rights were granted to farmers for three million acres of state land. Under this new land-distribution system, more than 100,000 small farms were created that now produce 65 per cent of the food for Cuba. Urban farming also flourished – 383,000 urban farms now produce 1.5 million tons of vegetables without using synthetic chemicals and supply 70 per cent of the vegetables for Cuban cities. These farmers apply organic technology, such as worm composting and reproduction of native microorganisms. They plant polycultures (diversified crops), practise crop rotation, and integrate animals into their agriculture. Cuban farmers also practice agroforestry, using trees and shrubs to reduce loss of soil and moisture and to recycle nutrients, thereby improving productivity and sustainability. As a result of these initiatives, Cuba's reliance on imported food continues to decrease, although the country still imports some meat, as well as significant amounts of cooking oil, cereals, rice, wheat, and powdered milk for human consumption, and corn and soybeans for livestock.

Despite efforts to discredit the agroecological food system in Cuba (see Avery 2009), today Cuba is able to feed its people, which is far more than can be said for most countries in the world that have embraced agribusiness and international markets. This is not to say that Cuba completely rejects monocultural industrial agriculture and biotechnology; indeed, experiments in transgenic crops are ongoing. However, in a time of food crisis, agroecology and sustainable approaches became more productive.

Cuba is fortunate that a significant number of scientists and other professionals live and work in the country, supported by numerous research centres and agrarian universities. The country also has a land base, much of it uncultivated until recently, that is large enough to produce food for its 11 million people (Funes-Monzote 2008). The participatory ideology of the farm organizations is to take into consideration the needs of the small farmers, and to provide avenues for sharing agricultural knowledge and innovation. All of these factors have contributed to the success of Cuba's agricultural revolution.

Besides food sovereignty, Cuba's agroecological strategy has also addressed energy sovereignty – the right for all people to access sufficient energy within ecological limits, using human and animal labour, windmills, and bioga,[5] along with technological sovereignty, which is "the capacity to achieve food and energy sovereignty by nurturing the environmental services derived from existing agrobiodiversity and using locally available resources" (Altieri & Funes-Monzote 2012: 5). Cuba also received an honourable mention from the World Food Council's Future Policy Award for its urban agriculture initiatives.

Out of necessity, Cuba returned to traditional agricultural practices that are efficient, resilient, and promote biodiversity. Cuba has thus become a model for other countries struggling to feed their populations. Yet industrial and biotech agriculture continues to entice agriculturalists in Cuba. According to Altieri & Funes-Monzote (2012), when times are good the lure of high-tech agriculture increases; however, when the situation reverses, Cubans revert to traditional, sustainable agroecology. Would this system work in other regions? Conditions would have to closely emulate those of Cuba – organization of the local farmers, sufficient land base, technological, scientific, and ecological know-how, and political will all ensured the success of this system in Cuba.

ENVIRONMENTAL COSTS OF INDUSTRIALIZED AGRICULTURE

The environmental costs of industrial agriculture and the inability to sustain this type of agriculture in the long term have implications for future food security. In particular, air, land, and water pollution, soil depletion, and diminished biodiversity present serious challenges for food producers. Release of greenhouse gases into the atmosphere from livestock facilities and over-use of fossil fuels is considered a major factor in global warming and climate change that is causing violent weather events, droughts and floods, and rising oceans – all of which threaten food security.

Monocultures erode soil faster than can be replenished, causing fertile farmland to lose nutrients and water-retention ability. Growing the same plants year after year depletes soil nutrients, creating a need for synthetic fertilizers, and pesticides to hold off weeds and insects. Heavy machinery compacts the soil, destroying soil structure and killing beneficial organisms. Monocultures also erode biodiversity among plants and animals, especially birds and insects (Horrigan, Lawrence, & Walker 2002).

Small-scale farming causes less harm to the environment by maintaining a balance with nature. It does not use synthetic fertilizers, employs crop rotation and recycles organic matter, uses simple technologies with little carbon footprint, and uses renewable forms of energy (human labour, animal manure). Small-scale farmers also market locally, reducing transport costs (Horrigan, Lawrence, & Walker 2002). Yet these traditional agricultural practices that maintain a balance have been dismissed by the FAO, which instead promotes agribusinesses that apply pesticides, herbicides, and chemical fertilizers to crops. These chemicals find their way into the groundwater and eventually poison farmland. Fertilizer run-off is also causing algal blooms; huge "dead zones" without oxygen have developed in the

"Concentrated animal feeding operations ... and other factory farms have been called 'a frontal assault on the environment with massive groundwater and air pollution problems.'" Dr. Peter Checke, professor emeritus of animal sciences at Oregon State University, quoted in Lallanilla (n.d.).

---

5 Gaseous fuel produced from decayed animal and plant matter.

Gulf of Mexico and the Baltic Sea, causing hypoxia and killing the aquatic life (Union of Concerned Scientists 2012). In the United States, pesticide run-offs have been linked to abnormalities in amphibians, a reduction in the number of honey bees, and immune problems in dolphins, seals, and whales (Rapetto & Baliga 1990). Agribusinesses and chemical corporations are well aware of the problems. A recent report on the burgeoning agribusinesses in Brazil suggests that a major challenge is to "conceal the use of pesticides [in light of] ... the growing demand for organic food" (Novais 2012).

Although over-exploitation of resources and waste-disposal problems have been linked to large populations and increased global consumption, industrial agricultural practices also contribute significantly to the crisis. Industrial agriculture consumes an enormous amount of water for irrigation systems, which in turn creates shortages for other needs (Horrigan, Lawrence, & Walker 2002). Global export of food products requires increased fossil-fuel use for transportation and running machinery, and refrigeration during transportation is contributing to ozone depletion. The need to construct a complex infrastructure, such as airports and ocean ports, damns, etc., has caused serious ecological damage in these areas. Thus, environmental degradation presents an increasing challenge for global food security.

HUMANITARIAN CONSEQUENCES OF FOOD INSECURITY

One of the "hunger myths"[6] is that over-population[6] and food scarcity cause world hunger. However, more than enough food is available for each person to consume four pounds of grains, fruits and vegetables, dairy, and meats every day (Poole-Kavana 2006). The problem is *access*; if the food is being exported, little remains for the local people. Distribution of what food there is, including foreign aid, is also a serious problem, especially among the poorest segments of society. Climate change is also blamed; however, climatic distress rarely accounts for starvation – it is merely the last straw in an already desperate situation.

The most obvious humanitarian impact of food insecurity is an inadequate caloric intake that leads to malnutrition, especially among children (Ramalingam, Proudlock, & Mitchell n.d.). Malnutrition is responsible for stunting the growth of children, learning problems in school, and susceptibility to disease and illness. Families in economic distress also have less to spend on health care, and children may be pulled from school to earn money for the family, leading to higher illiteracy and an uneducated populace. On a national level, if the nutritional needs of the people are not met, civil instability is inevitable, leading to conflicts, food riots, protests and demonstrations, and increased criminal activity. Many dispossessed people have migrated to the cities in search of work; this uncontrolled urbanization has led to appalling living conditions in makeshift shantytowns on the outskirts of cities in developing countries that cannot or will not provide the necessary infrastructure. Seldom do these dispossessed agriculturalists find employment to support their families.

Humanitarian aid is not the answer to world hunger. This is one of the biggest hunger myths of all, perpetrated on Westerners feeling guilty for their wealth and abundance. Most aid does not reach the truly hungry, but foreign grain companies become rich off the purchase of grain for aid agencies. Much of the monetary aid goes to the government elite

---

6 See Chapter 4 for a detailed discussion of the over-population myth.

to purchase arms and enrich their own lives; and, as discussed in Chapter 3, swamping a region with food aid hastens the destruction of local food production. If humanitarian assistance must be offered, then local experts or officials need to be consulted to design locally appropriate ways of delivery.

Economists identify externalities, such as social disruption, deterioration of rural communities, and environmental damage as hidden costs for developing nations (Horrigan, Lawrence, & Walker 2002), but there are also costs for people in developed nations in the form of taxation that pays for research into biotechnology, subsidization of transportation, communication, and energy infrastructures, foreign aid, and the enormous costs of mitigating the inevitable environmental degradation.

A CASE STUDY OF RESTORING FOOD SECURITY

The Brazilian city of Belo Horizonte, population 2.5 million, tackled the problem of food security using an integrated urban policy that addressed consumption needs, distribution issues, and food production. According to food scientists Cecilia Rocha and Iara Lessa (2009: 389), this city created a government-driven alternative food system that is flexible, focuses on both urban and rural players, and is committed to social justice and equitable access to food. The goal was zero hunger by increasing access to nutritious food for all citizens.

FIGURE 10.3 THE PEOPLE OF BELO HORIZONTE TOOK STEPS TO END HUNGER IN THEIR CITY

The organizers focused on three major plans of action that addressed the most urgent food security issues: 1) assisting poor families at risk to prevent and reduce malnutrition in children, pregnant and nursing women, and the elderly, and promoting healthy eating habits; 2) partnering with private food vendors to bring food to areas of the city with little access to commercial outlets (food deserts), and regulating the prices and quality of this food; and 3) increasing food production and supply by providing technical and financial incentives to small producers, forming links between rural producers and urban consumers, and promoting community gardens and other forms of urban agriculture.

In the 1990s, 18 per cent of Belo Horizonte's children younger than five suffered from malnutrition. The Zero Hunger strategy aimed to reduce food insecurity by providing greater access to food, strengthening family agriculture, generating more family income, and promoting partnerships between the private sector and civil society. Popular Restaurants (also known as Food and Nutrition Units) is one of the programs developed. Four units offer nutritious meals to the city's population at low cost. A second program, Popular Big Basket, uses mobile units to sell subsidized non-perishable food to lower-income families in areas of need, while School Meals serves meals to students in 218 public schools. These programs have been a resounding success in providing access to food for needy families. As well, the Straight from the Country and Country Store programs facilitate links between rural producers and urban consumers. These programs have increased farm income and helped rural families remain on their farms, while offering urban consumers affordable prices.

Participatory community involvement is promoted in an expansive urban agricultural endeavour. Agroecologically sustainable methods are used in community gardens (e.g., vegetables and medicinal plants), school gardens (e.g., vegetables for school meals), orchard projects (e.g., fruit trees planted in several areas), and workshops for teaching alternative planting methods. Forty-four community gardens and 60 school gardens were created, 1,600 fruit-tree seedlings were distributed, and 62 workshops on gardening were held for 1,300 people.

There have been challenges, such as the continuing socio-economic inequality in the city, the need for education on good nutrition practices, and sustainability – the programs are vulnerable to changing governments and priorities. Nonetheless, Rocha and Lessa (2009) credit the success of this food system to the commitment of the government, private sector, and civil society. Belo Horizonte, Brazil, is a model for communities large and small to take responsibility for their own food security.

Questions always arise regarding the sustainability of such endeavours without corporate involvement. This program has proven that citizens, with the aid of their local governments, can take control of their own well-being. The Belo Horizonte program is touted as "the world's most comprehensive policy that tackles hunger immediately and secures a healthy food supply for the future" (World Food Council n.d.: n.p.). In 2009, Belo Horizonte received the Future Policy Award presented by the World Food Council. This award is given to policies that "have a positive effect on the rights of future generations and that can be applied to other countries or regions around the world" (Ryerson University 2013: n.p.).

CONCLUSION

The Millennium Development Goals' mandate to halve world hunger by 2015 is unrealistic given the current food crisis and ongoing agribusiness policies and globalization processes. If these policies continue, the proportion of the world's population that lives in poverty and hunger will continue to rise. This reality has negative humanitarian consequences, as well as increasing the threat of political instability and environmental degradation.

Research into the impact of outside forces, such as foreign investment and agribusinesses, has been limited, leading to contradictory and contested evidence, solutions, and predictions for the future. Proponents of modernization and globalization claim that foreign investment benefits developing economies, while food sovereignty and anti-globalization supporters believe that foreign investment has far more negative consequences on developing countries and their people. Ultimately, agriculture for development and food sovereignty perspectives raise the question of whether agriculture should be used as a vehicle for economic growth and profit or to develop a source of food that is sustainable and accessible to local markets.

Improving conditions and productivity and introducing market economies may seem the pathway to economic development and prosperity, but these policies have a profit goal rather than a feeding goal. Indeed, many of these policies have actually exacerbated world hunger. According to McMichael and Schneider (2011:134), "industrial agriculture... exposes existing global food systems to short-term investment volatilities and long-term environmental and energy vulnerabilities. And it does this at the expense of preserving and enhancing systems of small-holder agriculture that could well be a significant part of the solution to hunger, displacement, and environmental and energy crises." Agriculture for export also has dramatic consequences for the sustainability of the environment, which in turn are affecting long-term food security.

On the other hand, the benefits of agribusiness and industrial agriculture are hard to ignore – even in the colonial era when the British built irrigation systems in India that increased production (Lappe & Collins 1977). Modernization of technology and equipment, safety guidelines for food production, improving water quality, and restrictions on pesticide use are all touted as benefits of modernizing agriculture. Whether these benefits trickle down to the actual farmers remains to be seen; however, efforts to improve equity in farming are ongoing.

The global food system is now controlled by a group of powerful transnational corporations and agribusinesses that have displaced millions of small-scale farms and created a global food crisis that threatens human rights in many parts of the world. Despite small triumphs, such as in Cuba and Brazil, this food crisis is bound to increase unless agricultural policies dramatically shift. Scientists are sounding the alarm and advocating a return to more sustainable agriculture that maintains a balance with the natural environment and more closely emulates the practices of small-scale farmers who, if given the opportunity to flourish, will feed the world, one community at a time.

QUESTIONS FOR CONSIDERATION AND CLASSROOM ACTIVITIES

1. Choose a developing nation and research the food-security issues it faces. Critically examine the steps taken to "feed the hungry." Is this strategy designed to feed the hungry or create profits for individuals and/or organizations?
2. Critically assess the motives of the World Bank or IMF in their financial-aid packages to a country of your choice. Pay particular attention to the conditions

and restrictions placed on the country in order to receive financial support, and the obstacles this country will face in repaying the loan.

3. Investigate whether your community has any programs to feed the needy. How can you, as a global citizen, assist in ensuring food security for the needy in your community, or in the global community?

4. "Marketing boards became another mechanism for extracting wealth from developing nations" (Lappe & Collins 1977). Investigate the accuracy of this statement.

5. Critically assess the short- and long-term impact of humanitarian aid in a country stricken with famine. In your opinion, is this aid a benefit or hindrance to their food security? Many opponents to aid offer other solutions rather than "handouts." Explore some of these solutions and determine if any of them are feasible.

6. What are the Millennium Development Goals? Are any of them likely to be achieved by the 2015 deadline? What factors have impeded the realization of these goals?

7. Choose an aid agency or NGO and investigate its food-aid programs. Are these programs really helping the people, and in what ways? In what ways are they hindering food security?

8. "The way we produce and process food now is not sustainable in the future." Investigate the accuracy or inaccuracy of this statement.

9. Identify the 25 hunger hotspots mentioned in this chapter. Have any of these nations managed to solve their food-security problem since 2010?

SUGGESTED READINGS

Kugelman, M., & Levenstein, S.L. (2012). *The global farms race: Land grabs, agricultural investment, and the scramble for food security.* Oakland, CA: Island Press.

This book presents a comprehensive examination of transnational corporations and private investors buying up hundreds of millions of hectares of farmland, and what this means for food security.

Rayfuse, R. (2012). *Challenge of food security: International policy and regulatory frameworks.* Cheltenham, UK: Edward Elgar Publishers.

Food security is addressed through an interdisciplinary development perspective. The root causes of food insecurity are discussed, as are sustainability, equitable distribution of food, and land grabs by multinational corporations. The legal and regulatory policies are an important component of this book.

Chapter 11

Ethnic Conflicts: What Are the Underlying Reasons and the Consequences of These Conflicts?

Key Terms: ethnic boundary markers, ethnic conflict, ethnic groups, ethnic identity, ethnicity, ethnic stratification, genocide, nation, nationality, race, refugees

---

INTRODUCTION

"We concluded – I concluded – that genocide has been committed in Darfur and that the government of Sudan and the Janjaweed[1] bear responsibility – and genocide may still be occurring." Secretary of State Colin Powell giving testimony before the Senate Foreign Relations Committee (Mayroz 2008: 367).

The above question is difficult to answer, given the many reasons behind ethnic conflict. Those of us who have not had first-hand experience in a conflict situation cannot understand what it means to harbour memories of wrongdoings passed down through generations, to be driven from our homes or lands, or to deal with daily discrimination and exploitation based on ethnicity or religion. These age-old resentments and a history of conflict and persecution can define a people and influence their perceptions of the world around them. Indeed, Davis (1992) suggests that war is embedded in the social experience of many societies where war, loss, and suffering have become integral parts of their cultures.

The question is also misleading because it suggests that conflict is due to ethnic differences, when in fact power struggles over territory, resources, and political dominance are more likely to cause conflict. Authoritarian states attempting to eliminate or destabilize ethnic groups[2] in order to access their resources and territory are a contributing factor in many twentieth-century conflicts. However to suggest that historical grievances, minority rights, and ethnic and religious intolerance do not play a part in these conflicts is also an oversimplification of the situation.

A fundamental question when addressing ethnic conflict is why some nations with ethnic diversity live in relative peace, while others are consumed with ethnic conflict (Wolff 2006). Regrettably, ethnopolitics is such a complex issue, and ethnic conflict is so dynamic in nature, that it is impossible to present a straightforward answer that addresses every conflict situation. Nevertheless, several significant factors will be addressed in the following discussion.

---

1 The *janjaweed* are bandits, criminals, demobilized Sudanese soldiers, young men from Arab tribes, tribal leaders, and fighters from Chad and Libya.

2 The term "ethnic group" is used to avoid fallacious terms such as "race."

Ethnic conflict is often predicated on scarcity of resources, as you will see in the discussion of the conflict in Darfur. Resource scarcity fits well with the instrumentalist theory of ethnic conflict where "participants ... hope to derive some material benefit from the conflict" (Bates 1982, quoted in Caselli & Coleman 2011: 8). Indeed, economists Francesco Caselli and Wilbur Coleman (2011) have developed a model that suggests if a region is economically developed and control over resources is equalized, then ethnic conflict will be reduced.

Resource scarcity, however, does not address every conflict situation. Political scientist James Fearon (1995: 21) suggests that a commitment problem has caused ethnic conflict in nations such as Azerbaijan, Georgia, Moldova, Ukraine, Estonia, Zimbabwe, South Africa, and Northern Ireland. This commitment problem arises when minority ethnopolitical communities become insecure without a third party (e.g., the Soviet Union) ensuring that they will not be exploited or oppressed by the ethnic majority. This is evident in post-Soviet Eastern Europe, where Armenians conflicted with the Azeri over the Nagorno-Karabakh region. The Armenians were confronted with having to become part of an independent Azerbaijan without having any credible guarantee that their physical or economic security would be protected (Fearon 1995). Thus, ethnic conflict often results from minority fears and the inability or unwillingness of ethnic majorities to guarantee their rights.

The quest for autonomy and independence, whether to protect resources or validate historical contentions, is also an important factor in ethnic conflict, as evidenced in the conflict between Tibetans and Han Chinese. Ethnic Tibetans have been struggling for years to gain "genuine autonomy" from the Han Chinese government. China claims full sovereignty over Tibet, while Tibetans believe they are an independent nation that the Chinese invaded in 1950. Reaching genuine autonomy would enable Tibetans to fully participate in "cultural, social, economic and political life, promoting both democracy and human rights in Tibet" (Davis 2008: 2); however, both sides believe their claims are legitimate.

One of the consequences of ethnic conflict is displaced persons, also known as refugees. **Refugees** are people who have been forced to flee their homes to escape persecution during conflicts and who have undergone "a violent 'rite' of separation" (Harrell-Bond & Voutira 1992: 6). Many refugees remain in a transient state that dramatically affects their legal, psychological, economic, and social status. Refugees and their adaptation to changing social and political conditions are addressed in this chapter. The conditions that lead to ethnic conflict will be explored through the ongoing genocidal conflict in Darfur, western Sudan. Given the complexity of ethnic conflict, this discussion will rely on the expertise and perspectives of several disciplines, including history, economics, political science, and anthropology.

THE NATURE OF ETHNICITY AND ETHNIC CONFLICT

To begin our discussion of ethnic conflict we will explore several relevant concepts. **Ethnicity** refers to a sense of identity based on cultural traits that have been passed down for generations and that possess meaning for a group of people (Fenton 2003). **Ethnic groups**, such as the Plains Cree of Canada or the Albanians of Montenegro, share a common identity, history, and territory of origin. Members of an ethnic group speak the same language, observe the same customs (e.g., dress, diet), and hold relatively the same beliefs and values. An ethnic group shares a memory of its cultural past and a sense of continuity from the past to the present. Its members see themselves as distinct and separate from other groups. For example, Indian immigrants to North America affiliate with other Indians, based on their state of origin (e.g., Kerala), rather than on India as an entire country, and the Roma (Gypsies of Europe) who until recently were nomadic, do not claim a homeland, but possess an ethnic identity based on their lifestyle (De Vos 1995). Today, there are approximately 5,000 ethnic groups in the world (Eller 1999), many of whom are seeking recognition as distinct nations.

Although sharing an identity based on ethnicity has a long history, the concept of **ethnic identity** is relatively new and the product of modern politics, involving state building, colonization, and globalization (Crawford 1998). Ethnic identity is determined by **ethnic boundary markers**, which are socially constructed in that they vary from one group to another, and tend to be quite elusive (De Vos 1995). They are also fluid, meaning the importance and purpose of certain markers (e.g., language) can change over time (Miyares & Airries 2007: 7).

Religion is one marker that may provide ethnic identity. Although the Serbs, Croats, and Bosniaks[3] consider themselves distinct ethnic groups, they speak the same language and have lived similar lives. It is religion that separates these three ethnic groups: the Croats are Roman Catholic, the Serbs, Orthodox Christian, and the Bosniaks, Muslim. Despite the importance of ethnic boundary markers based on religion, followers of the same religion do not necessarily constitute a distinct ethnic group. Many people the world over follow Islam: for example, the Samals of the Philippines, the Moors of Sri Lanka, and the Pashtun of Afghanistan are all Muslims, but they come from diverse ethnic backgrounds. Still, if a group of people self-defines as an ethnic group, then they are an ethnic group, regardless of what categories outsiders may assign.

Language is another powerful marker of ethnic identity. For the Acadians of maritime Canada, for example, language is an integral component of their ethnic identity, although they separate their culture from that of other French-speaking Canadians. Despite its importance as an ethnic identity marker, language is often the first marker to disappear among immigrants, usually by the third generation (Miyares & Airries 2007: 8). Physical appearance, such as the distinctive features of Han Chinese, may also serve as an ethnic boundary marker. Distinctive clothing and food, such as Sikh turbans (*dastar*) and Hamitic Bedouin *jalabiyya*,[4] or Ukrainian perogies and Mexican tacos, are symbols that make ethnic groups recognizable to outsiders. New ethnic groups may also arise, for example, Mexican, Peruvian, Chilean, and Guatemalan ethnic groups evolved out of the Spanish who immigrated to North and South America and mated with indigenous peoples already settled there.

Quite similar to the concept of ethnicity and ethnic groups is the idea of nation or nationhood. A **nation** is a community where people consider themselves "one people" based on common ancestry and history, religion and ideology, language, and territory of origin. Eller (1999: 144) believes that a nation must fulfill certain requirements to be called a nation: "a common culture, a consciousness of shared identity, and political organization toward a national goal." As an example, the people of Taiwan have owned a sense of identity

---

3 "Bosniak" is the correct term for the ethnic group living in southeastern Europe, mainly in Bosnia and Herzegovina. The term "Bosnian" is sometimes used in place of "Bosniak."
4 A long hooded robe.

different from mainland China for more than a century (Dreyer 2003). Indeed, most of the population identifies as Taiwanese rather than Chinese. Taiwan nationalism and the push for independence and nationhood are growing. Various factors have contributed to this emerging identity: occupations by the Spanish, Portuguese, and Dutch; Japanese colonization; close proximity to Polynesian cultures; American influence during World War II; isolation from mainland China; and a brutal policy of assimilation by Chinese ruler Chiang Kai-shek between 1948 and 1975. Today, the Taiwanese are seeking independent nation status.

Nationality is similar to ethnicity; however, nationality can encompass several ethnic groups that are politically unified (De Vos 1995). For example, Canada is a nation, and the citizens of Canada usually identify their nationality as Canadian, yet each person also possesses an ethnic identity such as Chinese, Ukrainian, or German. In other forms of nationhood, the Kurds of Iran consider themselves a nation, though they do not possess autonomy.

Race is a difficult term to define, partly because it is based on erroneous facts. Usually race refers to a group of people who have been categorized based on biological and behavioural traits. However, people cannot be definitively categorized into specific racial groups based on rigorous scientific data. According to Boas (1932), there is as much physical variation within races as between races, there are no clear-cut geographic or biological lines between races, and there are no correlations between races and cultural or mental characteristics. Thus, a northern European may be genetically more similar to a San from southern Africa than with someone from southern Europe. The only clear biological difference between populations is blood type, but blood types do not correspond to so-called racial categories. This means the concept of race is culturally constructed according to economic, political, and social agendas, rather than any biological reality.

Ethnic stratification, which is often the precursor to ethnic conflict, means placing groups of people in a hierarchy of superior versus inferior, based on ethnicity, race, religion, historical origins, occupation, wealth, etc. Ethnic stratification limits a target group's access to reasonable wealth, power, and prestige – three important components to the well-being of an ethnic group. In North America, indigenous peoples have a long history of conflict with Europeans who dispossessed them of their land, and in the United States in particular, African Americans have experienced generations of discrimination and exploitation. Although all of these examples are predicated on economic and political factors, there is also a powerful element of social, religious, and ethnic prejudice.

In a stratified society, people are ranked relative to other ethnic groups and face varying degrees of inequality and discrimination. In Canada, numerous ethnic groups have been viewed as inferior and undesirable – although the group or groups pinpointed as inferior change from one period to another. For example, when Ukrainians began immigrating to Canada at the end of the nineteenth century, Canadians of French and English descent were less than enthusiastic. An article appeared in the *Winnipeg Telegram* on May 13, 1901, expressing this aversion:

> "That there are few people who will affirm that Slavonic immigrants are desirable settlers or that they are welcomed by the white people of Western Canada. ... Those whose ignorance is impenetrable, whose customs are repulsive, whose civilization is primitive, and whose character and morals are justly condemned, are surely not the class of immigrants which the country's paid immigration agents should seek to attract. Better by far to keep our land for the children, children's children, of Canadians than to fill up the country with the scum of Europen." (Cheney 2000)

Discrimination, exploitation, and inequality breed resentment and hostile relationships between ethnic groups which given the right circumstances and incentives, can lead to ethnic conflict.

ETHNIC CONFLICT

Ter-Gabrielian (1999: 1) defines **ethnic conflict** as "a conflict between two or more ethnic groups, one of which possesses the actual state power." Much of the ethnic conflict today is traced to European colonialism in the nineteenth century, when political boundaries were created with little consideration for ethnicity or historic homelands. When European colonial powers granted independence to these colonies in the twentieth century, dominant or majority ethnic groups quickly seized power to the detriment of other ethnic groups – this is what happened in Rwanda. The Belgians took control of the country in 1912 and began favouring the Tutsi with education and employment, while excluding the supposedly lower-class and impoverished Hutus. When the Belgians left Rwanda, Hutu extremists seized power and, spurred on by the media and political manoeuvres of local and national leaders, massacred a million Tutsis (Bowen 1996).

Evidence of ethnic conflict and its ramifications are everywhere: the Irish Republican Army versus the British government; the Serbs' ethnic cleansing of Bosniaks; Palestinian and Israeli conflict; Kurdish separatist movements in Iraq and Turkey; and ethno-nationalist conflicts on the periphery of Russia. Although this is by no means a comprehensive list, the prevalence of ethnic conflicts worldwide is a sobering reality – what Brubaker (2004: 88) calls the "new world disorder."

Most modern states are pluralistic, which means that more than one ethnic group exists within its borders. The pluralism in Western states is fairly obvious, but even in smaller states ethnic diversity is pronounced. For example, 120 ethnic groups coexist in Tanzania, many of whom are experiencing an ethnic resurgence (Omari 1987). Although some pluralistic states such as Switzerland and Belgium have managed to maintain relative peace and harmony, pluralism often results in discord that can spill over into ethnic conflict. Yet this conflict is not entirely *ethnic* in nature, though it is often blamed on ethnicity; rather, it is more likely due to economic, religious, or political factors (often all three), such as claims to territory and resources – what Ter-Gabrielian (1999) terms "conflict of secession."

In conflict of secession, one or more ethnic groups wish to separate from the home state and create a new state with more autonomy and freedom. This form of ethnic conflict often escalates into open warfare, as in the case of the Tamil and Sudanese of Sri Lanka. An ethnic group may also seek political power or dominance over other ethnic groups within the state, in a "conflict of replacement" (Ter-Gabrielson 1999). In such a situation, one ethnic group wants to replace another at the centre of power. In this case, genocide is a very real possibility. The genocide in Rwanda is a good example of replacement conflict.

Genocide is the deliberate extermination of an ethnic group. Historic examples of genocide are numerous: in 1915, 1.8 million Armenians were murdered in the Ottoman Empire and the Caucasus; in the Soviet Union, Chechens, Tatars, and others were exterminated after World War II because of alleged collaboration with the Nazis; and, in 1971, up to three million Bengalis were killed by the Pakistani army, resulting in the secession of Bangladesh (Ter-Gabrielian 1999).

Genocide almost always has an economic or political motivation. The 1990s Serbian extermination of Bosniaks and Croats in the former Yugoslavia was based on political motivation, although the reasons for this ugly page in Eastern European history are complex.

Serbian president Slobodan Milosevic tapped into Serbian nationalism and their desire to expand their territory, while Croatia's President Franjo Tudjman played on Croatian nationalism. Both leaders sought to destroy the Yugoslavian civil identity and replace it with ethnic identities – a divide-and-conquer strategy. Thus, political manipulation created an atmosphere of distrust and fear in Yugoslavia in the early 1990s: Milosevic persuaded Serbs that all Croats were crypto-Nazi Ustashe, and Tudjman convinced the Croats that Serbs were Chetnik assassins bent on controlling the Balkans. Both leaders convinced their people that Bosniak Muslims were the front wave of an Islamic threat.[5] The media also played an influential role in inciting Serbian hatred that harkened back to Serb massacres perpetuated by the Croats during World War II (Bowen 1996). When Croatia, Bosnia, Slovenia, and Macedonia declared their independence from Yugoslavia in 1991, leaving only Serbia and Montenegro in Yugoslavia, the Serbs in Croatia and Bosnia rebelled, and a bloody war ensued (Brubaker 2004). By 1995, 200,000 people had died, half the population of Bosnia had become refugees, and the Serb population in Croatia was forced to flee (Crawford 1998). Bringa (1995: xvi) found that what hurt the most was neighbour turning on neighbour. The person next door became "a depersonalized alien, a member of the enemy ranks." Yet anthropologist Tone Bringa (1995: 3) discounts both the "age-old hatred" model of ethnic conflict and the "peaceful co-existence" approach. In the village where she lived, neither model fit: "there was both co-existence and conflict, tolerance and prejudice, suspicion and friendship." When the conflict was over, some Muslims returned to their villages, but the wounds from inter-communal violence take a long time to heal, and people remained socially distant.

GENOCIDE IN DARFUR

On September 9, 2004, United States Secretary of State Colin Powell described the Sudan government's policies toward the indigenous African people of Darfur as genocide – a term not used by the United States since the Holocaust of World War II (Welling 2007). As of 2010, the government-supported genocide in Darfur has resulted in an estimated 300,000 deaths and 2.7 million displaced persons (UN News Centre 2010). The American Anthropological Association (2004: n.p.) issued a strongly worded statement regarding the conflict: "the violence is systematic, sustained and grossly disproportionate to quelling the military threat posed by Darfur's rebel groups. ... Mass summary executions, the burning of entire villages, destruction of food stocks and livestock, and poisoning of wells, speak of an effort to destroy the entire basis of life of the targeted populations." This genocide has far-reaching political and humanitarian consequences, and the effects of this endemic violence and instability will be felt for generations to come.

To succinctly address the multidimensional socio-cultural, economic, political, and religious factors contributing to the Darfur conflict is as challenging as finding feasible solutions to the crisis. Social scientists have conducted numerous analyses of the crisis and

---

5 In the former Yugoslavia, the term "Muslim" referred to their religion but also represented a nation within Yugoslavia that set them apart from Serbs and Croats (Bringa 1995).

stress the importance of understanding the conflict within a historical and ecological context, as well as the ethnopolitical, economic, and social factors.

Darfur is an environmentally fragile region in western Sudan, bordering on Chad, Libya, and the Central African Republic. Seven million people of Arab Muslim and non-Arab African ethnic groups inhabit Darfur (World Savvy Monitor 2008). Although Sudan is a heterogeneous society, with myriad languages, ethnicities, and tribal affiliations, many languages are dying out because of the government's attempt to homogenize and "Arabize" the country.[6]

The largest non-Arab ethnic group is the Fur, who live in central Darfur, followed by the Zaghawa in the north, and the Masalit in western Darfur, though more than 40 other ethnic groups also live in the region (Mulaj 2008). This cultural diversity is due to an influx of people from neighbouring countries during the nineteenth century (Adam 2008) and Arab migrations in the seventh and eighth centuries.

In Darfur, most Africans are sedentary farmers, while most Arabs are nomadic pastoralists, and until recently relations between the groups were peaceful. Indeed, in a remarkable system of reciprocity, farmers provided pastoralists with agricultural products, pastoralists provided farmers with animal products. Intermarriage and sharing of languages ensued – some African groups, such as the Berti, speak Arabic, and some Arabs speak Fur (Adam 2008). However, three decades of drought and desertification have increased competition between the farmers and herders for scarce water and grazing lands (Wadlow 2005). The tribal system for mediating disputes broke down over increasing competition for the scarce resources (World Savvy Monitor 2008). This tension was exacerbated by the government of Sudan. Battles between African farmers and Arab pastoralists broke out in 1987–89, killing almost 3,000 people (Power 2004). Following the displacement of African farmers, few crops were grown or harvested, leading to food shortages. Yet suggesting the conflict is between pastoralists and farmers is misleading and diverts attention away from the underlying ecological and resource-shortage problems.

While it was formerly an independent sultanate, during World War I the British annexed Darfur to Sudan without considering whether the political borders would separate ethnic groups and tribes (Welling 2007). The northern Arab ruling class dominated Sudan and sought to economically and politically marginalize Darfur, a policy that increased following Sudan's independence in 1956. The people of Darfur received "less education, less development assistance, and fewer government posts" (Wadlow 2005: 2). This strategy began during colonialization, when administrators played different ethnic groups, tribes, and elites against each other in a pattern of favouritism and racist policies that contributed to the historic ethnic tension. When Sudan became independent, only the elite northern Arab Muslims and the southern Africans and Christians were involved in the political process; the African ethnic groups in Darfur were excluded (Adam 2008).

One of the main reasons for the genocide in Darfur is the Sudanese government's desire to acquire the region's land and resources, especially the oil in western Sudan. China, as Sudan's major investor in oil, has repeatedly supported Sudan and blocked United Nations resolutions in order to protect its oil interests (World Without Genocide 2011).

---

6 Despite the tendency to separate the Sudanese into Arabs and indigenous groups, it is important to recognize that all of the groups are indigenous to Sudan.

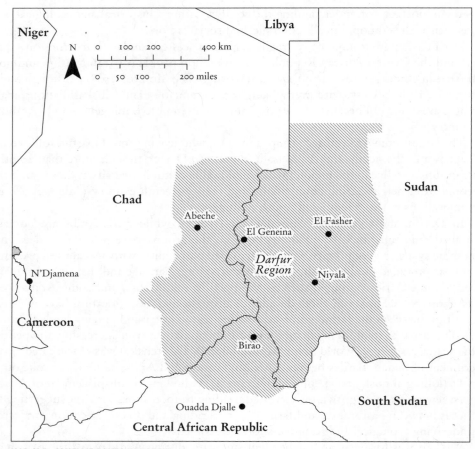

MAP 11.1 CONFLICT ZONES IN DARFUR

The Sudanese government's solution was to clear out the indigenous inhabitants, and free up the land and oil for development.

As early as 1977, the Sudan National Islamic Front and Umma Party singled out African ethnic groups, in particular the Fur, Kordofanis, and southern Sudanese, as inferior to elite Arabs. Following the 1985 overthrow of President Jaafar Numeiri, the military moved into the Darfur region and the deputy minister of defence began distributing weapons to local Arabs (Adam 2008). To defend the African population's rights to equal representation and fair distribution of goods and services, including health care and education, the secular Sudanese Liberation Army/Movement (SLA/M) and the Islamist Justice and Equality Movement (JEM) were created. During the 2000 peace negotiations between the North and South, the SLA/M and the JEM tried to draw the government's attention to their needs. When the Khartoum regime ignored their "Black Book" of

First, there is a reign of terror in this area; second, there is a scorched-earth policy; third there is repeated war crimes and crimes against humanity; and fourth, this is taking place before our eyes." Bertrand Ramcharan, acting United Nations High Commissioner on Human Rights, quoted in Wadlow (2005).

grievances, the rebels attacked the military base at El Fasher (Wadlow 2005). The Sudanese government responded by arming militias in Darfur, and recruiting the *janjaweed* ("devils on horseback") to raid and loot African villages. The *janjaweed* became the prime agents of genocidal violence in Darfur. This government strategy set off widespread "destruction, sexual violence, and displacement that by 2008 affected more than four million people in the region and over 1195 villages were destroyed" (US Department of State 2007, quoted in Apsel 2009: 241).

A great deal of propaganda was released by Sudan state media, especially under the rule of Omar al-Bashir, suggesting that the Fur were rebellious and must be militarily controlled for the stability and unity of the state (Apsel 2008), thus justifying the *janjaweed* campaign of murder and destruction that began in October 2002 (Burr & Collins 2006: 292). The government gave these bandits arms, uniforms, and equipment, and then bombed villages to lead the *janjaweed* to the preferred targets. The *janjaweed* were not paid for their efforts;[7] instead, they looted homes, crops, and livestock,

FIGURE 11.1 A DARFUR CAMP

captured slaves, and raped women and girls for payment. They burned crops, filled wells with sand, and displaced thousands of people who fled to safer regions, fulfilling the government's mandate. The *janjaweed* destroyed villages under the pretext that the inhabitants supported the Sudan Liberation Army or the Justice and Equality Movement.

Religion also played a role in the Darfur conflict (Adam 2008). The military and government elite attempted to impose an Islamic state ideology on all citizens to stamp out cultural pluralism, heterogeneity, and traditional family and societal structure (Apsel 2009). The non-Arab Muslims of Darfur were relegated to the category of "Other," and identified by Islamists

"Kaltoma Idris, 23, was inside her hut when the janjaweed arrived. Outside her sister was boiling water ... her recently born twins next to her. 'The janjaweed came and took the water and poured it over the babies.... They tied my sister up.' Idris fled out the back ... she saw children being thrown into flaming huts. Two hours later, she returned to find her sister still tied up. 'The babies were dead inside the pot.' She untied her sister. They took her babies and buried them.... Her sister later told her she was whipped and gang raped twice." Raghaven (2004).

in the government as a hindrance to former Libyan leader Moammar Ghadafi's vision of a pan-African Arab state (Adam 2008). Ethnic riverine Sudanese were appointed to "impose fundamental Islam on the syncretic Muslims of Darfur, who retain some animistic beliefs,

---

7 There is some debate on this issue. Mulaj (2008) suggests that the Sudanese government pays them stipends that are double what soldiers receive.

and make them all acceptable Arabs" (Markakis 1998: n.p.). Fuelled by Islamic zeal and the concept of *Alhizam Al'Arabi* (the Arab Belt), and fully armed, the Arabs targeted the Fur, killing, looting, burning shops, and rustling livestock.

Obviously, there are many social, political, historical, and cultural dimensions to the conflict in Sudan that cannot easily be resolved. It is equally obvious that the ruling government of Sudan has fostered and perpetuated genocide against the people of Darfur. Apsel (2009: 257) divides the cycle of violence in Darfur into several stages: During the first stage, the gestation period before 2002, people suffered from discrimination and neglect, while environmental degradation increased competition for scarce resources. The initial stage (2003–05) was the time of mass killings, destruction of villages, and displacement of millions of people. The slow motion stage (2005–08) saw periodic attacks on villages and refugee camps. Sexual violence and human-rights abuses were rampant during this period, and the displaced persons suffered from malnutrition, disease, and high mortality rates due to lack of security and few resources. The situation in Darfur remains extremely volatile with continuing political instability, land, water, and food shortages, a proliferation of arms in the possession of ruthless thugs, and an Arab-Muslim ideology that threatens the cultural diversity of the region.

The issue of humanitarian intervention has been raised numerous times, though little has been accomplished. Anthropologists have been vocal in their support of "a more vigorous international humanitarian response" as well as international pressure to bring peace to the region (American Anthropological Association 2004: n.p.), and they hold the Sudanese government accountable for its role in perpetuating and facilitating the conflict. However, any humanitarian intervention should come from African nations with support from Europe and the United States.

In January 2011, after two decades of civil war, the people of South Sudan voted in a referendum to separate from Khartoum-controlled northern Sudan (Avlon 2011). Whether this will lead to peace and security for the people of Darfur remains an open question.

REFUGEES AND THE HUMANITARIAN CRISIS

"We are not able to go back to our villages and we are not able to stay here safely, so we are not thinking about life now." Khaled Abdel Muti Ali, a displaced person in Abu Shouk camp on the outskirts of El-Fasher, North Darfur, quoted in Henshaw (2008: n.p.).

Populations of displaced persons are one of the tragic consequences of ethnic conflict. Indeed, an estimated 135 million people were uprooted in the twentieth century (*Jerusalem Post* 2009). Seventy-eight percent of the world's refugees come from ten countries: Afghanistan, Angola, Burundi, Congo-Kinshasa, Eritrea, Iraq, Myanmar, Palestine, Somalia, and Sudan (Human Rights Education Association n.d.). The preponderance of refugees has created a vast network of permanent international aid agencies. The most obvious form of aid is establishing refugee camps in "trouble spots" to accommodate displaced people. Conditions in these camps vary greatly, but most anthropologists agree that refugee camps are part of the problem, not the solution, because they disempower people and perpetuate a culture of dependency. Indeed, Harrell-Bond (1986) found that despite the goodwill and largesse attached to providing aid, refugees are often treated as villains and the aid workers as figures of authority, meaning the refugees have little power or control over their own welfare (Harrell-Bond & Voutira 1992). Aid workers also tend to homogenize refugees, giving little consideration to differing values, norms, and social organization among ethnic groups.

FIGURE 11.2 DARFURI REFUGEES IN BAHAI, CHAD

In Darfur, over one-third of the population is displaced by ongoing conflicts, and many more are directly affected by this population displacement. As a result, many refugee camps have been established in the Darfur region. These refugee camps are beneficial to the Sudanese government because they attract relief aid and create a pool of recruits for the Sudanese army and cheap labour.

Land degradation and water and firewood scarcity are serious problems around large camps, such as Abu Shouk near El Fasher (Apsel 2008), as is poor sanitation. Conditions continue to deteriorate even now: camps are crowded, and many refugees suffer from acute malnutrition and infectious diseases like yellow fever and malaria. Tensions run high over access to scarce resources within the camps, there is constant danger of conflicts with neighbouring communities, and women and children face sexual violence when they leave the camps in search of firewood. The camps are also recruiting grounds for various factions and militias. Loss of traditional family and societal structure, poverty, and trauma have resulted in increased violence in the camps, from rape to extortion (Apsel 2008).

"Beyond the short-term deprivations and degradations of becoming a refugee, and of sometimes being exploited by middlemen, lies the (possibly lifelong) traumatic reality of never belonging, of being permanently dispossessed of homeland and rights. The practical effects of what this entails are under-researched; recent findings, however, indicate that fear, depression, and the loneliness of having no roots — often being cut off from relatives, friends, community support, culture, and means of livelihood — can have profound effects which are sometimes only apparent in refugees and their children long after resettlement." (D'Souza 1981: 5)

CONCLUSION

This chapter began with the question, what are the underlying reasons for ethnic conflict? Obviously, ethnic conflict is a complex issue embedded in political, social, religious, and economic factors. Although ethnic groups are at the centre of these conflicts, the underlying reasons have little to do with ethnicity, and everything to do with power struggles over people, resources, and land, which is why these conflicts continue to be perpetuated around the world, and why solutions to ethnic conflict remain elusive.

The most devastating consequence of ethnic conflict is the displaced persons that lose their socio-economic and political status at the same time as they lose their "place." Throughout the twentieth century and into the twenty-first century, genocide has been perpetuated against ethnic groups – this is a global crisis, not a regional one. The conflict in Darfur is an example of the devastation that is wrought when state authorities seek to marginalize or destroy an ethnic group for economic gain, religious ideology, and/or ethnic imperialism. Indeed, the United Nations aptly describes the Darfur conflict as one of the "world's worst humanitarian crises" (AlertNet 2011: n.p.). Individuals in positions of power and celebrity, such as actor George Clooney, have tried to draw attention to the plight of the Darfurian people, but still the problems persist.

QUESTIONS FOR CONSIDERATION AND CLASSROOM ACTIVITIES

1. The question is often asked, whether conflict can be reduced if ethnic minority groups are encouraged to assimilate into mainstream society. Research the meaning and application of assimilation policy, and then respond to the following questions: Do you agree or disagree with a policy of assimilation? What would we gain if everyone identified with one homogenous "ethnic" group? What would we lose?
2. We have all heard a great deal about the harmful effects of racism and ethnic prejudice on the victims. But have you ever thought about the perpetrators – the people who hold these views, and how these attitudes affect their lives? In other words, have you ever met a happy bigot? Create a list of the ways in which racists limit their lives because of their views.
3. If more people become global citizens, do you think racism and bigotry will decrease?
4. What does ethnicity mean to you? Do you identify with an ethnic group? Why or why not?
5. Choose a nation and research its history of ethnic conflict. What are the underlying causes of this conflict? What level has this conflict reached, and have any of the issues been resolved?
6. Research the term "race." What criteria have been used to categorize people into different races? Why have these criteria failed to work for every group?
7. Locate a refugee camp (e.g., in Darfur) and research the economic, social, political, and religious systems found within this camp. How do these systems of culture enable the refugees to survive camp life? Are these systems as well developed as in cultures outside a camp environment?

8. Actor George Clooney has visited refugee camps in Darfur several times, and has been a vocal proponent for international aid in the region. What impact do you think his activism has had on the situation? What can you (i.e., you and your fellow students) do to help the people of Darfur?
9. Debate topic: should international military forces move into Darfur and "clear out" the *janjaweed*?
10. Why do you think the media has focused so little attention on the conflict in Darfur?

SUGGESTED READINGS

Bringa, T. (1995). *Being Muslim the Bosnian way*. Princeton, NJ: Princeton University Press.

This book is an ethnographic account of Bosnian Muslims living in a rural village near Sarajevo. Bringa focuses on religion as a boundary marker for ethnic identity, and the role of individual households in creating this identity. The issues of ethnicity and nationality are explored through the struggles of a small community dealing with the horrors of conflict and war.

Hecht, J. (2005). *The journey of the lost boys: A story of courage, faith and the sheer determination to survive by a group of young boys called "The Lost Boys of Sudan."* Jacksonville, FL: Allswell Press.

This award-winning book recounts the struggle of orphaned boys in war-torn southern Sudan, where their lives were in danger, walking a thousand miles to safety. This book also discusses the political and historical events that led to the civil war in Sudan.

Chapter 12

Human Migration: What Are the Socio-Economic and Political Implications of the Transnational Flow of People?

Key Terms: discrimination, globalization, human migration, human trafficking, immigrants/migrants, modern-day slavery, multiculturalism, racism, systemic racism, transnational communities

---

INTRODUCTION

"Politicians know all too well that migration serves vital economic interests, and cannot stop immigration even if they would want to, but do not dare to tell so to their voters. Their tough talk about reducing immigration is usually nothing more than a smokescreen to hide their inability and unwillingness to stop immigration." (de Hass 2012)

In 2007, the United Nations predicted that as many as 400,000 Africans and 1.2 million Asians would migrate to "rich" countries each year. This large-scale migration is expected to last until at least 2050 and will create "a global upheaval without parallel in human history" (MailOnline 2007: n.p.). Human migration in response to economic need, political instability, religious persecution, or environmental crisis has a long and convoluted history beginning during the industrialization era,[1] when many thousands of dislocated and impoverished Europeans fled to the Americas. However, the unprecedented human migrations of the twentieth and twenty-first centuries are a result of **globalization** processes, with far-reaching implications for both source and destination countries. Indeed, Moses (2006: n.p.) describes contemporary international migration as "globalization's last frontier."

Human migration refers to emigration from one place and immigration to another place (Fitzgerald 2006). Moving from one locality to another within the same country is internal migration, while international migration means crossing political borders. **Immigrants** are loosely categorized as political or economic immigrants, family-sponsored immigrants, refugees, sojourners (temporary residents, such as students or seasonal workers), and increasingly, environmental refugees/immigrants who are forced to leave a locality because of environmental disaster or degradation. Another category, not always included in a discussion of immigration, is the victims of human trafficking.

---

1 Humans have always migrated; however, in this discussion we are focusing on more recent large-scale migrations.

Human trafficking is "modern day slavery involving victims who are forced, defrauded or coerced into labour or sexual exploitation" (CIA World Factbook 2009: n.p.). Law professor Benjamin Perrin, in his book *Invisible Chains* (2010), brought to light sexual exploitation in Canada. He recounts how a Canadian teenager, only 14 years old, was auctioned over the Internet for men to purchase by the hour; how slave traders took a young woman from an African war zone and brought her to Edmonton to exploit her as a prostitute; and that a Quebec gang lured teenagers with false promises of job opportunities, and then sold them for sex to high-profile men in the community. Such stories of human trafficking have led some researchers to take a more applied approach, advocating for human rights and equality, such as improving working conditions and the treatment of migrant workers.

Social scientist Hein de Haas (2012) points out that economy is the prime motivator for migration. Migrants leave their home country in search of economic opportunities, while developed countries have a need for migrant workers, both skilled and unskilled, and both legal and illegal, for service-sector jobs such as cleaning, catering, agriculture, and factories – jobs that local workers tend to shun. However, the social factors that influence the decision to migrate and the evolving migration patterns must not be overlooked. For this reason, interdisciplinary research has become a cornerstone of migration research. Each discipline interested in large-scale migration offers its own theoretical perspectives and specialized forms of analysis (Boswell 2008), which augment the theoretical, conceptual, and methodological study of human migration. Concepts such as "social capital" from economics, "transnational spaces" from human geography, and "institutions" and "networks" from sociology all serve to enrich our understanding of the impact of globalization on human migration.

In this chapter we will situate international migration within the context of globalization processes. The multidimensional reasons for immigration flows, as well as the challenges facing immigrants and the source and destination countries will be addressed. Mass migration has resulted in an increase in discrimination against immigrants, including social exclusion and economic inequality; discriminatory policies toward African immigrants in France, the sex trade in Thailand, and human trafficking in Canada are featured in this chapter. International migration is a characteristic of the worldwide interconnectedness (globalization) of economies, technology, and perspectives; therefore, this discussion will draw on experts from sociology, political economy, immigration law, history, human geography, and anthropology.

THE NATURE OF HUMAN MIGRATION

Large-scale human migration has become the new world order, and with it come increasingly complex, multidimensional issues. Powerful push–pull factors trigger initial migration patterns. Push factors in countries of origin are often economic; limited economic opportunities, including low wages or unemployment, poor investment opportunities, and inadequate access to credit to start businesses may drive people to emigrate (Rosenblum & Brick 2011). Many migrants are fleeing war-torn, politically unstable countries with corrupt or authoritarian governments, while natural disasters and environmental collapse of regions may also uproot families. Indeed, the United Nations projects 50 million environmental refugees by the year 2020 (Heyer 2012). Once immigration is established in a destination country, chain migration may occur; social networks based on kinship and established communities already in the destination country facilitate migration for those still in the home country (de Haas 2010).

For source countries, emigration alleviates population pressures and unemployment, creating both diaspora networks that may lead to further migration and human capital accumulation (e.g., education and skills) if the migrant returns home. Immigrants send wealth to their home country through remittances to families, creating what Schiller (2009) calls a social field of networks that connect people across borders. Social remittances, in the form of ideas and behaviours, also have implications for the source country in that they may exacerbate culture change and create conflict between traditional societal norms and increased awareness of opportunities and lifestyles in other parts of the world. This transnational flow of people and ideas can have a dramatic effect on the sending society, encouraging a continuing transnational flow of enterprising people and creating a "culture of migration" (Massey et al. 1993).

> "Globalization's rhetoric of the increased freedom and interconnection in fact conceals bondage and displacement."
> Cruz (2008: 372)

Immigrants also respond to pull factors from the destination countries, such as secure employment, legal equality, political stability and safety, and limited government interference. Canada has become a destination of choice because of its relative political stability, low crime rate, economic vitality, universal health care, and a global reputation for embracing **multiculturalism.** Multiculturalism is a mechanism designed to peacefully manage a nation founded on ethnic diversity. However, as we will see, the degree to which this multiculturalism is welcomed or facilitated varies from one society to another. Differing perspectives on multiculturalism may also create disharmony in destination countries. On the one hand, ethno-nationalists champion a homogeneous, unilingual, and unicultural nation and claim that multiculturalism dilutes nationalism. In Europe, some fear that cultural diversity will destroy national symbols and icons and replace them with "foreign" cultural components. On the other hand, multiculturalists believe that ethnic, cultural, religious, and social diversity enhances the quality and variety of life in a nation.

One common factor in choosing a destination country is prior links to countries through colonialism, political influence, trade, cultural ties, or reciprocal investment. Migrants from the Caribbean, for example, tend to choose former colonial powers (e.g., Jamaicans immigrate to Britain) as their preferred destination (Castles 2000). Similarly, Koreans and Vietnamese choose the United States due to past military involvement in their countries. African migrants tend to prefer Europe, largely because of its geographic and language proximity, colonial ties, and its high standard of living (Katseli, Lucas, & Xemogiani 2006).

Virtually all Western countries are experiencing declining birth rates. These countries encourage immigration to replenish their population, and, more specifically, to replenish their aging workforces (Halli & Driedger 1999).[2] Humanitarian reasons also play a role; countries such as Canada have been inundated with requests to accommodate refugees and asylum seekers. The need for foreign investment may also determine government immigration targets. During the 1980s and 1990s, Hong Kong entrepreneurs and investors were encouraged to immigrate to Canada. In return, they created economic boons for major urban centres.

Despite the need for labour replenishment, immigration can cause unpredictable socio-economic changes in destination countries (Castles 2000), which may be viewed as a threat to national sovereignty and identity, and security. As a result, in the last half of the

---

2 In 2005, *Maclean's* reported that according to then foreign affairs minister Pierre Pettigrew, Canada needed 40 million people to offset the aging baby boomers heading into retirement (*Maclean's* 2005).

twentieth century many governments established restrictions on immigration, including country-of-origin quotas and favoured immigrants with credentials in preferred professions or financial and investment means. These closed-door policies began to hamper low-skilled, visible-minority populations from entering destination countries legally, and led to increased irregular (or illegal) immigration and human trafficking (Wickramasekara 2008). Resentment and fear of these influxes of irregular immigrants have caused discrimination and social disparity in some destination countries, such as the United States. Indeed, Archbishop Silvano Tomasi contends that the plight of irregular immigrants is a sign of the moral failure of the international community to protect and offer some hope to these desperate people (Tomasi 2008).

SOCIO-ECONOMIC, POLITICAL, AND CULTURAL CHALLENGES

Absorbing a large immigrant population into a destination country can present significant challenges for both the government and resident populations, as well as the immigrants themselves. Immigrants may hold different traditions, beliefs, and political views from residents of the host country. They often speak different languages, may look visibly different, and can overwhelm a region's infrastructure (e.g., transportation, education). Consequently, some citizens in destination countries may react negatively to an influx of immigrants who threaten the illusion of homogeneity and social cohesion (Castles 2000). Those who oppose immigration fear that immigrants will jeopardize their standard of living. Immigrants are often made scapegoats for unemployment and crime, the growing disparity between the rich and poor, the shrinking of the middle class, the reduction in availability of and quality of education, and the rising costs of housing and health care (Schiller 2009). Illegal immigration bears the brunt of most of this fear and angry rhetoric.

Some regions and nation-states have responded to public pressure by deporting illegal immigrants (e.g., Libya), building walls (e.g., Arizona, Israel), and setting sanctions against employers who hire illegal immigrants (e.g., South Africa). In Europe, anti-immigrant campaigns are gaining power, and this politicization of immigration often leads to social conflict. Attempts to stop irregular immigration tend to fail, as the push–pull factors override the danger, and as long as there is a need, immigrants will find a way. For example, in the last four decades, migration rates from Mexico, El Salvador, Guatemala, and Honduras have accelerated. Approximately 14 million immigrants from these four countries now live in the United States (Rosenblum & Brick 2011). Although typically looking for agricultural jobs in the American Southwest, today Mexicans work in construction, maintenance, food service, and manufacturing. Despite the need, since most of these immigrants do not have resident status, American immigration policy is focused on curtailing this irregular immigration. However, this trend is now shifting; according to the Pew Hispanic Center report, the economic downtown in the United States and increasing enforcement at the Mexico–United States border has caused the net migration of Mexicans to the United States to come to a standstill. As well, the number of Mexicans returning to Mexico, where the economy is on an upswing, is increasing dramatically (Esquivel & Becerra 2012). A new immigration bill endorsed by President Barack Obama was passed in June 2013, granting legal status to millions of undocumented foreigners (mainly Mexicans) and providing the opportunity for eventual citizenship. The bill also strengthens border security (Reuters 2013).

Despite trying to become part of their new country, visible minorities may still experience barriers that prevent them from accessing economic opportunities in destination countries – what Li (1988) calls **systemic racism** – much more commonly than "white" immigrants. Because of physical and behavioural differences (e.g., darker skin, religious beliefs), they are kept on the margins of society. Refugees are particularly vulnerable because of the political turmoil and hardships they have escaped, and because it is likely that they fled with few employable skills or economic resources. Anti-immigration discourse ignores the contributions that even low-skilled immigrants make to society by providing labour and services (Schiller 2009). Immigrants also improve neighbourhoods previously considered undesirable, create new businesses and industries, and restructure the social fabric of a region.

Following 9/11, fears of terrorist attacks have led to visible minorities from the Middle East being targeted as potential terrorists. This has made life more difficult for immigrants, especially in the United States and Europe, where immigration policies have shifted to security control (Spencer 2003). In Canada a 2005 survey[3] suggested that two-thirds of Canadians fear that immigrant groups will bring their ethnic conflicts to Canada with them, and they call for tough screening of potential immigrants to weed out terrorists. On a more positive note, 63 per cent of Canadians polled worry that concerns over terrorism could lead to a decline in civil rights for Canadians from Arabic or Islamic countries (Butler 2005).

> "Migrant workers can make their best contribution to economic and social development in host and source countries when they enjoy decent working conditions, and when their fundamental human and labour rights are respected." Statement by the Director-General of the ILO, Roundtable 3 on Globalization and Labour Migration, 2006 ECOSOC High-Level Segment, Geneva, 5 July 2006, quoted in Alsvik (2009: n.p.).

The common misconception that immigrants take jobs away from native-born citizens is refuted by economists. In the United States, for example, those states with high immigration rates enjoy lower unemployment rates and job creation because of increasing demands for goods and services (Soria 2005). Indeed, de Haas (2012: n.p.) states, "there is an incredibly close relationship between economic growth and immigration rates." A second misconception is that immigrants put pressure on an economy without giving anything back. However, immigrants "pay taxes, pay into Social Security and boost the economy with their added consumption" (Soria 2005: 301) by supporting services such as housing, education, transportation, and so on. This is certainly evident in Canada, where immigration results in a net increase in jobs (Kymlicka 2003: 205). The tendency to accuse immigrants of hurting the economy becomes particularly common during economic recessions, when immigrants are blamed for the economic woes of native-born citizens (Spencer 2003).

Technological innovations in communications and transportation have created **transnational communities.** This means immigrants and their descendants can maintain familial and cultural connections with their ancestral homeland, although most immigrants also become enculturated into their new society, creating a dual identity. For example, Chinese immigrants to Canada have a cultural identity that is neither Canadian nor Chinese, but Chinese Canadian, which enables them to maintain their Chinese heritage while adopting Canadian cultural elements (Ng 1999). Immigrants gravitate to those who are similar to them; hence, new immigrants often settle in urban centres where there are well-established

---

3 Taken by Innovative Research Group, The World in Canada: Demographics and Diversity in Canadian Foreign Policy (http://www.cdfai.org/PDF/The%20World%20In%20Canada%20Poll.pdf).

populations from the same country. These areas are known as ethnic enclaves. Balakrishnan and Hou (1999) found that residential segregation helps maintain cultural identity but also prolongs the sense of separateness from mainstream society and the process of integration.

Immigrants, for their part, must learn the official language, obey the laws of the land, find employment, and become involved in the community (Neuwirth 1999). The host country must ensure meaningful employment is available, and share the basic values, ideology, and traditions of the country with new immigrants. If immigrants are excluded from economic and social institutions, they will not adopt the host country's practices and norms, and will, out of a sense of preservation, try to maintain their traditional culture. Above all, immigrants need to be viewed as an asset, not a liability (Soria 2005).

Some destination countries view foreigners as solutions to short-term labour shortages, rather than permanent residents (Simmons 1999). Indeed, today some European countries are attempting to drastically curtail or even eliminate immigration from non-European countries. This selective immigration policy is predicated on **racism** and xenophobia, which are on the rise throughout Europe and North America. One dramatic example of this xenophobia and the ensuing discriminatory practices based on race is France.

DISCRIMINATION AGAINST IMMIGRANTS IN FRANCE

Immigration policies and integration strategies, as well as managing cultural diversity, have always been a challenge for France. Following the French Revolution, France adopted an assimilation policy toward the "Other" – more than half of France's population did not speak French at the time. To ensure every citizen was French, the country embarked on a long and difficult "self-colonizing" process (Malik 2012). The roots of the later integration model and secularism lie in the 1905 law that separated church and state (Well 2004: 2). The French constitution and integration model emphasize French identity rather than ethnic identity as the pathway to national unity. Despite these policies, which were designed to prevent **discrimination** while promoting integration of new arrivals into French society and equality for all, the country's history is fraught with tension between immigrants and other French citizens, and secularism has created a discourse that promotes religious and cultural intolerance.

According to the republican ideal, everyone is equal in France; religion, colour, etc., are irrelevant (Jennings 2000). However, in reality France's immigration policy perpetuates exclusion and refuses to acknowledge cultural groups or religions in the public sphere. The exclusion of Muslim populations is particularly noticeable as there are no Muslim state schools, no Muslim chaplains in the army, and employment ads often clearly state "whites only," "no coloureds," or "French nationals only" (Randall 2005). Terms such as "second generation" or "persons born in France of immigrant parents" are still used to distinguish immigrants from other French citizens (Hamilton, Simon, & Veniard 2004).

France views retention of ethnic identity as a deterrent to integration into French society and rejects multiculturalism as a threat to national identity, echoing a recent comment by Germany's Chancellor Angela Merkel that multiculturalism is dead. This runs counter to the desires of second-generation immigrant youth who want to preserve their cultural identity but who also proudly proclaim their French citizenship (Fuga 2008). As a consequence, France is raising a generation of dispossessed people who often become scapegoats for France's ills, and the exclusionary and discriminatory policies, both nationally and locally, have created a culture of tension. In October 2004, this tension sparked suburban riots (Chrisafis 2010). The catalyst was two young boys who were electrocuted while hiding from police in a power substation, but the root cause was the hopelessness of a generation of youth who are ghettoized, marginalized, and unemployed, even among those who are native-born French citizens (Kamber & Lacey 2005).

France is home to the largest Muslim community in Europe (Hamilton, Simon, & Veniard 2004), imported in the 1970s to meet labour-market needs. When French women began entering the job market in the 1970s, France no longer needed as many immigrant workers and so restrictive immigration policies were put in place: foreign graduates of French schools could no longer accept employment in France; waiting periods for family reunification doubled; spouses who were illegal before their marriage to a French citizen were denied residence; and asylum appeals were limited. These restrictive immigration policies created resentment, discontent, and strife, especially among visible-minority youth.[4]

> "We're French but we're not considered as real French people." (Chrisafis 2010: n.p.)

In a human-rights survey, three-quarters of the respondents blamed immigrants for increasing unemployment and crime in France, and for lowering educational standards. Forty per cent of the respondents agreed with forcible repatriation of the unemployed, and 22 per cent wanted forcible repatriation of all immigrants. The 2000 Eurobarometer found that only 31 per cent of French respondents supported laws outlawing discrimination against minorities (Randall 2005). These alarming statistics indicate a growing resentment toward immigrants.

Fear of cultural diversity in France has been exploited by politicians for political gain (Randall 2005). In February 2004, the government passed a bill banning religious symbols in public schools. Although the bill did not specifically target Muslim veiling, the intent was clear. This bill is one of many actions taken against immigrants in an effort to keep France secular (Hamilton, Simon, & Veniard 2004). Some, however, accuse the French government of being anti-Islamic rather than pro-secularist, and that they are indirectly legitimizing anti-Arab stereotypes and fostering racism. Others view the bill as the right step since it may provide an option to girls who do not want to wear the veil.[5]

Former president Nicolas Sarkozy won the French election in 2007 on a right-wing, anti-immigrant platform, attracting votes from the extreme right Front National party. Once elected, Sarkozy ordered the expulsion of 25,000 irregular immigrants. The police roundups of Roma, Muslims, and other minorities took place outside schools, metro stations, and businesses and created a backlash of protest from many French citizens. Some even hid children of illegal immigrants in their homes. The round-ups eerily resembled the time when the French collaborationist government deported 75,000 French citizens and Jewish refugees to Nazi concentration camps during World War II (Chrisafis 2010). Although President Nicholas Sarkozy

> "Sarkozy's constant talk of immigration and national identity chips away at you, but worse is the perpetual police stops and searches. Cops insult us, saying 'Get back to your own country, you're not welcome.' That's pretty hard to stomach when you're French." Fariz Allili, 21, son of an Algerian café owner, quoted in Chrisafis (2010: n.p.).

---

4 The term "visible-minority youth" is used here because many of the people experiencing serious economic, social, and religious discrimination in France are fourth- or fifth-generation French citizens, but the colour of their skin still sets them apart.

5 This is predicated on the assumption that Muslim women are forced to veil, which is far from true.

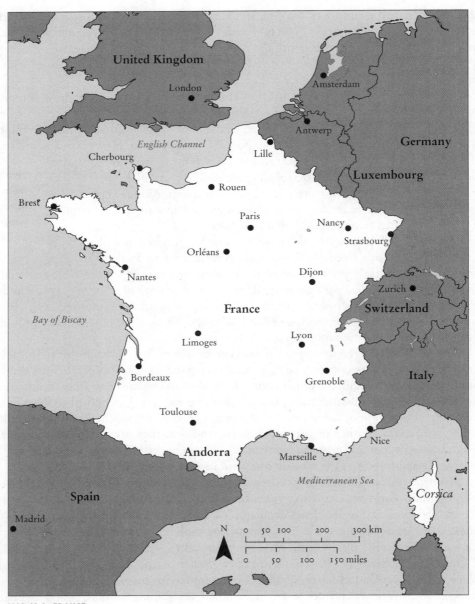

MAP 12.1 FRANCE

lost the 2012 election for numerous reasons, analysts suggest this was partly due to accusations of racism and Islamophobia and a backlash over his policies (Cross 2012).

HUMAN TRAFFICKING

Former United Nations secretary-general Kofi Annan has warned that forced labour and exploitation are among "the most egregious [organized] violations of human rights" (UNODC 2000). Human trafficking across international borders now surpasses drugs and arms trafficking in incidence, cost to human well-being, and profitability to the criminal traffickers (Schauer & Wheaton 2006). Worldwide, more people now live in slavery than during the slave-trade era (Perrin 2010). Trafficking, then, has become a global problem and is a form of transnational organized crime that flourishes because of the demand for "free labour, sexual services, child soldiers and human organs" (Oosterman 2010: n.p.). Restrictive immigration policies in destination countries are also credited with channelling low-skilled immigrants into irregular migration that can lead to trafficking.

According to the United Nations International Labour Organization, globally an estimated 12.3 million people are living in forced labour or sexual exploitation situations (The Evangelical Fellowship of Canada 2009). These victims are coerced, threatened with harm to their families, locked up in inhumane conditions, and have their passports confiscated. The consumers are employers of trafficked labour (e.g., "johns," or home owners who employ household staff), and the products are human beings (e.g., prostitutes, domestics). Traffickers, then, are the intermediaries between vulnerable victims and unscrupulous employers (Wheaton, Schauer, & Galli 2010).

Profit is the driving force behind trafficking and is a response to poverty, war and conflict, dislocation from homeland, social and cultural exclusion, and limited access to education or employment in source countries (UNODC 2008: 75). Women are most often sexually exploited, while men are sold into bonded labour, and children are forced to beg or enter the sex trade. Others work in agriculture, domestic service, factories and workshops, mining, land clearance, and selling in a market (Bales 2005). Most victims of **modern-day slavery** are low skilled: traffickers prey on those who cannot immigrate legally. Some are kidnapped, others misled about opportunities, and still others – children – sold by their desperate families. Victims of slavery suffer physical injury from beatings and abuse and psychological trauma, including post-traumatic stress disorder, anxiety, depression, and alienation.

"Looking in a victim's eye and telling her that the Police will do everything they can, but it is now up to the law and the court system to make sure that these guys will never hurt her again can be really scary to rely on." Timea Nagy, survivor of trafficking, now educator and advocate, in an email message to Canadian Members of Parliament, Sept. 30, 2009, quoted in Oosterman (2010: n.p.)

Canada and the United States are often viewed as lands of freedom, but an illegal economy that plunges vulnerable people, mostly women and children, into a nightmare of slavery and exploitation thrives beneath the surface. Slavery has been illegal in Canada since 1807 and the United States since 1865, yet people continue to be bought and sold in both countries. Thousands of Canadian citizens are trafficked to other countries for forced labour and sexual exploitation; others, usually irregular immigrants, are trafficked through Canada into the United States; and a third group, foreigners, are trafficked into Canada every year (Stirk 2009). Internally, traffickers recruit Canadian girls for the sex trade by

"Human trafficking is a form of modern-day slavery and a priority of the RCMP.... Public awareness is the first step towards putting an end to this horrific crime that robs one person's freedom to benefit another." Inspector Steve Martin, RCMP, news release, quoted in Byrne (2010: n.p.)

using coercion, deception, and force. These traffickers use both Craigslist's erotic service section and Facebook to buy and sell sexual services. Internationally trafficked victims are shipped into Canada from Asia and Africa, and then they are forced to pay off inflated "debts" by selling their bodies or forced labour in sweatshops. This modern-day slavery is a thriving business in Canada – one victim can earn as much as $280,000 for their "owner" in a year (Online Press Conference 2010).

What can be done to prevent trafficking or rescue the victims? The United Nations has adopted a common-sense approach to dealing with human trafficking: 1) prevent trafficking; 2) prosecute traffickers; and 3) protect victims. The United Nations Protocol established strategies, including media campaigns in source regions to inform people of the dangers inherent in agreeing to be smuggled[6] into another country, and improving economic opportunities for people in their own countries (General Assembly 2004). Most experts suggest that diminishing demand (e.g., from sex consumers) is the most effective way to stop trafficking. In Sweden, for example, the purchase of sexual services is now penalized as "male sexual violence against women and children" (Oosterman 2010: n.p.). Consequently, the rate of trafficked victims in Sweden has dropped dramatically. Prompt prosecution of traffickers may also slow trafficking. Proponents advocate changing the definition of "victim" to include sex workers as victims of trafficking.

"Police are no longer willing to look at these cases as simply prostitution cases, which is historically how they have been dealt with and often dismissed by many people.... Now they're being recognized for what they are, which is serious allegations of child sex trafficking." UBC law professor Ben Perrin, interviewed on CTV News (2011.)

In Canada, human trafficking has become an offence under the Criminal Code, and advocacy against this underground illegal economy is being promoted in the media to create more public awareness. Yet Perrin (2010) believes that Canada needs a national action plan to end human trafficking. "While traffickers have playbooks to teach each other tactics to exploit victims, there's no such government plan," says Perrin. "Canada needs to protect and provide services for victims, and ensure that the perpetrators of these crimes are brought to justice" (Online Press Conference 2010: n.p.).

Elsewhere in the world, particularly in Asia, the situation is dire. In Thailand, for example, trafficking of children into the sex trade is an ongoing problem, although the demographics have changed somewhat (Arnold & Bertone 2002). As the economy has improved, there has been a gradual decline in the number of Thai women entering the sex trade, but an increase in girls and women trafficked into the country or from the hill tribes of northern Thailand. The sex industry in Thailand is directly linked to sex tourism: men from Europe, North America, and Japan travel to Thailand to engage in sex with children. Although some prostitution in Bangkok is "voluntary," others are trafficked within and into Thailand. Many of the young women come from Myanmar; they have agreed to work as prostitutes in Thailand in the hopes of a better life than the violence, rape by military personnel, and poverty they face in Myanmar. Once in Thailand, however, they are physically or psychologically coerced into working in conditions they did not expect. Girls from Yunan province in China are sent to south Thailand where demand for light-skinned girls

---

6 Smuggling means illegally crossing a border; however, smuggled individuals may then find themselves trafficked – forced into indentured servitude to pay off inflated debts.

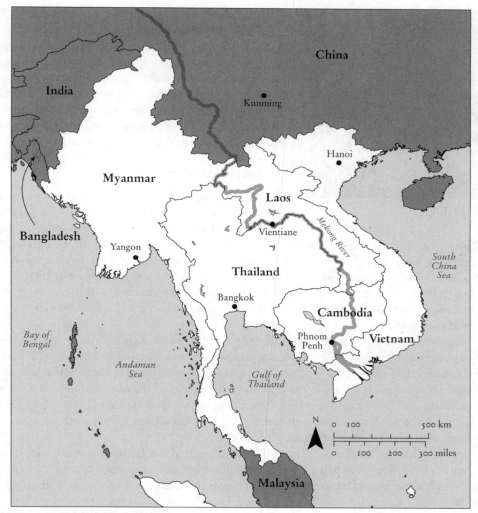

MAP 12.2 MEKONG RIVER BASIN

is high. Girls from Myanmar are sent to northern Thailand, while those from Laos and Cambodia go to Bangkok and northeast Thailand.

The police, government, and NGOs in Thailand are working to stop the sex trade. Social movements against trafficking, prostitution, and sex tourism are well established and organized, and the under-classes, who usually do not have a political voice, are participating in these movements. Campaigns have been launched to prosecute foreigners who have sex with children; however, if a child between the ages of 12 and 15 is paid for the sex, it is considered consensual in Thailand, and foreign "consumers" are granted bail, after which they quickly leave the country. Therefore, a great deal of work needs to be done to end sex tourism in Thailand (Arnold & Bertone 2002).

FIGURE 12.1 A YOUNG PROSTITUTE

Can human trafficking be stopped? According to Bales (2005), if poverty, corruption, population explosions, environmental destruction, conflict and international debt are eradicated, and laws and legislation are enforced, then yes, human trafficking can be stopped. But these are lofty goals, so obviously, other solutions are needed, such as reducing demand and prosecuting those who traffic in human beings.

CONCLUSION

The future belongs to those nations that recognize migration as a global reality and are prepared to transform their societies into multicultural, collaborative, and inclusive societies that recognize their responsibility as part of the international community to protect the human rights of immigrants and displaced persons. Until immigrants are granted social, economic, religious, and political equality, social discord is likely to continue in destination countries. Leaders must work creatively with the key players to find equitable solutions to prevent conflict that could destroy the social fabric of their societies.

Economic and political change is an integral component of globalization, and is closely tied to people movements. Attempts to regulate immigration have met with limited success, and short-sighted immigration policies have created an environment for irregular immigration that encourages exploitation and human-rights abuses of the most vulnerable – women and children, and low-skilled workers. According to Wickramasekara (2008: 1247), "there is an imperative need for fresh approaches and bold initiatives to promote international labour mobility for the welfare of the global community."

Although many of the misconceptions and much of the ignorance at the root of discrimination have given way to a growing social maturity and acceptance among increasingly global citizens, we would be naive to assume that intolerance and bigotry have disappeared from Western countries, a case in point being France, where attitudes toward immigrants appear to be regressing. Exclusionary rhetoric portrays immigrants as unskilled, threatening, and disruptive invaders, thereby dehumanizing people when they are at their most vulnerable. In the twenty-first century, a major challenge for the international community will be to build bridges, not fences, and to embrace a global labour market that does not trample on the human rights of desperate people in search of a better life.

QUESTIONS FOR CONSIDERATION AND CLASSROOM ACTIVITIES

1. Put yourself in the shoes of a new immigrant. You have moved to a foreign country, are unable to speak the language, and must find a place to live, a job, and necessities, such as food and water, with a limited supply of money. Outline your strategy for surviving, and then becoming comfortable in your new surroundings. What assistance would you welcome from the locals?

2. Here's a second scenario. You are in a foreign country. The people stop and stare at you because you look different (e.g., skin colour, height), they make fun of you and laugh at you, and when you approach someone for help, they walk away with an impatient shrug at your feeble attempt to speak their language. Analyze why they are responding to you this way. How would these responses make you feel? How should they have responded?

3. If you moved to another country, would you try to hold on to your cultural practices and values or would you adopt (assimilate into) your new country's culture? Depending on your answer to this question, how can you expect any more from people immigrating to your country?

4. Investigate how Canadian immigration policies have restricted the ability of immigrants to settle comfortably into Canadian society. Choose an immigrant group and discuss how they have coped with the restrictions placed on them. What could the government and the people of Canada do to help them integrate into Canadian society?

5. Develop a definition of multiculturalism and then create a class debate on the positive and negative aspects of this policy. Why do you think some Europeans are rejecting multiculturalism? What is the alternative? How will life be different for immigrants if multicultural policies are changed?

6. Interview a newly arrived immigrant student using prepared questions, in order to write a personal narrative about his/her experiences with discrimination in your country. Read this narrative to the class.

7. In groups of three or four students, search for job ads on the Internet that possess discriminatory and/or inflammatory information in them. Now "clean up" the ads, using inclusive, culturally sensitive language.

8. How can you, as a global citizen, ensure that human trafficking is not happening in your community?

SUGGESTED READINGS

Parrenas, R. (2005). *Children of global migration: Transnational families and gendered woes.* Stanford, CA: Stanford University Press.

This is the story of children left behind when migrant workers seek employment in foreign countries. The author uses interviewing and ethnographic research to uncover their story. Unlike many academic books, this book brings the human side of migration to the reader.

Perrin, B. (2010). *Irresistible chains: Canada's underground world of human trafficking.* Toronto: Viking Canada.

An engaging examination of the underground economy flourishing in Canada that provides sex services or forced labour. This book offers an insightful introduction to the sex trade in Canada and the actions needed to stop sex exploitation.

Chapter 13

Global Conflict: Is the World Safer Because of Military Intervention, and What Are the Consequences of Militarism?

Key Terms: Cold War, ecoterrorism, global citizens, imperialism, internationalized intrastate armed conflicts, just war, militarism, military industrial complex, neoconservatives

---

INTRODUCTION

"On April 4, 1967 Martin Luther King called the United States government 'the greatest purveyor of violence in the world today' ... 'the deadly Western arrogance that has poisoned the international atmosphere for so long.' ... 'a nation that continues year after year to spend more money on military defense than on programs of social uplift' and a nation that suffers from 'spiritual death.'" King 1967, quoted in Greenwald (2013: n.p).

Since the end of World War II the major world powers – France, the United Kingdom, Russia (formerly USSR), and the United States – have repeatedly sent their military forces to intervene in civil conflicts in developing nations. Whether these powers were assisting the government or rebel forces depended on their economic and political interests. Proponents suggest that military intervention is necessary to ensure peace and stability and that it serves as an effective way to curtail conflict. Opponents believe that military interference in another nation's affairs is exacerbating global conflict and precipitating so-called terrorist acts against these powers. Indeed, some opponents even suggest that military intervention by external powers is creating economic and political crises around the world.

Although brief reference is made to earlier conflicts and geopolitics, this discussion will focus primarily on internationalized state-based armed conflicts in the post–Cold War era. **Internationalized intrastate armed conflicts** (also referred to as external military interventions) are those conflicts where at least one of the parties is a legally recognized state government, and where at least one external military force is fighting on the side of one of the warring parties (Human Security Report Project [HSRP] 2012). Various schools of thought address armed conflict. In this chapter we will apply militarism and **just war** ideologies to investigate the underlying reasons for armed interventions by major powers. **Militarism** is both an ideology that promotes a strong military force to defend national and international interests, and a mindset that glorifies warfare. A prime example of militarism is the United States, where the moral imperative of spreading justice, democracy, and freedom around the world is used to rationalize military intervention.

The objectives of this final chapter in *Global Issues*, then, are to investigate armed conflict around the world, and to question Western assumptions that military and weapons proliferation, and military intervention in the affairs of other nations, are necessary and just. To that end, the United States, as arguably the leading perpetrator of Western **imperialism** and the leading proponent of military intervention, is a major focus in this discussion. Several questions are addressed: Is the world safer because of military intervention by powerful nations? What motives drive American military expansion despite the end of the Cold War? What are the national and international consequences of global armed conflict? The information presented in this chapter is not meant to demonize the United States, nor militarism; however, this is a critical examination that presents a bleak picture of the motives and consequences of militarism. Experts from the fields of geopolitics, political science, international relations, economics, justice and law, and history, as well as investigative journalists and anti-war politicians and activists, inform this discussion.

THE NATURE OF GLOBAL CONFLICT

Conflict is not a new phenomenon, although the regions with hotly contested armed conflicts have shifted over time. When the **Cold War** ended, militarism should have declined, at least in Western nations previously caught up in Cold War geopolitics. However, throughout the latter half of the twentieth century, internationalized intrastate armed conflicts actually increased. Indeed, many of the deadliest conflicts involved external military forces and resulted in twice as many battle deaths as other conflicts. There also appears to be a strong correlation between external military involvement and conflict intensity, although whether the former causes the latter remains unclear (HSRP 2012).

Since the end of World War II in 1945, at least 250 major conflicts have been fought and over 23 million people have been killed, with tens of millions of other people displaced from their homes and communities (Global Issues Overview n.d.). In the three decades following World War II, East and Southeast Asia and Oceania were the most conflicted regions in the world. The main conflicts were the Chinese Civil War, the Korean War, and wars in Indochina, including the Vietnam War. In the 1980s, the Middle East (e.g., Iran and Iraq) and North Africa erupted in conflict, while in the 1990s sub-Saharan Africa (e.g., Ethiopia, Angola) became a hotbed for armed conflict.

More recently, Sri Lanka, Afghanistan, Pakistan, Libya, and Iraq have experienced deadly conflicts (HSRP 2012). Some of these conflicts, most notably in Afghanistan, Iraq, Somalia, the Democratic Republic of Congo (DRC), and Libya, are internationalized intrastate armed conflicts, as were the earlier United Nations (led by the United States) and Chinese interventions in Korea in 1950, the American intervention in Vietnam in 1965, and the Soviet intervention in Afghanistan in 1979 and Iran in 1981. Not all military interventions come from major powers; for example, Cuba stepped into Angola in the 1970s and 1980s, and the Socialist Republic of Vietnam played a role in the Cambodian civil war in the 1970s and 1980s (HSRP 2012). The most recent example of external military intervention occurred in January 2013, when France launched aerial attacks on Islamist rebel groups in northern Mali to halt their southward advance (Masters 2013).

Several issues plague external military intervention. First, there is the lack of a mechanism for making the intervening powers accountable to the citizens of the target nation for their security policies (or lack thereof) and the consequences of their actions, which seldom benefit the people (Chandler 2002). Second, what is or is not a "just war" is determined by the major powers that may have political and military, as well as economic, interests that influence their decision to intervene (Nikolic-Ristanovic 2008: 102). Third, some underlying reasons for conflict are long term and difficult to resolve, unless members of the global community, including major powers, are willing to make changes. According to Kristina Rintakoski, executive director of the Crisis Management Initiative, many conflicts are caused by struggles against inequality, resource competition, particularly the politics of oil, and climate change (Shah 2009). These processes have increased the wealth of Western powers, but worsened poverty and economic inequality in developing nations, and have created tensions and the potential for conflict.

"It's a messy world out there, and there will always be some trouble somewhere that people will want Uncle Sam to fix." Robert and Renee Belfer professor of international relations at Harvard University, quoted in Stephen M. Walt (2011).

An alternative to making war is keeping and building peace. The United Nations is charged with monitoring political developments, peacekeeping, and peacebuilding on a global scale. Yet the UN, as well as the European Union, African Union, Organization of American States, and Arab League, have a mixed record of success and tend to be reactive rather than preventative (Masters 2013). Peacekeeping suffers from a lack of funding, personnel, and equipment. For example, in 2011, the United States budget for peacekeeping was $7.23 billion – less than one per cent of its military budget – and only 20 American troops served on a peacekeeping operation in 2012. Despite these shortcomings there have been successes, such as in East Timor and Liberia, although they do not attract much media coverage, and the United States does fund operations such as the Multinational Forces and Observers (Masters 2013).

REASONS FOR MILITARISM

Militarism and external military intervention are complex subjects, riddled with competing economic and political agendas, despite the number of global conflicts having stabilized at 30 to 40 per year (HSRP 2012).[1] In this section we will address the reasons behind military intervention in the conflicts of other nations, in particular why the United States continues what some analysts call an imperialist agenda of military expansion.

One reason for external military intervention is to protect the political and ideological interests of major powers, therefore making the war a just cause. For example, American containment policies against the expansion of communism during the Cold War caused several conflicts, including the Vietnam War. Another "just war" rationale is to provide humanitarian relief to a beleaguered people (Nikolic-Ristanovic 2008: 102), for example, the 2011 intervention in Libya. The United States and other major powers called on the international community to prevent a civilian massacre in Libya, based on reports of an imminent massacre, and previous actions by Moammar Qaddafi including the 1996 massacre in Abu Salim. Under the

---

1 The number of present-day conflicts varies considerably depending on source. For example, Project Ploughshares counted 26 active armed conflicts in 2011, as well as a series of pro-democracy movements known as the Arab Spring (Project Ploughshares 2013).

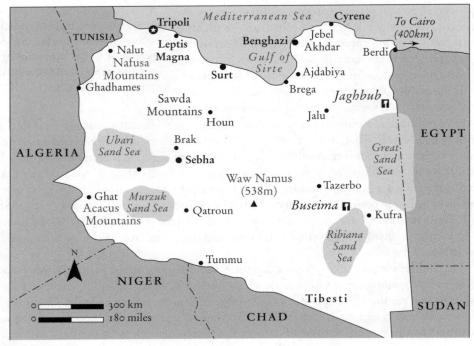

MAP 13.1 LIBYA

"Intervention in the name of humanitarianism or democracy is likely to create more problems than it solves; any use of force no matter how well intentioned, potentially can lead to chaos and this contemporary revival of imperialism is likely to impair the capacity of states to provide for political order...." (Welsh 2002: n.p.).

auspices of the Responsibility to Protect[2] doctrine, military intervention was approved by the Security Council to protect Libyan citizens. Whether this intervention was warranted remains unclear; however, the campaign in Libya changed course mid-mission and became a war effort to assist the rebel army in overthrowing the government, and eventually led to the assassination of Moammar Qaddafi (Lobe 2013). Thus, "responsibility to protect" can be used to legitimize Western militarism while ignoring the economic and social needs of the people (Tadjbakhsh & Chenoy 2007: 37).

A powerful motivator for external military intervention is protecting or enhancing foreign interests. Developed nations are becoming increasingly dependent on energy resources that are found in "conflict-heavy" developing nations (Shah 2009). According to activist Courtenay Barnett (2006: n.p.), energy acquisition is becoming an increasing source of global conflict, and appears to increase the willingness of military powers to intervene in the affairs of developing nations if they have oil reserves. Indeed, oil now dominates and guides American foreign policy. As an example, despite the many reasons given for the Iraqi War, and the "faulty" intelligence regarding weapons of mass destruction, ultimately

---

2 The Responsibility to Protect doctrine was endorsed by the UN General Assembly in 2005 and addresses the possibility of Security Council–mandated military interventions to protect civilians from becoming casualties of war (HSRP 2012).

the United States was protecting its oil interests. Iraq became part of the "oil war mechanism" – where attempts by major powers to dominate oil sources guide foreign-policy decisions in what has been called a modern-day neo-colonial war.

> "Empires are costly. Running Iraq is not cheap. Somebody's paying. Somebody's paying the corporations that destroyed Iraq and the corporations that are rebuilding it, in both cases, they're getting paid by the U.S. Taxpayer." (Chomsky 2005: 56)

Domestically, supporting the arms and munitions industry is another economic reason for militarism. In 1961, President Eisenhower expressed concern over the **"military industrial complex"** in the United States and the destabilizing effects of capitalist militarism on the democratic processes of the country (NPR staff 2011). Militarism enables corporations (defence contractors) that produce armaments to earn enormous profits. These wealthy and powerful corporations exert a great deal of influence over the American political system and often have key supporters in the government, such as former vice-president Dick Cheney, who was CEO of Halliburton, an oil and gas corporation, from 1995 to 2000. The United States is also the largest arms dealer, selling $66 billion worth of arms (compared to Russia, which sold $4.8 billion worth) to countries that are hostile to one another, for example, India and Pakistan, India and China, Israel and Egypt and Saudi Arabia (Lindorff 2012). Besides the ethics of arms dealing, these sales encourage conflict. Thus, Big Business and governments are often joined in partnership, while taxpayers pay the bill for research and development subsidies (Du Boff 1989). Noam Chomsky (2007) calls this "Pentagon system" a covert form of "corporate welfare." Today the arms industry is so large and diverse that any budget cuts would have dramatic economic implications for employees and communities throughout the United States. Indeed, economic considerations and jobs have forced American politicians into supporting the arms industry (Parry 2013).

UNITED STATES MILITARISM

Martin Luther King's words of condemnation in the opening quotation in this chapter still resonate today. Indeed, given ongoing American militarism, they are even more apt in the twenty-first century than in the mid-

> "... the international community has demonstrated its incapacity in resolving conflicts and building sustainable peace in many countries and regions of the world." President Martti Ahtisaari of Finland, quoted in Shah (2009: n.p.).

twentieth century. According to Greenwald (2013), the belief that the United States has not only the right but the duty to intervene militarily in the conflicts of other countries and to benefit politically and economically from these actions informs the country's foreign policy.

The roots of American militarism lie in 1947 with the passing of the National Security Act and the beginning of the Cold War (Goodman 2013b). The power and influence of the Pentagon and the military in foreign policy and national security grew over the next four decades, leading to the Defense Reorganization Act of 1986, through which the Joint Chiefs of Staff were appointed the primary military advisers to the president, the secretary of defense, and the National Security Council. Following the Korean War, weapons industries began to grow in the United States and a large standing army was kept on permanent duty (NPR 2011).

With the end of the Cold War, and the fall of the Berlin Wall, the Union of Soviet Socialist Republics (USSR), and the Warsaw Pact, American defence planners needed justification for expanding the military budget. They lobbied for an American presence and global military dominance to prevent hostile actions or a build-up of weapons "of

"When American power declines, the institutions and norms of American power will decline too." Robert Kegan of Carnegie Endowment for International Peace, quoted in Goodman (2013b.)

mass destruction." Any suspicion, accurate or not, as in the case of Iraq in 2003, has been used for defence budget increases (Goodman 2013b). Between 1945 and 2002, the United States undertook 200 military actions, not counting those completed in secret (Vidal 2002). The United States has more than 700 military bases spread around the world,[3] while most other countries have none. America can deploy 11 aircraft carriers, while China has one – highlighting the dramatic disparity of military power (Goodman 2013a).

The recent history of American militarism is fraught with military campaigns that either backfired or failed miserably: John F. Kennedy used the CIA against Cuba; Lyndon B. Johnson escalated the Vietnam War in 1965; Richard Nixon continued the escalation and fought a secret war in Cambodia; Gerald Ford used military force to free the US freighter *Mayaguez* (although the crew had already been released); George H.W. Bush authorized the first Gulf War; George W. Bush launched the Iraq and Afghanistan wars; and Barack Obama escalated the war in Afghanistan, using drone attacks (Goodman 2013b).

"In the councils of government, we must guard against the acquisition of unwarranted influence, whether sought or unsought, by the military-industrial complex. The potential for the disastrous rise of misplaced power exists, and will persist." Speech by President Dwight Eisenhower (1961)

Economically, the proportion of the United States budget that is allocated for defence is staggering. In 2012, $673 billion was budgeted for the military, $166 billion for military activities in other government departments (e.g., the nuclear weapons program), and $440 billion was paid in interest on loans for previous wars and military expenditures, for a total of $1.3 trillion dollars – nearly 50 per cent of the United States' entire budget (Lindorff 2012). Defence, homeland security, and intelligence spending in the United States have reached unprecedented levels in the twenty-first century (Goodman 2013a). Indeed, it surpasses the defence budgets of all other countries combined (Goodman 2013b). Ironically, America's spending on the military is making Americans poorer and less secure.

Former CIA analyst Melvin A. Goodman (2013b) suggests that American **neoconservatives** are committed to militarism. Neoconservatives advocate using political-economic-military superiority to expand America's influence around the world, to remove any challenges to the United States' pre-eminence, and to use military power at any provocation to protect American interests. Neoconservatives rose to "power" by exaggerating the Soviet threat in the 1970s and 1980s, and by hyping the threat from Iraq in 2002–03 (Parry 2013).

The answer to the question of how the neoconservative faction procures budget increases for defence given the lack of a real and substantiated threat and burgeoning economic woes lies with the media and their ability to promote the "just war" cause. Despite the role that media can play in informing the public and giving increasing visibility to current situations, such as human-rights abuses, media outlets have been accused of exaggerating the threat that other nations or non-state groups (e.g., al-Qaeda) pose (Nikolic-Ristanovic 2008), or the potential for massacres (e.g., claims of mass slaughter of Kosovo Albanians). They regularly portray "enemy" states as a real and present danger and promote the necessity for the American military to be ready to protect the nation. American news outlets

---

3 The number of bases that the Americans actually have is unknown, and estimates vary widely, depending on the source.

(e.g., FOX, CNN, ABC) distort the intentions and motivations of other nations to convince the American public that the military and any military action is necessary for their security, and that American militarism is a force for global good, freedom, democracy, and human rights. Indeed, political columnist David Sirota (2013: n.p.) accuses the US of having a "culture that portrays bloodshed as the most effective problem solver" and notes that the public has heard it so often they too believe that killing is the only effective way of achieving peace – in other words, a theology of militarism.[4] Currently, pro-military propaganda in the West is reiterating the dangers from nuclear facilities in North Korea, and portraying Kim Jong-un, the leader of North Korea, as unpredictable and irrational. This type of media hype incites fear and hatred in order to justify future military expenditures and to rationalize military interventions.

> "We [Americans] have the most expensive and lethal military force in the world, but we face no existential threat" (Goodman 2013a).

An important component of American foreign policy is the politicizing and militarization of intelligence that became entrenched in President Ronald Reagan's era (Parry 2013). This intelligence service identifies threats, manipulates information, and spreads militaristic propaganda via the media. Ultimately, this feeds the military industry. Despite no measureable security benefits from deployments in Vietnam, Iraq, and Afghanistan, and great financial and social costs, today the military is urging more forces for "trouble spots" at a time when defence budget cuts are on the table. According to Goodman (2013b), the "War on Terror" is the most recent demonstration of unilateral and hegemonic power. This perceived threat was used to send military forces to Pakistan, Libya, Somalia, and Yemen, as well as building secret facilities in Ethiopia, Djibouti, the Seychelles, and the Arabian Peninsula for drone aircraft. The United States has also stationed thousands of troops in the demilitarized zone between North and South Korea, to protect East Asia.

The United States habitually opposes any agreements or conventions that promote moderate actions in the global community (Goodman 2013b). For example, the International Criminal Court that tries human rights offenders, such as former Yugoslav president Slobodan Milošević, was not ratified by the United States because American soldiers and leaders could find themselves on trial. Other examples of American intractability include the League of Nations in 1919 and the ban on landmines, which would jeopardize the American deployment of landmines on the border between North and South Korea.

Whether the United States is justified in its militarism is beyond the scope of this chapter, but there is little doubt that its enormous military force is ready to deal with any international crises. For example, as North Korea increases its threatening rhetoric against the United States, Japan, and South Korea, having the American missile defences on alert is likely a prudent move, and perhaps a deterrent, given that the full extent of North Korea's nuclear capabilities is unknown (Bulletin Staff 2013).

CONSEQUENCES OF MILITARISM

Armed conflict has many consequences beyond the obvious loss of life and property. In many cases the ecosystem of a region is deliberately destroyed in what is now called **eco-terrorism**. The United States used Agent Orange to destroy the flora in Vietnam, thereby

---

4 Interestingly, most of the critical analysis of American military intervention originates with investigative journalists (outside the established papers).

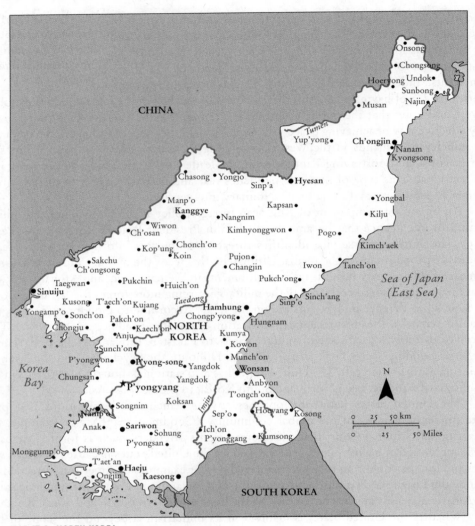

MAP 13.2 NORTH KOREA

jeopardizing the country's food sources. A second example of ecoterrorism is the more recent destruction of 800 Kuwaiti oil wells by the Iraqi military, which caused air pollution from soot and oil lakes that left hundreds of square kilometres of land uninhabitable. Birds, plants, and marine life suffered, as did the quality of water in the Persian Gulf from oil run-off and toxic wastes in sunken ships. This environmental damage also had economic implications for fishermen, drastically reducing their yield. Water desalination plants, power plants, and industrial facilities along the Gulf Coast were also endangered (Ali n.d.).

Heavy bombs can destroy the flora, fauna, and soil in large regions. The American forces first used heavy bombs, also known as DU weapons – depleted uranium (nuclear waste products) – in the 1991 Persian Gulf War, then in Bosnia and Herzegovina in

1994–95, Kosovo in 1999, and today in Afghanistan and Iraq. The dust cloud created by a DU bombing is chemically toxic and radioactive, and spreads with the wind. When inhaled by humans or animals, it causes birth defects, cancer, degenerative diseases, paralysis, and even death. DU cannot be removed from the land and air and continues to decay into more radioactive waste for thousands of years (WorldCentric.org 2013). Although heavy bombs have a disastrous effect on the environment, "ordinary" bombs and cluster bombs also destroy property and the ecosystem, while land mines create uninhabitable conflict zones and military facilities create toxic waste sites.

The social costs of military action are equally devastating. One of the primary reasons for food shortages around the world is civil strife (WorldCentric.org 2013). Food supplies, local markets, land, and even the farmers themselves are destroyed during conflicts, and food relief is often commandeered by the military. Funding that should be applied to educational and medical research and facilities is used for military spending. The social costs of this redirection of taxpayers' money can be tragic. In Eisenhower's prophetic speech he warned that the military establishment had joined forces with the arms industry and that an arms race would take much-needed funding away from education and hospitals. For example, Washington, Detroit, and Philadelphia have higher infant-mortality rates than Jamaica or Costa Rica, and African-American infant-mortality rates are higher than in Nigeria (analyst Holly Sklar, quoted in Peters 1992: 3). If defence funding were redirected to maternal care, these statistics would change dramatically. According to Democracy Now! (2010), life expectancy in the US has fallen to 49th in the world.

FIGURE 13.1 CONFLICT CAUSES EXTENSIVE ECOLOGICAL DAMAGE

Civilians are the main casualties of war – as many as 90 per cent of the deaths in a given conflict area are civilians, and many of them are children – what Donald Rumsfeld called collateral damage (Chandler 2002: 171). More and more evidence suggests that external military intervention increases civilian casualties. Dislocated and dispossessed people, numbering in the millions, live in refugee camps, awaiting either asylum or an end to the conflict. Yet Goodman (2013b) charges that major powers tend to ignore civilian deaths, destruction of local economies, schools, hospitals, and vital infrastructure. This callous disregard for innocent life may have led Iraqi civilians to join militias and insurgent groups, and recent indiscriminant drone attacks in Afghanistan have been accompanied by a "rise in al-Qaida recruits, proving that, in predictable 'blowback' fashion, the attacks may be creating more terrorists than they are neutralizing" (Sirota 2013: n.p.).

"Every gun that is made, every warship launched, every rocket fired signifies, in the final sense a theft from those who hunger and are not fed, those who are cold and are not clothed." President Dwight Eisenhower, in a 1953 address to newspaper editors, quoted in Lindorff (2012).

FIGURE 13.2 MILITARY INTERVENTION CAUSES HUMAN TRAGEDY

"Drones are a lot more civilized than what we used to do ... I think it's actually a more humane weapon because it can be targeted to specific enemies and specific people." Senator Angus King (I-Maine) justifying drone attacks, quoted in Sirota (2013: n.p.)

"Libya has gone from being a tyrannical state to being barely a state at all ... descent into worse chaos cannot be ruled out." Robert Kaplan, senior fellow at the Center for a New American Security, quoted in Lobe (2013: n.p.)

Targeted killings, including drone strikes and kill/capture special operations, are justified as a counterterrorism tactic when pursuing al-Qaeda and Taliban terrorists. The United States government is in a state of armed conflict with these groups and believes it has a right to self-defence according to Article 51 in the United Nations charter (Masters 2013). Targeted killings, in particular drone strikes, are especially criticized for civilian deaths, although actual death statistics from American sources and target countries vary considerably. Drone attacks in Pakistan have caused increasing tensions between Pakistan and the United States. On the other hand, targeted killings put fewer Americans in harm's way and are less expensive than conventional weapons and troops on the ground.

As mentioned earlier, the original reason for the Security Council agreeing to military intervention in Libya was to protect civilians. However, the battle heated up, and Britain, France, and the United States took more aggressive action geared toward regime change (Lobe 2013). Some would say the positive consequences of this action were getting rid of a ruthless dictator and restoring oil production. However, this mainly benefits major powers looking for a secure source of oil. It also meant they no longer had to deal with Moammar Qaddafi and his anti-imperialist agenda, including his attempts to establish the gold dinar, which would have threatened Western bank profits. However, following the military intervention, Libya descended into political chaos, with a weak central government and a security vacuum in most of the country. With the shift to regime change from civilian protection in Libya, relations between the United States and Russia and China cooled, the latter two feeling they were deceived by both the Security Council and the United States (Lobe 2013).

Thus, military intervention can lead to destabilization of an already unstable political situation and can also have repercussions for other parts of the region. In the Libyan case, Tuareg mercenaries looted Qaddafi's arsenal, before returning home to northern Mali where they routed the army and overthrew the government. French and Chadian troops had to intervene to re-establish the government, although only part of the country has as yet returned to order.

CONCLUSION

Martin Luther King (1967) believed that "ending US militarism and imperialism was not merely a moral imperative, but a prerequisite to achieving any meaningful reforms on American domestic life." He urged Americans to show "allegiances and loyalties which are broader and deeper than nationalism and speak for the voiceless" (Greenwald 2013) – in other words, become **global citizens**. King's words of wisdom still resonate today – he urged an end to war and violence for the sake of the American people – that violence against other nations is what drives so many people to want to do harm to the United States.

> "We can be a nation that declares its war over, that declares itself at peace and goes about vigorously and energetically using intelligence and diplomacy and well-resourced work to protect us from future attacks." Chris Hayes of MSNBC, quoted in Sirota (2013: n.p.)

As mentioned earlier in this chapter, there are opposing views on whether militarism is a deterrent or catalyst for civil conflict. The HSRP (2012: n.p.) found that external military intervention increases the risk of conflict escalation and strongly "correlates with intensified and prolonged conflicts." Evidence also suggests that negotiating, diplomacy, and peacekeeping are more effective in ending global conflicts. Yet the primary source of peacekeeping – the United Nations – is neglected and woefully underfunded. Analysts outside the neoconservative realm appear to agree that deployment of American troops to Vietnam, Iraq, and Afghanistan over the past four decades has not improved national security. In fact, "there is no nation on earth that poses any military threat to the U.S." (Lindorff 2012: n.p.), nor could these military actions ever stop a sneak attack by terrorists. Indeed, it appears that America is becoming increasingly vulnerable as it flexes its military muscle.

There is a great deal of highly critical rhetoric against American militarism. On one level this is important, because it alerts the public to inconsistencies and hidden agendas within the American foreign policy and the consequences of military intervention in other countries. However, critics should not forget that the United States is the first on the scene when an international crisis transpires. As well, conflicts between countries have decreased over the past 60 years, mainly due to "collective security agreements, a balance in nuclear weapons, and increasing economic interdependence" (Masters 2013). Nevertheless, militarism, as an ideology and a practice, has undermined the standing of the United States around the world.

Is it fair to demonize America? No, not America, but those driving the United States war machine – defence contractors and energy multinationals – who continue to control American foreign policy and are complicit in military actions. The American public (and others within the American media sphere) has been fed a steady diet of war and fearmongering against various "enemies," to the point where many cannot deny war, nor look positively on alternatives to continuing American imperialism and violence. Yet protests against American military intervention are growing in America, as witnessed on the tenth anniversary of the 2003 invasion of Iraq. Civil-liberties and human-rights groups are protesting civilian deaths from targeted killings and the lack of accountability from the American military forces (Masters 2013). There is also a growing outcry against military spending at the expense of education and social programs and crumbling infrastructures.

Are there alternatives to militarism, especially for the United States? Would diplomacy and negotiations, and non-interference in economic and other components of developing nations bring global security? What about the military industry and the economic impact of disbanding it? Would military withdrawal risk a secure supply of oil? These are all valid questions when considering the reasons and consequences of militarism. The future? There is very little evidence that militarism as an ideology and the "just war" doctrine are changing in the United States, and armed conflict, whether national or international, is jeopardizing the well-being of the fragile global community. The answer to the question, is the world safer because of militarism and military intervention, is a resounding no.

QUESTIONS FOR CONSIDERATION AND CLASSROOM ACTIVITIES

1. Critique this statement: The belief that the United States has not only the right but the duty to militarily intervene in the conflicts of other countries informs the country's foreign policy and is predicated on imperialism.
2. In your opinion, what would happen to world security if the United States disbanded most of its military and destroyed its weapons of mass destruction?
3. Class debate or research paper: Is militarism making the world a safer place? Cite examples to prove your point.
4. In the analysis of the media's role in military propaganda, most television media appear to promote militarism, while print media (outside the establishment) appear to critically challenge it. Find out why.

SUGGESTED READINGS

Goodman, M.A. (2013). *National insecurity: The cost of American militarism*. San Francisco: City Lights Publishers.

This is a timely book on militarism that pulls no punches. Highly recommended reading for all students interested in uncovering the real reasons behind militarism.

Klare, M.T. (2002). *Resource wars: The new landscape of global conflict*. New York: Holt Paperbacks.

Although this book is more than 10 years old, the subject matter is very much current. The author is an international security expert who clearly outlines the resource crises we will face in this century and the international conflicts and instability that may occur due to competition over dwindling supplies of oil, natural gas, minerals, and water.

CONCLUSION

The topics discussed in this volume were chosen to offer a glimpse into contemporary global society, and to address this question: "Why is it important to understand the world around us?" In part, this question refers to our growing awareness that the knowledge and insights of social scientists should be applied to find solutions to, or at the very least to understand, the problems that confront human existence. Social sciences, such as anthropology, challenge us to question our beliefs and practices and to ask if there are other ways of living as undeniable as our own. To that end, in this concluding section of *Global Issues* we will briefly examine the growing value of becoming a global citizen.

THE VALUE OF GLOBAL CITIZENSHIP

The study of global issues presents the world to students and can stoke their imagination about other ways of living and being. As an example, investigating female circumcision and *purdah* raises the question of whether these practices promote gender inequality or if this is merely a narrow Western perception. In *Global Issues*, readers have been encouraged to view these customs through the eyes of the practitioners, and to understand their cultural meaning. To understand another's point of view when it comes to sensitive issues like gender equality or ethnic conflict is difficult, but this is when the true value of a global perspective becomes obvious. The goal of *Global Issues* has not been to change readers' opinions, but to help them recognize that these issues are not one-dimensional, and that not everyone agrees with the Western way of life.

Many of us live in cultural environments other than our own – it is one of the most valuable experiences an individual can undertake, and for young people this may become a rite of passage into adulthood and global citizenship. Yet all of us have questions about our sense of place and identity; this struggle is particularly evident in the question of human sexuality and marriage practices. People struggle with changing traditional definitions and extending rights to ways of life formerly considered deviant. The concept of body image also raises some important questions – why are humans, especially females, so obsessed with an "ideal" body? On a global scale, many communities are struggling to preserve their heritage languages and promote the importance of linguistic diversity. In these discussions and others, the ambiguity and intolerance toward those who own a different identity, and our suspicions and even rejection of cultural diversity, are all clearly evident.

Thus, global awareness may teach young people to *appreciate* cultural diversity, rather than merely *tolerate* it. On an individual level, this change in attitude is particularly relevant when we live in a country where immigration from diverse parts of the world is common. Appreciating cultural diversity makes us more comfortable when interacting with people who look different, speak different languages, practise different customs, and hold different beliefs.

THE VALUE OF GLOBAL ISSUES

The study of global issues has much to offer, both in knowledge and perspective. For example, social media has changed the way people mobilize for social, economic, or political activism, and likely will continue to have an impact on the socio-political stage for some time to come. Throughout *Global Issues* we have critically examined Western interference in global issues, whether in the guise of international aid, the overt attempts to change cultural practices such as female circumcision, encouraging birthrate reductions in developing nations to ensure adequate resources for developed nations, or military intervention.

As discussed earlier, the sharing of knowledge and understanding of cultural diversity are central goals of global awareness, and the importance of understanding someone else's point of view and acknowledging that there are many ways of living has been emphasized. We have given consideration to the moral, ethical, and political questions posed, such as the true nature of resource depletion, which should make us examine our own consumptive behaviour. This is what makes *Global Issues* so relevant. Through the lens of social sciences we view other people and the way they live as deserving of the dignity and respect that we ourselves expect. Although not the answer to all our difficulties, this perspective promotes understanding, acceptance, and appreciation of the amazing cultural diversity in our global community.

FINAL REFLECTIONS

Writing *Global Issues* has been a journey of discovery. As an anthropologist, I have always been interested in international affairs, particularly as they impact local cultural groups and especially women and children, but researching this book led me in directions I had never travelled. For example, I began the research on population control thinking that we do have a population problem, albeit with many other factors contributing to the world's ills, only to discover that most of the problems blamed on over-population in developing nations are actually due to over-consumption in developed countries. As well, my perspective on female circumcision has undergone many transformations over the years, including as I wrote this book. My attitude has shifted from outright rejection of the practice as a human-rights abuse to recognition that practices that possess such deep meaning deserve my understanding, if not acceptance.

My perspective on *purdah* and *hijab* has also changed through time; the women I met and grew to know and like in Egypt did not feel oppressed – they wore *hijab* and followed the customs of their family and community just as we do. I found their sense of inner beauty and self-worth refreshing. Two chapters in *Global Issues* hold a special meaning for me and my lived experiences. First, I was living in Egypt at the time of the "revolution" and witnessed first-hand the power of cell-phone technology and social media. Second, I taught TCKs at Cairo American College and grew to understand the unique challenges they faced on a daily basis, yet I also recognized the incredible experiences and opportunities they enjoyed because of their cross-cultural lives.

While writing *Global Issues*, I frequently encountered articles, often under the auspices of organizations such as the United Nations, that advocated global governing bodies and laws to ameliorate many of the global issues discussed in this book. Indeed, globalization versus local culture is a theme running throughout *Global Issues*. I question whether global governing bodies are the solution or whether such bodies become part of the larger problem. Who would control a global governing body and draft its laws – those countries that possess most of the economic and political power, or everyone? How would this body be any different from current "global" institutions such as the World Bank, International Monetary Fund or various United Nations organizations – all of which have exacerbated problems in developing countries to the benefit of developed countries. This came home to me when investigating the underlying reasons for militarism – greed and hegemony – and the horrific consequences of these ideologies.

Societies no longer exist in isolation – this became evident with the rise of grassroots people-power campaigns using social media to effect change and address global socio-economic and political problems. These advocates are aware of the problems and issues we face, and they have chosen to use their global citizenship to demand change. Global issues belong to us all, and whether we act or not will have a long-lasting impact on us and those who come after us. Ultimately, this is why we need to know about the world beyond our borders, and this is why we need to understand global issues.

In his anti-war speech on April 4, 1967, Martin Luther King denounced "the Western arrogance of feeling that it has everything to teach others and nothing to learn from them." In *Global Issues*, I have strived to fight against this cultural imperialistic attitude. Indeed, I feel the world has everything to teach *us*.

GLOSSARY

advocacy   Supporting, influencing, or recommending certain actions, such as developing immigration policies.

agribusiness   A broad concept that describes corporate agricultural enterprises that are involved in the production, manufacturing and processing, and transportation and distribution of crops and livestock for economic gain.

agriculture for development   A plan to increase agricultural productivity via modernization of agricultural practices, instigated by the World Bank.

applied linguistic anthropology   Providing solutions to linguistic issues, such as revitalization programs.

biculturalism   A sense of belonging to more than one culture, usually after a person has lived in another culture.

blogosphere   A network of connected blogs, which are personal journals online.

body adornment/body modification   Decoration (e.g., tattoos, jewellery, painting) or modification (piercings, cuttings, and branding) of the human body.

body dissatisfaction   Negative feelings about one's own body – its size, shape, etc.

body image   A culturally defined image of beauty that influences the way people view their bodies.

body politics   The struggles for power and control through the body, as well as the way society regulates the body.

carrying capacity   The number of people who can be supported on a given piece of land.

civic media   Using social media to garner attention and encourage action from a global audience.

civil society   A society where violence is relatively absent and people live in peace rather than fear of oppression. May also refer to those elements of society not associated with government or business.

climate change   Long-term changes in weather patterns, for example, global warming.

clitoridectomy   A female circumcision ritual where part or all of the clitoris is removed, as well as part or all of the labia minora.

Cold War   Political and military tension between NATO, particularly the United States, and the Eastern Bloc, particularly the USSR.

conflict   A struggle or battle between two or more parties. Conflicts can be political, social, religious, or based on access to economic resources.

consumerism   The acquiring and consuming of resources, such as food.

contract farming   An agreement between the grower of food and the corporate buyers.

cross-cultural comparison   The comparison of a cultural trait (e.g., ritual) in many cultures to develop hypotheses about human behaviour.

cultural diversity   The distinct traditions, beliefs, and language of different cultures.

cultural identity   The culture to which individuals feel they belong, based on their upbringing, residence, heritage, customs, and language.

cultural imperialism   Promoting a nation's values, beliefs, and behaviour above all others.

cultural marginality   When people are marginalized on the edge of society for some reason, such as ethnicity.

cultural relativism   The principle that each culture and its practices are unique and valid in their own right, and must be viewed within the context of that culture.

cultural sensitivity   Being respectful toward other ways of thinking, believing, and living.

culture   The shared ideals, values, and beliefs that people use to interpret, experience, and generate behaviour. Culture is shared, learned, based on symbols (e.g., language), and integrated.

culture change   The process of changing the behaviour, technology, or beliefs within a culture.

culture shock   A feeling of disorientation, confusion, and irritability that results from living in an unfamiliar foreign environment.

cyberpunks   Individuals who embed technology and science fiction into their lives.

democratic divide   The division of people or societies based on one or more criteria, such as wealth.

dependency theory   When wealthy nations extract resources from poor countries, making them poorer and more dependent on assistance for food security.

developed nations   Industrialized countries that have well-developed economic infrastructures. A fair portion of their populace enjoys a high standard of living.

developing nations   Nations that are still developing their economic and industrial infrastructures. Their populace usually has a low standard of living.

development   Usually refers to assistance given to developing countries to create infrastructures (e.g., education, health care, business)

development and modernization approach   The theoretical perspective that change, such as the eradication of female circumcision, will not come from outside forces, but rather from large-scale social changes, for example, women becoming more empowered in their communities through access to education and employment.

discrimination   Differential access to resources and opportunities based on gender, age, sexual orientation, disabilities, or ethnic identity.

eating disorders   Severe disturbances in normal eating behaviour and attitudes toward food and body image.

ecoterrorism   Deliberate acts of violence against the environment or wildlife, usually to cause harm to the people living in that area.

emigration   *See* immigration

enculturative forces   Various forces that serve to enculturate children, e.g., parents, schools, government, etc.

endangered language A language that has few speakers and is in imminent danger of disappearing.

engaged anthropology Using anthropological knowledge and insights to participate in and contribute to public debate on cultural issues and to disseminate anthropological findings to a general audience (public anthropology).

ethics/ethical dilemma The rules that anthropologists and other social scientists follow when conducting research. The primary rule is to "do no harm." Researchers have an obligation to protect the privacy of their study group, uphold the integrity of their discipline, and meet the needs of their funding agency, which causes conflicting loyalties.

ethnic boundary markers Those indicators or characteristics, e.g., dress, that identify individuals as belonging to a particular ethnic group.

ethnic cleansing *See* genocide

ethnic conflict A conflict between ethnic groups due to ethnic nationalism or economic and political power plays.

ethnic group A group of people with shared ancestry, cultural traditions, and practices, and a sense of common history.

ethnic identity The identity we possess based on our membership in an ethnic group.

ethnicity Refers to a group of people who take their identity from a common place of origin, history, and sense of belonging.

ethnic stratification Institutionalized inequality with differential access to wealth, power, and prestige based on ethnic identity.

ethnocentrism The attitude that one's own culture is superior to all others.

ethnoscape A landscape or transnational distribution of group identity that is not limited by location.

expatriates/expats People who live in a country other than the one in which they were born, but who retain citizenship in their natal country.

family People who consider themselves related through kinship: nuclear, extended, single, blended.

fatness A vague term to indicate more body fat than required for good health.

female circumcision/female genital cutting The removal of all or part of a female's external genitalia for religious, traditional, or socio-economic reasons. Female genital mutilation is the Western term to exemplify disapproval of this procedure.

feminist/queer critics Critics who suggest that marriage, whether homosexual or heterosexual, is an institution of patriarchal societies designed to control behaviour.

flashmobs A group of people who gather quickly to perform a function, such as a political protest, and then disperse.

food security Reliable, regular access to enough nutritious food to sustain an individual or a population.

food sovereignty A perspective that promotes biodiverse traditional agricultural practices to supply nutritious food to the local population rather than exporting it.

gay assimilationists *See* lesbian and gay assimilationists

gender/gender identity A cultural construct to differentiate between men and women and their social identity, status, and roles in society. Some cultures also have a third gender (e.g., Two-Spirits).

gender inequality Unequal treatment, status, or access to resources based on gender.

gender stratification   Usually refers to the situation wherein women have unequal access to resources, opportunities, and prestige because of their gender.

genocide/ethnic cleansing   The deliberate extermination of one cultural group by another, usually to gain economic and/or political control over a region.

global citizens/citizenship   Understanding of one's roles and responsibilities in global society. Involves awareness of issues and actions to improve the quality of life of other citizens.

global economy   The interdependence (globalization) of markets, trade, and foreign investment.

global issues   Concerns that affect the global populace and require cooperation from all nations to resolve.

globalization   Worldwide integration of economies, assisted by global transportation, communication, and information technology.

global nomads   People who live and work in countries other than their own.

global population   The sum total of the people who live in the world.

heritage languages   Languages that have a long history within a speech community.

heterosexuality   Sexual attraction between individuals of opposite sex.

hijab   A head covering for Muslim women.

homophobia   A fear and dislike of people who are homosexual.

homosexuality   Sexual attraction between individuals of the same sex.

human migration   The movement of people either internally or across national borders in search of a new place to live.

human rights   A set of guidelines adopted by the United Nations General Assembly in 1948 to ensure the equal treatment of all people, regardless of gender, age, or ethnicity, including the right to health, safety, and security.

human trafficking   The illegal selling or trading of people for sexual exploitation and forced labour, a form of modern-day slavery.

identity   A person's perception of their place – as a person and as part of a group.

immigrants   People who have left their home country and moved to another country, usually for economic or political reasons.

immigration/emigration/migration   The movement of people from one place to another, be it to a new country, from rural regions to urban centres, or from one region to another.

imperialism   Maintaining economic and political dominance through military force.

indigenous people   Members of cultures who self-identify as the original inhabitants of the land based on a long history of occupation.

industrial agriculture   Large-scale agriculture that uses complex machinery, and chemicals and fertilizers. Unsustainable in the long term.

inequality   A situation in which individuals or groups have unequal access to wealth, power, and status.

internationalized intrastate armed conflict   Conflict where at least one of the parties is a legally recognized state government, and where at least one external military force is fighting on the side of one of the warring parties.

just war   The concept that some wars are necessary to fight, often in the name of national or international security or to stop human-rights abuses.

language   A complex system of communication, using mutually understood sounds.

language isolate   A language that has no known relationship with any other languages.

language loss   Usually refers to a language becoming extinct.

language nests   Immersion programs that teach young children their heritage languages.

language retention/revitalization   *See* revitalization

language shift   When a speech community changes to using another language.

lesbian and gay assimilationists   A perspective that supports same-sex marriage on the basis that gays will receive legitimacy and social respectability if they are allowed to marry.

linguicism   Linguistic prejudice or discrimination against a particular language.

linguistic anthropology   The study of how people use language to interact with each other and transmit culture.

linguistic diversity   The number of different languages spoken today, the linguistic version of biodiversity.

linguistic homogenization   The elimination of linguistic diversity and creation of one global language.

linguistics   The scientific study of language from a historical and descriptive perspective.

market-based agribusiness   A system of agriculture that promotes foreign investment in agriculture and joining an international market economy rather than local production and markets.

marriage   The joining of two or more people to form a conjugal bond.

migration   *See* immigration

militarism   An ideology that supports a strong military force in order to defend a nation or promote national economic and political interests on the international scene.

military industrial complex   The partnership between government, the arms industry, and military organizations, predicated on huge profits from the proliferation of weapons and arms sales.

missionism   The process of converting people to another belief system.

modern-day slavery   *See* human trafficking

modernization   The process of making other societies over in the image of the West by changing their social, economic, political, and religious systems.

modernization theory   The perspective that foreign investment and aid, and international trade coupled with agribusiness, will improve the economy of developing nations.

Modern Primitives   A countercultural movement that uses neo-tribal rituals and body modifications.

multiculturalism   The philosophy that people can maintain their distinctive cultural traditions, values, and beliefs while still participating in mainstream society.

multifunctional approach   Advocates protection of land and biodiversity, improving the position of subsistence farmers, and growing food that meets the needs of the local people.

nation   A cultural group that shares the same language, religion, history, territory, and ancestry. Examples include groups such as the Plains Cree, but the term can also refer to an independent state, such as Canada.

nationalism   A sentiment or consciousness of belonging to a nation.

nationality   Membership in a particular state based on birth.

neoconservatives A right-wing conservative group that favours big government and military intervention in foreign countries, and generally supports traditional institutions such as heterosexual marriage.

netizens A new form of citizenship that uses the Internet to solve socio-political problems.

NGOs Non-government organizations involved in humanitarian aid and development.

one-child policy A 30-year-old policy in China that allows couples to have only one child.

oppression Cruel or unjust treatment of individuals or societies that prevents them from reaching their full potential. The most common kind of oppression is based on gender.

over-consumption Consumption of more goods and services than is necessary to meet basic needs. Another term for greed.

over-population Too many organisms for a given resource base.

participatory media People actively participating in media, including creating content.

participatory politics People participating in the political system, taking part in the decision-making processes, and at times directing policy through social media and networking.

patriarchal society A male-dominated society.

pharaonic circumcision The removal of the clitoris, labia minora, and most or all of the labia majora. These cut edges are stitched together using thorns or other materials, leaving a small opening for urine and menstrual flow. This stitching is known as infibulation.

population control policies Usually refers to the practices of state governments that control the size and spacing of birth.

population pressure Various criteria based on population size that can cause harm to the natural and social environments.

population theory Various theories that tend to place blame for the world's ills on the poor in developing countries because their birthrates are higher than in developed countries.

purdah A Muslim tradition of secluding women, either within their homes or beneath concealing clothing.

queer subculture A term sometimes used to refer to gay and lesbian subcultures.

race A misleading concept used to place individuals and populations into categories based on broad biological and/or behavioural traits that do not hold up to scientific scrutiny.

racism Dislike of an individual or group based on colour of skin, ethnic origin, etc. May also involve discriminatory practices, such as employment restrictions. Racism is a misnomer since there is only one race – the human race.

refugees Individuals seeking asylum from political, economic, social, or religious strife.

reproductive rights The right to choose how many children to have and when to have them.

reverse culture shock Symptoms of culture shock experienced upon return to one's home country.

revitalization Efforts to keep endangered languages alive by teaching them to the younger generation.

rite of passage Rituals that mark important stages in an individual's life, for example, puberty.

ritual   Organized actions that have historical/traditional value.

same-sex marriage   Civil marriage between individuals of the same sex.

self-discrepancy theory   The perspective that everyone has an image of themselves, beliefs about how they should appear, and ongoing efforts to meet this ideal.

sexuality   Our sexual identity or orientation, the types of sexual practices, and our interest in having sexual relationships.

small-scale/subsistence farming   Farmers who grow crops to meet the needs of their families and the local market.

smart mobs   Groups of people who communicate, organize, and cooperate via mobile devices.

social change   Changes in the structure and organization of a society.

social comparison theory   Gaining our status and sense of self-worth through comparisons to others.

social conservatives   Those who believe that same-sex marriage will destroy the fabric of society, confuse gender roles, decrease family stability, and cause more infidelity.

social media   Social interaction and social mobilization facilitated by mobile devices (e.g., cell phones).

social network/networking   Individuals or organizations tied together by similar values, ideas, friendship, interests, or political activism.

sojourners   Temporary residents in a foreign country.

speech communities   A group of people who share the same language and concerns for the vitality of the language. They usually live in the same community, but can be dispersed.

subculture   Segments of a population that are distinct from mainstream culture due to ethnicity, class, religion, or behaviour.

***sunna* circumcision**   Female circumcision where only the clitoral prepuce (hood) is removed.

symbolic capital   An intangible value, such as the prestige of having many children.

symbolic circumcision   Circumcision rituals that do not involve the actual removal of any genitalia, for example, circumcision by words practised in some parts of Kenya.

systemic racism   Discrimination embedded in the systems of a culture that limits access to resources and opportunities for people of a certain "race."

Third Culture Kids (TCKs)   Young people who have lived significant portions of their lives in a foreign country.

transcultural/transnational identity   The fusion of two or more cultural identities, often found in global nomads.

transcultural literacy   The ability to be comfortable in a foreign environment, awareness of global citizenship, and language proficiency.

transnational/transnational communities   Groups of people that transcend political or geographical borders to form communities, e.g., online communities.

universalism   In opposition to relativism, suggests that there are universal human rights that must be followed, regardless of culture, sex, or religion.

xenophobia   Fear or dislike of strangers, often predicated on physical appearance or religious beliefs.

LESSON PLANS AND WEBSITES

Chapter 1

1. "Teen told she can't wear headscarf in JROTC parade," from http://www. firstamendmentcenter.org/teen-told-she-cant-wear-headscarf-in-jrotc-parade. An interesting news article that should generate discussion in class. Debate question: Should Demin Zawity have been allowed to wear her head scarf?

2. **The Islam Project, from http://www.islamproject.org/education/D04_Hejab_secularism. htm.** Lesson plans include handouts with historical information, case studies, as well as other sources and activities that can be used in classrooms.

Chapter 2

1. *National Geographic News,* "Reporter's Notebook: Female circumcision in Africa," from http://news.nationalgeographic.com/news/2002/02/0219_020219_circumcision.html. *National Geographic* provides relevant information on female circumcision that can assist in developing a class discussion or debate on the merits of programs to eradicate female circumcision.

2. **Radio Australia, 23 January 2013, "Debate in Indonesia over UN plan to ban female circumcision,"** from http://www.radioaustralia.net.au/international/radio/program/ asia-pacific/debate-in-indonesia-over-un-plan-to-ban-female-circumcision/1077806. This debate should create class discussions regarding the validity of the protest as well as the contentions regarding Islam and female circumcision.

3. **Prevention toolkit, from http://www.rutgerswpf.org/sites/default/files/Prevention-Girls-Circumcision-teaching-toolkit-2009.pdf.** A prevention toolkit directed toward students at all grade levels, including advanced high school and first-year university.

4. **A Teacher's Guide for nursing students. Training modules from http://www.who.int/ gender/other_health/teachersguide.pdf.** Provides extensive content and related information and activities on female circumcision in module format from WHO. This site provides a Western perspective only and could serve as a resource for examining Western bias.

Chapter 3

1. Developing a Global Perspective for Educators, from http://www. developingaglobalperspective.ca/tag/ngo/.
   Students will find an enormous amount of information on NGOs and non-profits that may generate research projects that evaluate the usefulness of these NGOs.

2. NGO Organizations, by UNODC, from http://www.unodc.org/ngo/list.jsp.
   Students should choose an NGO from the comprehensive list provided on this website and research its mandate, current projects, and success rate, using independent sources.

Chapter 4

1. *2012 World Population Data Sheet*, Population Reference Bureau, from http://www.prb. org/Educators/LessonPlans/2012/WorldPopulationDataSheet.aspx.
   Some useful information on population statistics and activities to begin an examination of world populations. Enrichment for university students needed.

2. *World in the Balance*, NOVA, from http://www.pbs.org/wgbh/nova/worldbalance/.
   Numerous interactive sites that discuss issues relevant to population growth. These sites provide information to begin the discussion on population growth. These lessons will likely need enrichment for university students.

Chapter 5

1. AAA Science NetLinks, Endangered Languages, from http://sciencenetlinks.com/lessons/ endangered-languages/.
   This site contains several lesson plans and student activities in linguistics and endangered languages at a fairly advanced level. Some enrichment is necessary for university students.

2. The American Forum for Global Education, The Globalization of Language, from http:// www.globaled.org/curriculum3.html.
   This website provides several relevant articles about endangered languages, followed by activities on endangered languages, English dominance in global affairs, and saving endangered languages. For senior high-school and university students these activities will need to be enriched.

3. Research project using resources from Simon Fraser University, B.C., from http://www. sfu.ca/vpresearch/links.html.
   Students will investigate the materials on this and other websites to learn about what is happening in language revitalization in Canada, and then design, conduct, and write a research-based paper.

4. Disappearing Languages, interactive map of language hotspots, from http://travel. nationalgeographic.com/travel/enduring-voices/.
   This site may be used in an interactive lesson for the entire class.

5. *Ethnologue*, Languages of the World, from http://www.ethnologue.com/statistics/size.
   A detailed table of language size. This site can be used for several types of research projects on individual languages, languages of specific countries, or to gain a perspective on the most dominant languages in the world versus the most endangered ones.

6. Vistawide World Languages and Cultures, from http://www.vistawide.com/languages/ language_statistics.htm.
   This site offers some interesting facts about world languages. Highly recommended introductory source of information on languages. Also provides links to other valuable information on languages.

Chapter 6

1. Healthy Body Image, Purdue University, from http://www.extension.purdue.edu/
   extmedia/CFS/CFS-737-W.pdf.
   A vast array of lessons for high-school students that will require some enrichment for
   university students.

2. Gender Stereotypes in Children's Cartoons, from http://cla.calpoly.edu/~jrubba/495/
   paperss98/paper1.html.
   This study informs students on the pervasiveness of stereotyping, even from a young age. Have
   students read the study, then design their own study of stereotyping in a media format, e.g.,
   soap operas, action movies, etc.

3. Declaration of Self-Esteem, in Part 5 of Barbara A. Cohen's *The Psychology of
   Ideal Body Image as an Oppressive Force in the Lives of Women*, from http://www.
   healingthehumanspirit.com/pages/body_img5.htm.
   Have students read this self-esteem declaration and then write a commentary. If it is a small
   class, some students can read their comments to generate a class discussion.

Chapter 7

1. Gay Rights Lesson Plans, from http://blog.gale.com/speakingglobally/projects/
   gay-rights-lesson-plans/.
   A series of lessons on gay rights, including gays in the military, gay marriage around the world,
   and gay-rights activism. Also includes numerous links to gay-rights issues. Lessons are suitable
   for senior high-school and introductory university-level students.

2. Teaching and Learning about Gay History and Issues, from http://learning.blogs.nytimes.
   com/2011/11/22/teaching-and-learning-about-gay-history-and-issues/.
   Numerous lesson plans and resources on gay and lesbian issues, including defining a family,
   gay communities, gay marriage, and civil rights.

3. "Missouri teacher planning same-sex wedding is fired," from http://www.
   democraticunderground.com/1002365155.
   This article should generate discussion and a class debate on gay teachers in school.

Chapter 8

1. *Researching digital media and social change: A theory of practice approach*, by John Postill,
   from http://johnpostill.com/.
   Provides information on researching digital media and social change within a given
   organization, collective, field of practice, or neighbourhood and can be used to guide group
   activities and research projects. Students can choose a familiar or exotic example and develop a
   research design.

2. Acceptable social networking, from http://www.commonsensemedia.org/educators/
   curriculum/cyberbullying/lessons/9-12/acceptable_social_networking/.
   High-school lessons and class activities, but the lessons are applicable to college students if
   enriched.

3. Technology and social networking lesson plans for adults, from Purdue University
   Extension: http://www.four-h.purdue.edu/downloads/volunteer/Tech%20and%20
   Social%20Network%20Lesson%20Plan.pdf
   A plethora of relevant lessons for young people and adults.

Chapter 9

1. **TCK: The Official Home of Third Culture Kids, from http://www.tckworld.com/.**
   A detailed article on Third Culture Kids with links to additional resources. Class discussions and research projects can be developed from this information.

2. **"Why third culture kids need corporate support," from http://www.expatica.com/fr/ employment/employment_information/Third-Culture-Kids-corporate-support-_16555. html.**
   An information site that explores what corporations can do to make living abroad a successful experience. This article should generate brainstorming about ways in which corporations and educational institutions can assist TCKs in adjusting.

Chapter 10

1. **Oakland Institute, "Foreign Corporations Scramble To Buy African Land Raising Food Security Concerns," from http://www.oaklandinstitute.org/ foreign-corporations-scramble-buy-african-land-raising-food-security-concerns.**
   This is an excellent resource for students researching food-security issues, foreign investment, and transnational acquisition of farmland in developing nations.

2. **Food Insecurity Lesson Plan by Kate McGinnis, Pulitzer Center on Crisis Reporting, from http://pulitzercenter.org/sites/default/files/Food Insecurity Lesson Plan.pdf.**
   This lesson plan provides a step-by-step guide and background information for examining food security in Nigeria, India, and Guatemala, from a scientific and social-science perspective. Video and radio broadcast links are provided. Some enrichment required for university students.

3. **No More Turning Away Lesson Plans, from http://www.nomoreturningaway.org/index. php?option=com_content&task=view&id=29&Itemid=53.**
   A series of lesson plans designed for all age groups, including adults, which examines the issues of food security. Some of the links and information must be viewed critically, as they often promote a Western perspective or agenda.

Chapter 11

1. **A Dissection of Ethnic Conflict, from http://www.pbs.org/pov/film-files/pov_ nomoretears_lessonplan_lesson_plan_0.pdf.**
   Critical analysis of ethnic conflict. This lesson plan should be used in conjunction with the film *No More Tears Sister: An Anatomy of Hope and Betrayal*. This 52-minute film recreates the struggles of human-rights activist Dr. Rajani Thiranagama, who remained in her war-torn homeland of Sri Lanka to expose human-rights violations. These lessons will need to be enriched for university students.

2. **Lesson on Ethnic Discrimination, from http://www.un.org/cyberschoolbus/discrim/ ethnicity1.asp.**
   These lesson plans explore discrimination that is based on ethnicity. Have students complete the lessons. For an enrichment exercise, have students design another lesson to teach students in middle school about the repercussions of discrimination.

3. **World Affairs Council of Pittsburgh, from http://www.worldpittsburgh.org/resources.jsp? pageId=2161392240601289549172297.**
   The lesson plan are not online but available through the web page. Global education and transnational security issues are two of the topics.

Chapter 12

1. **PBS Teachers resource**, from http://www.pbs.org/teachers/socialstudies/inventory/immigration-912.html.
   A wide range of lessons on immigration that can be used in many course disciplines and that can be enriched for university students. Includes both interactive and offline activities.

2. **Canadian Council for Geographic Education**, "Going Down the Road," from http://www.ccge.org/resources/learning_centre/lesson_plans_docs/migration/NS_S_GoingDowntheRoad.pdf.
   Well-developed lesson plans for Canadian students studying the migration of human populations and settlement in Canada.

3. **Migration Citizenship Education**, Learning Projects, from http://migrationeducation.de/33.3.html.
   Two lessons are particularly appropriate: the United Nations lesson plan on refugees and the *National Geographic* lesson plan on migration: Why People Move.

Chapter 13

1. **Peace and Conflict, International Baccalaureate**, from http://peernet.pearsoncollege.ca/sites/default/files/documents/Peace_and_conflict_lesson_plans_Eng.pdf.
   This site contains a plethora of lesson plans for older students. Of particular note for this chapter are "Personal and Global Conflict," "Leadership and Global Citizenship," "What is Terrorism?", and "Five Dimensions of Conflict." These lessons are geared to senior high-school students and older.

2. **International Conflict, Global Envision**, from http://www.globalenvision.org/forteachers/29/1206.
   These lesson plans are designed for high-school students but can be enhanced for university students. Examples of lessons: "Chemical and Biological Warfare," "Rwanda: A Nation Recovering and Rebuilding," and "Darfur and the Janjaweed."

REFERENCES

To the Instructor

Ostler, N. (2001). Endangered languages – lost worlds. *Contemporary Review, 279*(1631), 349–55.

Introduction

Bhargava, V. (2006). Introduction to global issues. In V. Bhargava (Ed.), *Global issues for global citizens. An introduction to key development challenges* (pp. 1–28). Washington, DC: World Bank Publications. https://openknowledge.worldbank.org/bitstream/handle/10986/7194/3745 20Global011OR0OFFICIAL0USE0ONLY.pdf?sequence=1

ClimateChangeConnection (2013). What causes climate change? http://www. climatechangeconnection.org/science/Climate_causes.htm

Geertz, C. (1973). *Person, time, and conduct in Bali. The interpretation of cultures.* New York: Basic Books.

——. (1984). Distinguished lecture: Anti anti-relativism. *American Anthropologist, 86*(2), 263–278. http://dx.doi.org/10.1525/aa.1984.86.2.02a00030

Haviland, W.A., Fedorak, S., & Lee, R.B. (2009). *Cultural anthropology* (3rd Cdn. ed.). Toronto: Nelson Education.

Messer, E. (1993). Anthropology and human rights. *Annual Review of Anthropology, 22*(1), 221–249. http://dx.doi.org/10.1146/annurev.an.22.100193.001253

Overing, J. (Ed.). (1985). *Reason and morality.* New York: Tavistock Publications.

Shah, A. (Fall 2011–Spring 2012). Women's empowerment through economic development: Gujarat, India. *Perspectives on Global Issues. Global Citizens Engaging Global Issues, 6*(1), 24–28. Center for Global Affairs' Student Academic Journal. http://www.perspectivesonglobalissues. com/current-issue/

Chapter 1: *Purdah:* Is the practice of female seclusion and wearing *hijab* oppressive to women or an expression of their identity?

Ali, M.C. (n.d.). The question of hijab: Suppression or liberation? The Institute of Islamic Information and Education. http://media.isnet.org/off/Islam/woman/Hijab/HijabSupLib. html.

Amin, C.M. (2002). *The making of the modern Iranian woman: Gender, state policy, and popular culture, 1865–1946.* Gainesville: University Press of Florida.

Arnett, S.P. (2001). Purdah. *Women's history resource site.* King's College History Dept. http:// departments.kings.edu/womens_history/purdah.html

Barr, J., Clark, I., & Marsh, M. (n.d.). *The veil and veiling: Women, the visual arts, and Islam.* http:// www.skidmore.edu/academics/arthistory/ah369/finalveil.htm

BBC News. (2011, December 12). Canada bans veils at citizenship oath ceremony. http://www.bbc.co.uk/news/world-us-canada-16152122

Bishr, H. (n.d.). Pro-hijab campaign in EU parliament. http://www.ummah.com/forum/showthread.php?43637-Pro-hijab-Campaign-in-EU-Parliament

Bonvillain, N. (1998). *Women and men: Cultural constructs of gender*. Upper Saddle River, NJ: Prentice Hall.

Boone, J. (2010, April 30). Afghan feminists fighting from under the burqa. *The Guardian*. http://www.guardian.co.uk/world/2010/apr/30/afghanistan-women-feminists-burqa

Brooks, G. (1994). *Nine parts of desire: The hidden world of Islamic women*. New York: Anchor Books.

Bullock, K. (2001). You don't have to wear that in Canada. http://www.themodernreligion.com/women/hijab-canada.htm

Capeloto, A. (2004). Hijab campaign: Women don scarfs in solidarity with female Muslims. https://groups.google.com/forum/#!topic/soc.men/Q-3BacWoCow

Cohen, L., & Peery, L. (2006). Unveiling students' perceptions about women in Islam. *English Journal*, 95(3), 20–26. http://dx.doi.org/10.2307/30047039

Cunningham, E. (2010, March 27). Despite ban, Gaza men still style women's hair. *The National*. http://www.thenational.ae/news/world/middle-east/despite-ban-gaza-men-still-style-womens-hair

Debré, J. (2003). *La laïcité à l'école: Un principe républicain à réaffirmer*. Rapport No. 1275, 2 vols. Paris: Assemblée Nationale.

de Souza, E. (2004). Introduction. In E. de Souza (Ed.), *Purdah: An anthology* (pp. 1–21). Oxford: Oxford University Press.

Fernandez, S. (2009). The crusade over the bodies of women. *Patterns of Prejudice*, 43(3–4), 269–286. http://dx.doi.org/10.1080/00313220903109185

Fernea, E.W., & Fernea, R.A. (2000). Symbolizing roles: Behind the veil. In J. Spradley & D.W. McCurdy (Eds.), *Conformity and conflict: Readings in cultural anthropology* (10th ed., pp. 233–240). Boston: Allyn and Bacon.

Geissinger, A. (2009). Hijab: An issue of global concern for the Islamic movement. http://www.crescent-online.net/2009/09/hijab-an-issue-of-global-concern-for-the-islamic-movement-1776-articles.html.

Hammami, R. (1990). Women, the hijab and the intifada. *Middle East Report*, 164/165, 24–28. http://dx.doi.org/10.2307/3012687

Hasan, M. (2010). Her dark materials. *New Statesman*, 139(5003), 20–23. http://www.questia.com/library/1G1-229229017/her-dark-materials

Hoodfar, H. (1989). A background to the feminist movement in Egypt. *Bulletin of Simone de Beauvoir Institute*, 9(2), 18–23.

Hoodfar, H. (1991). Return to the veil: Personal strategy and public participation in Egypt. In N. Redclift & M.T. Sinclair (Eds.), *Working women: International perspectives on labour and gender ideology* (pp. 23–50). London: Routledge.

Hoodfar, H. (1993). The veil in their minds and on our heads: The persistence of colonial images of Muslim women. *Resources for Feminist Research*, 22(3/4), 5–18.

Hoodfar, H. (2003). More than clothing: Veiling is an adaptive strategy. In H. Hoodfar, S. Alvi, & S. McDonough (Eds.), *The Muslim veil in North America: Issues and debates* (pp. 3–39). Toronto: Women's Press.

Hughes, L.A. (2007, July 2). Unveiling the veil: Cultic, status, and ethnic representations of early imperial freedwoman. *Material Religion*, 3(2), 218–241. http://dx.doi.org/10.2752/175183407X219750

IRNA (2005). Pro-hijab campaigners lobby in European parliament. http://www.irna.ir/en/news/view/menu-234/0505100391115018.htm

Islamonline.net (2005). Pro-hijab campaign in the parliament. http://www.prohijab.net/english/islam-online-article 3.htm

Keddie, N., & Baron, B. (1991). *Women in Middle Eastern history: Shifting boundaries in sex and gender*. New Haven, CT: Yale University Press.

Khan, S. (1999). *A glimpse through purdah: Asian women—Myth and reality*. Oakhill, UK: Trentham Books.

Lindholm, C., & Lindholm, C. (2000). Life behind the veil. In E. Ashton-Jones & C. Lindholm (Eds.), *The gender reader* (p. 252). Boston: Allyn and Bacon.

MacLeod, A.E. (1991). *Accommodating protest: Working women and the new veiling in Cairo*. New York: Columbia University Press.

Mahmood, S. (2003). Ethical formation and politics of individual autonomy in contemporary Egypt. *Social Research, 70*(3), 837–866.

Martin, M. (2010). In Egypt, Muslim women may lose right to wear veil. *NPR*. http://www.npr.org/templates/story/story.php?storyId=123889613

Mernissi, F. (2011). *The veil and the male elite: A feminist interpretation of women's rights in Islam*. New York: Addison-Wesley Publishing Company.

Mullally, S. (2011). Civic integration, migrant women and the veil: At the limits of rights? *Modern Law Review, 74*(1), 27–56. http://dx.doi.org/10.1111/j.1468-2230.2010.00835.x

Mustafa, N. (n.d.). Hijab (veil) and Muslim women. *Islamic Information and News Network*. http://www.islamawareness.net/Hijab/hijab_women.html

Nashat, G. (1988). *Women in the ancient Middle East. Restoring women to history*. Bloomington, IN: Organization of American History.

Paulsell, S. (2011, July 12). Veiled voices: Faith Matters. *Christian Century, 128*(14), 33. http://www.christiancentury.org/article/2011–06/veiled-voices

Read, J.G., & Bartkowski, J.P. (2000). To veil or not to veil? A case study of identity negotiations among Muslim women in Austin, Texas. *Gender & Society, 14*(3), 395–417. http://dx.doi.org/10.1177/089124300014003003

Risinger, M. (2012, January 6). Redefining the burqa: A reflection from Afghanistan. *Gender across borders: A global voice for gender justice*. http://www.genderacrossborders.com/2012/01/06/redefining-the-burqa-a-reflection-from-afghanistan/

Saldanha, A. (2010, September 9). Palestine: For Gaza students, no graduation without hijab. *Global Voices*. http://globalvoicesonline.org/2010/09/09/palestine-for-gaza-students-no-graduation-without-hijab/.

Shilandari, F. (2010, September). Iranian women: Veil and identity. *A forum on human rights and democracy in Iran*. http://www.gozaar.org/english/articles-en/Iranian-Woman-Veil-and-Identity.html.

Shirazi, F. (2001). *The veil unveiled: The hijab in modern culture*. Gainesville: University Press of Florida.

Talvi, S.J.A. (2002). The veil: Resistance or repression? *Alternet*. http://www.alternet.org/story/14826/the_veil%3A_resistance_or_repression/?page=4

van Santen, J.C.M. (2010). 'My "veil" does not go with my jeans': Veiling, fundamentalism, education and women's agency in northern Cameroon. *Africa, 80*(2), 275–300. http://dx.doi.org/10.3366/afr.2010.0205

Women in World History Curriculum (2011). Historical perspectives in Islamic dress. *Women in the Muslim world: personalities and perspectives from the past*. http://www.womeninworldhistory.com/essay-01.html

Young, W.C. (1996). *The Rashaayda Bedouin: Arab pastoralists of Eastern Sudan*. Toronto: Harcourt Brace College Publishers.

Zahedi, S. (n.d.). Hijab harassment. *Islam for today*. http://www.islamfortoday.com/hijabcanada5.htm

Chapter 2: Female Circumcision: Is this practice a violation of human rights or a cherished cultural tradition?

Abusharaf, R.M. (2006). "We have supped so deep in horrors": Understanding colonialist emotionality and British response to female circumcision in Northern Sudan. *History and Anthropology, 17*(3), 209–228. http://dx.doi.org/10.1080/02757200600813908

Ahmadu, F. (2000). Rites and wrongs: An insider/outsider reflects on power and excision. In B. Shell-Duncan & Y. Hernlund (Eds.), *Female "circumcision" in Africa: Culture: controversy, and change* (pp. 283–312). London: Lynne Rienner Publishers.

Al Jazeera English. (2011, May 25). *People & Power* broadcast.

Althaus, F.A. (1997). Special report. Female circumcision: Rite of passage or violation of rights? *Family Planning Perspectives, 23*(3), 1–9. http://www.guttmacher.org/pubs/journals/2313097.html

Amnesty International (1997). Female genital mutilation in Africa: Information by country. http://www.amnesty.org/en/library/index/ENGACT770071997

Asad, T. (1996). On torture, or cruel, inhumane and degrading treatment. *Social Research*, *63*(3), 1081–1109.

Assaad, M.B. (1980, January). Female circumcision in Egypt: Social implications, current research, and prospects for change. *Studies in Family Planning*, *11*(1), 3–16. http://dx.doi.org/10.2307/1965892 Medline:7376234

Blackburn-Evans, A. (2002). Women's rites: Janice Boddy explores a shocking tradition in northern Sudan. *Edge*, *3*(2). http://www.research.utoronto.ca/edge/fall2002/leaders/boddy.html

Boddy, J. (1982). Womb as oasis: The symbolic content of pharaonic circumcision in rural northern Sudan. *American Ethnologist*, *9*(4), 682–698. http://dx.doi.org/10.1525/ae.1982.9.4.02a00040

Coleman, D.L. (1998). The Seattle compromise: Multicultural sensitivity and Americanization. *The Economist* (1999, February 13). 350(8106): 45. *Duke Law Journal*, *47*(4), 717–783. http://dx.doi.org/10.2307/1372912

El Dareer, A. (1982). *Woman, why do you weep? Circumcision and its consequences*. London: Zed Press.

Equality Now. (1996, April 1). United States: Female genital mutilation and political asylum – The Case of Fauziya Kasinga. http://www.equalitynow.org/take_action/asylum_action91

Erickson, A., Hayes, M., Sabatke, S., Vargo, R., & Wall, J. (2001). *Ethics in anthropology: Public presentation of anthropological material*. University of Minnesota. http://www.d.umn.edu/~lbelote/Senior_Seminar/PublicAnth-ethics_in_anthropology.htm

Ginsburg, F. (1991). What do women want? Feminist anthropology confronts clitoridectomy. *Medical Anthropology Quarterly*, *5*(1), 17–19. http://dx.doi.org/10.1525/maq.1991.5.1.02a00030

Gordon, R. (1991). Female circumcision and genital operations in Egypt and the Sudan: A dilemma for medical anthropologists. *Medical Anthropology Quarterly*, *5*(1), 3–14. http://dx.doi.org/10.1525/maq.1991.5.1.02a00010

Gruenbaum, E. (1982). The movement against clitoridectomy and infibulation in Sudan: Public health policy and the women's movement. *Medical Anthropology Newsletter*, *13*(2), 4–12. http://dx.doi.org/10.1525/maq.1982.13.2.02a00020

––––––. (2000). Is female "circumcision" a maladaptive cultural pattern? In B. Shell-Duncan & Y. Hernlund (Eds.), *Female "circumcision" in Africa: Culture, controversy, and change* (pp. 41–54). London: Lynne Rienner Publishers.

––––––. (2005, September–October). Socio-cultural dynamics of female genital cutting: Research findings, gaps, and directions. *Culture, Health & Sexuality*, *7*(5), 429–441. http://dx.doi.org/10.1080/13691050500262953 Medline:16864214

Hernlund, Y. (2000). Cutting without ritual and ritual without cutting: Female "circumcision" and the re-ritualization of initiation in the Gambia. In B. Shell-Duncan & Y. Hernlund (Eds.), *Female "circumcision" in Africa: Culture, controversy, and change* (pp. 235–252). London: Lynne Rienner Publishers.

Hills-Young, E. (1943). *Female circumcision in the Sudan: The surgical seal of chastity*. Durham University Library Special Collections Archive: SAD #631/3/36G...S437.

Howell, S. (2010). Norwegian academic anthropologists in public spaces. *Current Anthropology*, *51*(S2), S269–S277. http://dx.doi.org/10.1086/652907

Johnson, M.C. (2000). Becoming a Muslim, becoming a person: Female "circumcision," religious identity, and personhood in Guinea-Bissau. In B. Shell-Duncan & Y. Hernlund (Eds.), *Female "circumcision" in Africa: Culture, controversy, and change* (pp. 215–234). London: Lynne Rienner Publishers.

Leonard, L. (2000). Adopting female "circumcision" in southern Chad: The experience of Myabé. In B. Shell-Duncan & Y. Hernlund (Eds.), *Female "circumcision" in Africa: Culture, controversy, and change* (pp. 167–192). London: Lynne Rienner Publishers.

Londoño Sulkin, C.D. (2009). Anthropology, liberalism and female genital cutting. *Anthropology Today*, *25*(6), 17–19. http://dx.doi.org/10.1111/j.1467-8322.2009.00700.x

Low, S.M., & Merry, S.E. (2010). Engaged anthropology: Diversity and dilemmas: An introduction to supplement 2. *Current Anthropology*, *51*(S2), S203–S226. http://dx.doi.org/10.1086/653837

Lutkekaus, N.C., & Roscoe, P.B. (1995). *Gender rituals: Female initiation in Melanesia.* New York: Routledge.

Mackie, G. (2000). Female genital cutting: The beginning of the end. In B. Shell-Duncan & Y. Hernlund (Eds.), *Female "circumcision" in Africa: Culture, controversy, and change* (pp. 253–282). London: Lynne Rienner Publishers.

Martinez, S. (2005). Searching for a middle path: Rights, capabilities, and political culture in the study of female genital cutting. *Ahfad Journal, 22*(1), 31–44.

Masland, T. (1999, July 5). The ritual of pain. In Uganda, tradition overpowers a United Nations drive against female genital mutilation. *Newsweek,* 61.

Morsy, S.A. (1991). Safeguarding women's bodies: The white man's burden medicalized. *Medical Anthropology Quarterly, 5*(1), 19–23. http://dx.doi.org/10.1525/maq.1991.5.1.02a00040

Moruzzi, N.C. (2005). Cutting through culture: The feminist discourse on female circumcision. *Critical Middle Eastern Studies, 14*(2), 203–220. http://dx.doi.org/10.1080/10669920500135587

Obermeyer, C.M. (2003, September). The health consequences of female circumcision: Science, advocacy, and standards of evidence. *Medical Anthropology Quarterly, 17*(3), 394–412. http://dx.doi.org/10.1525/maq.2003.17.3.394 Medline:12974204

Orubuloye, I.O., Caldwell, P., & Caldwell, J.C. (2000). Female circumcision among the Yoruba of southwestern Yoruba: The beginning of change. In B. Shell-Duncan & Y. Hernlund (Eds.), *Female "circumcision" in Africa. Culture, controversy, and change* (pp. 73–94). London: Lynne Rienner Publishers.

Rahlenbeck, S., Mekonnen, W., & Melkamu, Y. (2010, June). Female genital cutting starts to decline among women in Oromia, Ethiopia. *Reproductive Biomedicine Online, 20*(7), 867–872. http://dx.doi.org/10.1016/j.rbmo.2010.01.009 Medline:20400376

Sargent, C. (1991). Confronting patriarchy: The potential of advocacy in medical anthropology. *Medical Anthropology Quarterly, 5*(1), 24–25. http://dx.doi.org/10.1525/maq.1991.5.1.02a00050

Shandall, A.A. (1967). Circumcision and infibulation of females: A general consideration of the problem and a clinical study of the complications in Sudanese women. *Sudan Medical Journal, 5*(4), 178–212. Medline:12259304

Shell-Duncan, B. (2001, April). The medicalization of female "circumcision": Harm reduction or promotion of a dangerous practice? *Social Science & Medicine, 52*(7), 1013–1028. http://dx.doi.org/10.1016/S0277-9536(00)00208-2 Medline:11266046

_____, & Hernlund, Y. (2000). Female "circumcision" in Africa: Dimensions of the practice and debates. In B. Shell-Duncan & Y. Hernlund (Eds.), *Female "circumcision" in Africa: Culture, controversy, and change* (pp. 1–40). London: Lynne Rienner Publishers.

_____, Obiero, W.O., & Muruli, L.A. (2000). Women without choices: The debate over medicalization of female genital cutting and its impact on a Northern Kenyan community. In B. Shell-Duncan & Y. Hernlund (Eds.), *Female "circumcision" in Africa: Culture, controversy, and change* (pp. 109–128). London: Lynne Rienner Publishers.

Shweder, R.A. (2009). Disputing the myth of the sexual dysfunction of circumcised women: An interview with Fuambai S. Ahmadu. *Anthropology Today, 25*(6), 14–17. http://dx.doi.org/10.1111/j.1467-8322.2009.00699.x

Thomas, L. (2000). Ngaitana. I will circumcise myself: Lessons from colonial campaigns to ban excision in Meru, Kenya. In B. Shell-Duncan & Y. Hernlund (Eds.), *Female "circumcision" in Africa: Culture, controversy, and change* (pp. 129–150). London: Lynne Rienner Publishers.

Toubia, N. (Ed.) (1988). *Women of the Arab world: The coming challenge.* Papers of the Arab Women's Solidarity Association Conference. Atlantic Highlands, NJ: Zed Books.

_____, & Izette, S. (1998). *Female genital mutilation: An overview.* Geneva: World Health Organization.

Chapter 3: International Aid: What benefits do NGOs provide developing countries, and how can their presence generate new challenges?

Baldauf, S. (2005, April 1). A new breed of missionary: A drive for conversions, not development, is stirring violent animosity in India. *The Christian Science Monitor,* 1. http://www.infotrac.galegroup.com

Black, M. (1996). *Children first: The story of UNICEF, past and present*. Oxford: Oxford University Press.

Bock, J.G. (2010, December 6). Rising from the rubble. *America: The National Catholic Review*. http://www.americamagazine.org/node/149954

Boyden, J. (1997). Childhood and the policy-makers: A comparative perspective on the globalization of childhood. In A. James & A. Prout (Eds.), *Constructing and reconstructing childhood: Contemporary issues in the sociology of childhood* (pp. 190–229). London: Routledge Falmer.

Burr, R. (2006). *Vietnam's children in a changing world*. New Brunswick, NJ: Rutgers University Press.

Cudd, A.E. (2005). Missionary positions. *Hypatia, 20*(4), 164–182. http://dx.doi.org/10.1111/j.1527-2001.2005.tb00542.x

Doucet, I. (2011, January 13). The nation: NGOs have failed Haiti. *NPR*. http://www.npr.org/2011/01/13/132884795/the-nation-how-ngos-have-failed-haiti

Fraser, B. (2005, October 1). Getting drugs to HIV-infected children in Cambodia. *Lancet, 366*(9492), 1153–1154. http://dx.doi.org/10.1016/S0140-6736(05)67464-8 Medline:16200691

Goyet, C.V., Sarmiento, J.P., & Grünewald, F. (2011). Health response to the earthquake in Haiti. January 2010. Lessons to be learned for the next massive sudden-onset disaster. Pan American Health Organization for World Health Organization. http://reliefweb.int/sites/reliefweb.int/files/resources/Full_Report_3342.pdf

Ishkanian, A. (2004). *Anthropological perspectives on civil society and NGO development in a post-socialist context*. Paper presented at NGO Study Group Seminar "Ethnography of NGOs: Understanding Organization Processes," Oxford. http://www.intrac.org/data/files/resources/291/Anthropological-Perspectives-on-Civil-Society-and-NGO-Development.pdf

Lewis, D. (2005). *Anthropology and development: The uneasy relationship*. London: LSE Research Online. http://eprints.lse.ac.uk/253/

Lindsay, R. (2010, March 29). Haiti's excluded. *The Nation*. http://www.thenation.com/article/haitis-excluded#axzz2ZFxaa8Ri

Lonely Planet. (2011). *Map of Uganda*. http://www.lonelyplanet.com/maps/africa/uganda/

Macola, G. (2005, July). [Review of book *The steamer parish: The rise and fall of missionary medicine on an African frontier* by C.M. Good.] *Journal of African History, 46*, 36.

Partners in Health (2009–2012). *Our history*. http://www.pih.org/pages/partners-in-health-history

Panchang, D. (2012, July 4). Waiting for helicopters? Cholera, prejudice and the right to water in Haiti. *Truthout*. http://truth-out.org/news/item/10154-waiting-for-helicopters?-cholera-prejudice-and-the-right-to-water-in-haiti

Pupavac, V. (2000). *The infantilisation of the South and the UN Convention on the Rights of the Child*. Nottingham: Student Human Rights Law Centre.

Rohde, D. (2005, January 22). Mix of quake aid and preaching stirs concern. *The New York Times*. http://www.infotrac.galegroup.com

Sampson, S. (2002). Weak states, uncivil societies and thousands of NGOs. Western democracy export as benevolent colonialism in the Balkans. In S. Resic (Ed.), *Cultural boundaries of the Balkans* (pp. 27–44). Lund, Sweden: Lund University Press. http://www.anthrobase.com/Txt/S/Sampson_S_01.htm

Smith, D.J. (2010). Corruption, NGOs, and development in Nigeria. *Third World Quarterly, 31*(2), 243–258. http://dx.doi.org/10.1080/01436591003711975

Spoerri, M. (2012, February 13). Outrage over Egypt's arrest of NGO workers, but US would have done the same. *The Christian Science Monitor*. http://www.csmonitor.com/Commentary/Opinion/2012/0213/Outrage-over-Egypt-s-arrest-of-NGO-workers-but-US-would-have-done-the-same

Stephenson, C. (2005). Nongovernmental organizations (NGOs). *Beyond Intractability*. http://www.beyondintractability.org/bi-essay/role-ngo/

Thielke, T. (2005). For God's sake, please stop the aid. *Spiegel Online International*. http://www.spiegel.de/international/spiegel/spiegel-interview-with-african-economics-expert-for-god-s-sake-please-stop-the-aid-a-363663.html

———. (2008). Developmental aid workers are killing Africa. *Spiegel Online International*. http://www.spiegel.de/international/world/opinion-developmental-aid-workers-are-killing-africa-a-557723-2.html

Tishkov, V. (2005). An anthropology of NGOs. *Eurozine*. http://www.eurozine.com/articles/2005-06-01-tishkov-en.html

Tomasek, K.M. (1999). [Review of *Mary Lyon and the Mount Holyoke missionaries* by A. Porterfield.] *Journal of Interdisciplinary History, 30*(1), 143–145. http://dx.doi.org/10.1162/jinh.1999.30.1.143

Tran, M. (2013, January 10). The lack of national plan heightens the struggle to rebuild unstable Haiti. *The Guardian*. http://www.guardian.co.uk/global-development/2013/jan/10/lack-national-plan-struggle-rebuild-haiti

Valentin, K., & Meinart, L. (2009). The adult North and the young South: Reflections on the civilizing mission of children's rights. *Anthropology Today, 25*(3), 23–28. http://dx.doi.org/10.1111/j.1467-8322.2009.00669.x

Wilder, A., & Morris, T. (2008). 'Locals within locals': Cultural sensitivity in disaster aid. *Anthropology Today, 24*(3), 1–3. http://dx.doi.org/10.1111/j.1467-8322.2008.00581.x

Zanotti, L. (2010). Cacophonies of aid, failed state building and NGOs in Haiti: Setting the stage for disaster, envisioning the future. *Third World Quarterly, 31*(5), 755–771. http://dx.doi.org/10.1080/01436597.2010.503567 Medline:20821882

Chapter 4: Population Growth: Is the world over-populated, and should governments have the right to control birthrates?

Aird, J. (1994, July–August). The China model. *PRI Review, 4*(4), 1.

Alter, L. (2010, April 27). The coming population crash: An upbeat and optimistic outlook [Book review]. *Treehugger*. http://www.treehugger.com/culture/the-coming-population-crash-an-upbeat-and-optimistic-outlook-book-review.html

Anagnost, A. (1995). A surfeit of bodies: Population and the rationality of the state in post-Mao China. In F.D. Ginsburg & R. Rapp (Eds.), *Conceiving the new world order: The global politics of reproduction* (pp. 22–41). Berkeley: University of California Press.

Batabyal, A.A., & Beladi, H. (2004). On the tradeoff between cultural sensitivity and aggregate size in population control policy. *Applied Economics Letters, 11*(7), 401–404. http://dx.doi.org/10.1080/1350485042000204697

Bulte, E., Heerink, N., & Zhang, X. (2011). China's one-child policy and 'the mystery of missing women': Ethnic minorities and male biased sex ratios. *Oxford Bulletin of Economics and Statistics, 73*(1), 21–39. http://dx.doi.org/10.1111/j.1468-0084.2010.00601.x

Canada Immigration and Refugee Board. (2007, June 26). China: Treatment of "illegal," or "black," children born outside the one-child family planning policy; whether unregistered children are denied access to education, health care and other social services (2003–2007). The UN Refugee Agency. http://www.unhcr.org/refworld/docid/46c403821f.html

Clark, T. (2008, July 1). Plight of the little emperors. *Psychology Today*. http://www.psychologytoday.com/articles/200806/plight-the-little-emperors

CWAC (n.d.). *Population growth. Impacts on the environment*. http://www.cwac.net/population/index.html

Durning, A.T. (1994). The conundrum of consumption. In L.A. Mazur (Ed.), *Beyond the numbers: A reader on population, consumption and environment* (pp. 40–47). Washington, DC: Island Press.

Eberstadt, N. (2010). The demographic future: What population growth—and decline means for Global Economy. *Foreign Affairs*. http://www.foreignaffairs.com/articles/66805/nicholas-eberstadt/the-demographic-future

The Economist. (2011, July 21). Only and lonely: China's most populous province launches a public criticism of the one-child policy. http://www.economist.com/node/18988926

The Economist. (2013, Mar 16). Monks without a temple. http://www.economist.com/news/china/21573579-china-may-have-begun-long-end-game-its-one-child-policy-experts-say-it-cannot-end-soon

Ehrlich, P.R. (1971). *The population bomb*. New York: Ballantine Books.

Engels, F. (1844). Outlines of a critique of political economy. *Marx and Engels in Malthus: Selections from the writings of Marx and Engels dealing with the theories of Thomas Robert Malthus.* London: Lawrence and Wishart. http://www.marxists.org/archive/marx/works/1844/df-jahrbucher/outlines.htm

FAO (n.d.). *Population growth and the food crisis.* http://www.fao.org/docrep/U3550t/u3550t02.htm

Firth, L. (Ed.). (2012). *Population growth and migration.* Cambridge: Independence Educational Publishers.

Frazer, E. (1996). *Thailand: A family planning success story.* Context Institute. http://www.context.org/iclib/ic31/frazer/

Government of Maharastra Public Health Department (2000, May 9). State population policy. http://www.maha-arogya.gov.in/policies/default.htm

Greenhalgh, S. (2003a, June). Science, modernity, and the making of China's one-child policy. *Population and Development Review, 29*(2), 163–196. http://dx.doi.org/10.1111/j.1728-4457.2003.00163.x

————. (2003b). Planned births, unplanned persons: "Population" in the making of Chinese modernity. *American Ethnologist, 30*(2), 196–215. http://dx.doi.org/10.1525/ae.2003.30.2.196

Gribble, J.N. (2012, July). Fact Sheet: Unmet need for family planning. *World population data sheet 2012.* http://www.prb.org/Publications/Datasheets/2012/world-population-data-sheet/fact-sheet-unmet-need.aspx

Gross, R.M. (1995). Buddhist resources for issues of population, consumption, and the environment. In H. Coward (Ed.), *Population, consumption, and the environment: Religious and secular responses* (pp. 155–172). Albany: State University of New York Press.

Hartmann, B. (1995). *Reproductive rights of women and the global politics of population control.* Cambridge, MA: South End Press.

Haub, C. (2012 July). Fact sheet: World population trends 2012. Population Reference Bureau. http://www.prb.org/Publications/Datasheets/2012/world-population-data-sheet/fact-sheet-world-population.aspx

Hinrichsen, D., & Robey, B. (2000). *Population and the environment: The global challenge.* Actionbioscience.org. http://www.actionbioscience.org/environment/hinrichsen_robey.html

Iyer, S. (2002). Religion and the decision to use contraception in India. *Journal for the Scientific Study of Religion, 41*(4), 711–722. http://dx.doi.org/10.1111/1468-5906.00156

Johnson, K. (1996). The politics of the revival of infant abandonment in China, with special reference to Hunan. *Population and Development Review, 22*(1), 77–98. http://dx.doi.org/10.2307/2137687

Laurent, G. (2012, June 26). *Combating deforestation in Haiti.* Canada Haiti Action Network. http://www.canadahaitiaction.ca/content/combating-deforestation-haiti

Lutz, W., Sanderson, W., & Scherbov, S. (2001, Aug 2). The end of world population growth. *Nature, 412*(6846), 543–545. http://dx.doi.org/10.1038/35087589 Medline:11484054

Moorhead, J. (2012, July 11). Melinda Gates challenges Vatican by vowing to improve contraception. *The Guardian.* http://www.guardian.co.uk/world/2012/jul/11/melinda-gates-challenges-vatican-contraception

Mosher, S.W. (2006, Winter). China's one-child policy: Twenty-five years later. *Human Life Review, 32*(1), 76–101. http://www.humanlifereview.com/index.php?option=com_content&view=article&id=42:chinas-one-child-policy-twenty-five-years-later&catid=31:2006-winter&Itemid=6 Medline:17111544

Nakra, P. (2012, Summer). China's "one-child" policy. The time for change is now! *World Future Review.*

PBS Newshour (2012, March 15). What's causing water shortages in Ghana, Nigeria? http://www.pbs.org/newshour/bb/globalhealth/jan-june12/westafrica_03-15.html

People and Planet (2011, March 10). Population and human development—the key connections. http://www.peopleandplanet.net/?lid=25990&section=33&topic=44

Population Connection. (2009). Rising emissions, growing numbers of people: Demography and climate change. Population Connection fact sheet. www.populationconnection.org

Raulkari, M., Toledo, V.J., & Harvey, M. (n.d.). *Lack of sustainable agriculture: Biggest threat to the environment*. WWF Global. http://wwf.panda.org/about_our_earth/about_freshwater/freshwater_problems/thirsty_crops/

Richards, L. (1996). Controlling China's baby boom. *Contemporary Review, 268*(1560), 5.

Rodriguez-Trias, H. (1995). Foreword (pp. xi–xiv). *Reproductive rights of women and the global politics of population control*. Cambridge, MA: South End Press.

Shah, H. (2012). Women's empowerment through economic development: Gujarat, India. In M. Tamontano (Ed.), *Perspectives on global issues: Global citizens engaging global issues, 6*(1): 25–39.

Tobin, K.A. (2004). *Politics and population control: A documentary history*. Westport, CT: Greenwood.

Tran, M. (2012, July 11). Rich countries pledge 2.6bn for family planning in global south. *The Guardian*. http://www.guardian.co.uk/global-development/2012/jul/11/rich-countries-pledge-family-planning-women

Tucker, P. (2006, Sept–Oct). Strategies for containing population growth. http://patricktucker.com/2010/04/01/strategies-for-containing-population-growth/

United Nations Department of Economic and Social Affairs/Population Division (2004). *World Population to 2300*. http://www.un.org/esa/population/publications/longrange2/WorldPop2300final.pdf.

Web of Creation (n.d.). Problem: Fresh water and oceans in danger. http://www.webofcreation.org/Earth%20Problems/water.htm.

Weiss, K.R. (2012, July 22). Fertility rates fall, but global population explosion goes on. *Los Angeles Times*. http://www.latimes.com/news/nationworld/world/population/la-fg-population-matters1-20120722-html,0,7213271.htmlstory

Wilkinson, M. (2007, October 26). *The Sydney Morning Herald*. http://www.smh.com.au/articles/2007/10/25/1192941241428.html

Wirth, T.E. (1995). The human factor. *Sierra, 80*(5).

Yardley, J. (2010, August 21). India tries using cash bonuses to slow birthrates. *The New York Times*. http://www.nytimes.com/2010/08/22/world/asia/22india.html

Zhang, D.D., Lee, H.F., Wang, C., Li, B., Zhang, J., Pei, O., & Chen, J. (2011). Climate change and large-scale human population collapses in the pre-industrial era. *Global Ecology and Biogeography, 20* (4), 520–531. http://dx.doi.org/10.1111/j.1466-8238.2010.00625.x

Chapter 5: Heritage Languages: Are they an endangered species?

Abbi, A. (2009). Endangered languages, endangered knowledge: Vanishing voices of the Great Andamanese of India. *Biocultural Diversity Conservation*. http://www.terralingua.org/bcdconservation/?p=125

Baloy, N.J.K. (2011). We can't feel our language. *American Indian Quarterly, 34*(4), 515–548.

Binion, S., & Shook, O. (2007). Endangered languages: Voices on the brink of extinction. *World Literature Today, 81*(5), 12–14.

Boroditsky, L. (2011, February). How language shapes thought. *Scientific American, 304*(2), n.p.

Černý, M. (2010). Language death versus language survival: A global perspective. *Beyond globalization: Exploring the limits of globalization in the regional context* (pp. 51–56). http://conference.osu.eu/globalization/publ/06-cerny.pdf

Charny, I.W. (1999). A proposed definitional matrix for crimes of genocide. In I.W. Charny (Ed.), *Encyclopedia of genocide* (pp. 7–9). Santa Barbara, CA: ABC-CLIO.

Crystal, D. (2000). *Language death*. Cambridge: Cambridge University Press. http://dx.doi.org/10.1017/CBO9781139106856

Fillmore, L.W. (2000). Loss of family languages: Should educators be concerned? *Theory into Practice, 39*(4), 203–210. http://dx.doi.org/10.1207/s15430421tip3904_3

Fishman, J. (1991). *Reversing language shift: Theoretical and empirical foundations of assistance to threatened languages*. Clevedon, UK: Multilingual Matters.

———. (1996). What do you lose when you lose your language? In G. Cantoni (Ed.), *Stabilizing indigenous languages* (pp. 80–91). http://www.eric.ed.gov/PDFS/ED428922.pdf

Francis, N., & Nieto Andrade, R. (1996). Stories for language revitalizations in Nahuatl and Chichimeca. In G. Cantoni (Ed.), *Stabilizing indigenous languages* (pp. 162–173). http://www.eric.ed.gov/PDFS/ED428922.pdf

GaelicMatters.com (2011). *The Gaelic revival – past and present*. http://www.gaelicmatters.com/gaelic-revival.html

Gallegos, C., Murray, E.W., & Evans, M. (2010). Research note: Comparing indigenous language revitalization: Te reo Māori in Aotearoa New Zealand and Mapudungun in Chile. *Asia Pacific Viewpoint*, *51*(1), 91–104. http://dx.doi.org/10.1111/j.1467-8373.2009.01418.x

Goswami, R. (2003, July 31). Globalization challenges Asian languages. *Asia Times*. http://www.atimes.com/atimes/Global_Economy/EG31Dj01.html

Gray, R. (2012, February 18). Internet may save endangered languages. *The Telegraph*. http://www.telegraph.co.uk/technology/internet/9090885/Internet-may-save-endangered-languages.html

Harrison, K.D. (2008). *When languages die: The extinction of the world's languages and the erosion of human knowledge*. Oxford: Oxford University Press.

Haspelmath, M. (1993). In memoriam: Ubykh (Tevfik Esenç). *Circassian World*. http://www.circassianworld.com/new/language/1262-tevfik-esenc-ubykh.html

Haynes, E. (2010). *Heritage briefs*. Center for Applied Linguistics. http://www.cal.org/heritage/pdfs/briefs/what-is-language-loss.pdf

Khemlani-David, M. (1991). The Sindhis in Malaysia—Language maintenance, language loss or language death? Paper presented at the International Conference on Bilingualism and National Development. http://www.eric.ed.gov/PDFS/ED357632.pdf

Krauss, M.E. (1992). The world's languages in crisis. *Language*, *68*(1), 4–10. http://dx.doi.org/10.1353/lan.1992.0075

———. (1998). The condition of Native North American languages: The need for realistic assessment and action. *International Journal of the Sociology of Language*, *132*(1), 9–21. http://dx.doi.org/10.1515/ijsl.1998.132.9

———. (n.d.). A loss for words. *Diversity in the age of globalization*. Earthwatch Institute. http://www.wadsworth.com/anthropology_d/special_features/ext/earthwatch/alfw.html

Laukaitis, J. (2010). The politics of language and national school reform: The Gaelic League's call for an Irish Ireland, 1893–1922. *American Educational History Journal*, *37*(1), 221–235.

Lemkin, R. (1944). *Axis rule in occupied Europe: Laws of occupation, analysis of government, proposals for redress*. Washington, DC: Carnegie Endowment for International Peace, Division of International Law.

López-Goñi, I. (2003). Ikastola in the twentieth century: An alternative for schooling in the Basque country. *History of Education*, *32*(6), 661–676. http://dx.doi.org/10.1080/0046760032000151483

McMahon, T.G. (2008). *Grand opportunity: The Gaelic revival and Irish society, 1893–1910*. Syracuse, NY: Syracuse University Press.

Messieh, N. (2012). National Geographic brings endangered languages into the digital age, one dictionary at a time. *TNN Media*. http://thenextweb.com/media/2012/02/19/national-geographic-brings-endangered-languages-into-the-digital-age-one-dictionary-at-a-time/

Mexicoinsider.com (2008). Language in Mexico. http://www.mexinsider.com/language-in-mexico.html

Munro, M. (2012, February 17). "Talking dictionary" could help dying languages survive. *Vancouver Sun*. http://www.vancouversun.com/life/Talking+dictionary+could+help+dying+languages+survive/6171976/story.html

Nahir, M. (1988). Language planning and language acquisition: The "great leap" in the Hebrew revival. In C.B. Paulston (Ed.), *International handbook of bilingualism and bilingual education* (pp. 275–296). Westport CT: Greenwood Press.

Nettle, D., & Romaine, S. (2000). *Vanishing voices: The extinction of the world's languages*. Oxford: Oxford University Press.

Ostler, N. (2001). Endangered languages – lost worlds. *Contemporary Review*, *279*(1631), 349–355.

Ottenheimer, H.J. (2009). *The anthropology of language: An introduction to linguistic anthropology* (2nd ed.). Belmont, CA: Wadsworth, Cengage Learning.

Raymond, J. (1998, September 14). Say what? Preserving endangered languages. *Newsweek*, *132*(11).

Reyhner, J. (1999). Some basics of language revitalization. In J. Reyhner (Ed.), *Revitalizing indigenous languages* (pp. 5–20). Flagstaff: Northern Arizona University.

Sampat, P. (2002). Our planet's languages are dying – worldview. *USA Today (Society for the Advancement of Education)*.

Solash, R. (2010, February 19). Silent extinction: Language loss reaches crisis levels. Radio Free Europe. http://www.rferl.org/content/Silent_Extinction_Language_Loss_Reaches_Crisis_Levels/1963070.html

Swarthmore News. (2012). K. David Harrison. http://www.swarthmore.edu/x12040.xml.

van Driem, G. (2007). Endangered languages of South Asia. In M. Brenzinger (Ed.), *Handbook of endangered language* (pp. 303–341). Berlin: Mouton de Gruyter. http://www.himalayanlanguages.org/files/driem/pdfs/2007EndangeredLggsSouthAsia.pdf

VOGA (n.d.). Vanishing voices of the Great Andamanese. http://www.andamanese.net/media.html

Wilson, K., & Peters, E.J. (2005). You can make a place for it: Remapping urban First Nations spaces of identity. *Society and Space*, *23*, 399.

Yamamoto, A.Y. (1998). Retrospect and prospect on new emerging language communities. In N. Ostler (Ed.), *Endangered languages: What role for the specialist?* (pp. 113–120). Bath, UK: Foundation for Endangered Languages.

_____, Brenzinger, M., & Villalón, M.E. (2008). A place for all languages: On language vitality and revitalization. *Museum International*, *60*(3), 60–70. http://dx.doi.org/10.1111/j.1468-0033.2008.00653.x

Zuckermann, G., & Walsh, M. (2011). Stop, revive, survive: Lessons from the Hebrew revival applicable to the reclamation, maintenance and empowerment of aboriginal languages and culture. *Australian Journal of Linguistics*, *31*(1), 111–127. http://dx.doi.org/10.1080/07268602.2011.532859

Chapter 6: Body Image: How does body image affect identity and status, and how has the transnational flow of Western ideals of beauty impacted other cultures?

Altabe, M., & O'Garo, K. (2002). Hispanic body images. In T.F. Cash & T. Pruzinsky (Eds.), *Body image: A handbook of theory, research, and clinical practice* (pp. 250–256). New York: The Guilford Press.

Anorexia 10 (2006, December 12). *Tips for anorexics*. http://www.anorexia10.com/anorexia/tips-for-anorexics-2/

Bonetti, D. (n.d.). [Review of *Modern Primitives*.] www.researchpubs.com/books/primprod.php.

Bourdieu, P. (1977). *Outline of a theory of practice*. Cambridge: Cambridge University Press. http://dx.doi.org/10.1017/CBO9780511812507

Brewis, A.A. (1999). The accuracy of attractive-body-size judgment. *Current Anthropology*, *40*(4), 548–552. http://dx.doi.org/10.1086/200052

Bruch, H. (1978). *The golden age: The enigma of anorexia nervosa*. New York: Vintage.

Brumberg, J.J. (1989). *Fasting girls: The surprising history of anorexia nervosa*. New York: New American Library.

Cash, T.F., & Pruzinsky, T. (Eds.). (2002). *Body image: A handbook of theory, research, and clinical practice*. New York: Guilford.

Counihan, C.M. (1999). *The anthropology of food and body: Gender, meaning, and power*. New York: Routledge.

Crook, M. (1991). *The body image trap: Understanding and rejecting body image myths*. Vancouver: International Self-Counsel Press.

Cudd, A.E. (2005). Missionary positions. *Hypatia*. http://www.infotrac.galegroup.com

Cyberpunkreview.com. (2006, June 8). *Experiences in body modification*. http://www.cyberpunkreview.com/cyberpunked-living/experiences-in-body-modification/

Edut, O. (1998). Introduction. In O. Edut (Ed.), *Adios, Barbie: Young women write about body image and identity*. Seattle: Seal Press.

Feminism and Women's Studies. (2012). *Body image and "eating disorders."* http://feminism.eserver.org/real-and-ideal-body-image.txt

Ferguson, C.J., Munoz, M.E., Contreras, S., & Velasquez, K. (2011). Mirror, mirror on the wall: Peer competition, television influences, and body image dissatisfaction. *Journal of Social and Clinical Psychology*, *30*(5), 458–483. http://dx.doi.org/10.1521/jscp.2011.30.5.458

Gillen, M.M., & Lefkowitz, E.S. (2011). Body size perceptions in racially/ethnically diverse men and women: Implications for body image and self-esteem. *North American Journal of Psychology*, *13*(3), 447–467.

Gilman, S.J. (1998). Klaus Barbie, and other dolls I'd like to see. In O. Edut (Ed.), *Adios, Barbie: Young women write about body image and identity* (pp. 14–21). Seattle: Seal Press.

Gordon, R.A. (2000). *Eating disorders: Anatomy of a social epidemic* (2nd ed.). Oxford: Blackwell.

Hesse-Biber, S. (1996). *Am I thin enough yet? The cult of thinness and the commercialization of identity*. New York: Oxford University Press.

Higgins, E.T. (1987, July). Self-discrepancy: A theory relating self and affect. *Psychological Review*, *94*(3), 319–340. http://dx.doi.org/10.1037/0033-295X.94.3.319 Medline:3615707

Holmberg, C.B. (1998). *Sexualities and popular culture*. Thousand Oaks, CA: Sage Publications.

Jenks, C. (2003). *Transgression*. London: Routledge.

Kaplan-Myrth, N. (2000). Alice without a looking glass: Blind people and body image. *Anthropology & Medicine*, *7*(3), 277–299. http://dx.doi.org/10.1080/713650612

Kawamura, K.Y. (2002). Asian American body images. In T.F. Cash & T. Pruzinsky (Eds.), *Body image: A handbook of theory, research, and clinical practice* (pp. 243–249). New York: The Guilford Press.

Kenlie. (2011, June 16). Guest blog – The invisible (horrible, lazy, unattractive) fat person. All the Weigh. http://alltheweigh.com/2011/06/guest-blog-the-invisible-horrible-lazy-unattractive-fat-person/

Klesse, C. (2007). Racializing the politics of transgression: Body modification in queer culture. *Social Semiotics*, *17*(3), 275–292. http://dx.doi.org/10.1080/10350330701448561

Lee, S. (2001). Fat phobia in anorexia nervosa: Whose obsession is it? In M. Nasser, M.A. Katzman, & R.A. Gordon (Eds.), *Eating disorders and cultures in transition* (pp. 40–65). New York: Brunner-Routledge.

Littlewood, R. (2004, December). Commentary: Globalization, culture, body image, and eating disorders. *Culture, Medicine and Psychiatry*, *28*(4), 597–602. http://dx.doi.org/10.1007/s11013-004-1069-3 Medline:15847055

Mackenzie, M. (1991). [Review of the books *Fasting girls: The emergence of anorexia nervosa as a modern disease*; *Fasting girls: The surprising history of anorexia nervosa*; *¡Que Gordita! A study of weight among women in a Puerto Rican community*; and *Never too thin: Why women are at war with their bodies*.] *Medical Anthropology Quarterly*, *5*(4), 406–410. http://dx.doi.org/10.1525/maq.1991.5.4.02a00080

Mirante, E. (2006, September 28). The dragon mothers polish their metal coils. *Guernica*. http://www.guernicamag.com/features/the_dragon_mothers/

Nichter, M., & Vuckovic, N. (1994). Fat talk: Body image among adolescent girls. In N. Sault (Ed.), *Many mirrors: Body image and social relations* (pp. 109–131). New Brunswick, NJ: Rutgers University Press.

Orbach, S. (2001, June 24). Give us back our bodies. *Observer*. http://www.guardian.co.uk/politics/2001/jun/24/Whitehall.uk

Pike, K.M., & Borovoy, A. (2004, December). The rise of eating disorders in Japan: Issues of culture and limitations of the model of "westernization." *Culture, Medicine and Psychiatry*, *28*(4), 493–531. http://dx.doi.org/10.1007/s11013-004-1066-6 Medline:15847052

Ping, W. (2000). *Aching for beauty: Footbinding in China*. Minneapolis: University of Minnesota Press.

Pitts, V.L. (2000). Visibly queer: Body technologies and sexual politics. *Sociological Quarterly*, *41*(3), 443–463. http://dx.doi.org/10.1111/j.1533-8525.2000.tb00087.x Medline:19569274

_____. (2003). *In the flesh: The cultural politics of body modification*. Basingstoke, UK: Houndsmill.

Rasmussen, S.J. (2010, December). Remaking body politics: Dilemmas over female fatness as symbolic capital in two rural Tuareg communities. *Culture, Medicine and Psychiatry*, *34*(4), 615–632. http://dx.doi.org/10.1007/s11013-010-9193-8 Medline:20835886

Sargent, J. (n.d.). *Anorexia nervosa: Judy's story*. http://www.angelfire.com/ms/anorexianervosa/

Sault, N. (1994). Introduction: The human mirror. In N. Sault (Ed.), *Many mirrors: Body image and social relations* (pp. 1–28). New Brunswick, NJ: Rutgers University Press.

Simmons, A.M. (1998). Where fat is a mark of beauty. *Los Angeles Times.* Reprinted in E. Angeloni (Ed.), *Annual Editions Anthropology: 05/06 (2005).* Dubuque, IA: McGraw-Hill/Dushkin.

The Talk. (2012, March 21). CBS.

Trampe, D., Stapel, D.A., & Siero, F.W. (2007, January). On models and vases: Body dissatisfaction and proneness to social comparison effects. *Journal of Personality and Social Psychology, 92*(1), 106–118. http://dx.doi.org/10.1037/0022-3514.92.1.106 Medline:17201546

Vale, V., & Juno, A. (1989). *Modern primitives.* San Francisco: RE/Search Publications.

van Esterik, P. (2001). Commentary. In M. Nasser, M.A. Katzman, & R.A. Gordon (Eds.), *Eating disorders and cultures in transition* (pp. 20–21). New York: Brunner-Routledge.

Young, W. (1994). The body tamed: Tying and tattooing among the Rashaayda Bedouin. In N. Sault (Ed.), *Many mirrors: Body image and social relations* (pp. 58–75). New Brunswick, NJ: Rutgers University Press.

Chapter 7: Same-Sex Marriage: What are the socio-economic, religious, and political implications of same-sex marriage and changing family structure?

American Anthropological Association (AAA). (2004, February 26). Statement on marriage and the family. http://www.aaanet.org/issues/policy-advocacy/Statement-on-Marriage-and-the-Family.cfm

AngusReidPublicOpinion. (2013, February 19). Half of Americans would allow same-sex marriage. http://www.angus-reid.com/polls/48671/half-of-americans-would-allow-same-sex-marriage/

Awom, U., & Ukaibe, C. (2011, November 1). Nigeria: Same sex marriage, a taboo. AllAfrica. http://allafrica.com/stories/201111010623.html

Baird, R.M. & Rosenbaum, S.E. (Eds.). (1997). *Same-sex marriage: The moral and legal debate.* Amherst, NY: Prometheus Books.

Baskerville, S. (2006). Politics and same-sex marriage. *Society, 44*(1), 60–66. http://dx.doi.org/10.1007/BF02690469

BBC News. (2013, June 4). Gay marriage. http://www.bbc.co.uk/news/uk-18407568

Bonvillain, N. (1998). *Women and men: Cultural constructs of gender* (2nd ed.). Upper Saddle River, NJ: Prentice Hall.

Burns, K. (Ed.). (2005). *Gay marriage.* Farmington Hills, MI: Thomson Gale.

Cathcart, T. (2012, February 27). Gay marriage bill gains momentum, public support. *The DePaulia.* http://faculty.usfsp.edu/jsokolov/2410gaymar1.htm

Chacha, B.K. (2004). Traversing gender and colonial madness: Same-sex relationships, customary law and change in Tanzania, 1890–1990. In *Gender activism & studies in Africa* (pp. 129–151). http://www.codesria.org/IMG/pdf/GA_Chapter-8_chacha.pdf

CNNWorld. (2009, December 21). Mexico City legalizes same-sex marriage, adoptions. CNN World. http://articles.cnn.com/2009-12-21/world/mexico.gay.marriage_1_same-sex-civil-unions-union-between-two-people-legalizes?_s=PM:WORLD

Demian. (2005). Marriage traditions in various times and cultures. http://www.buddybuddy.com/mar-trad.html

Duggan, L. (2002). The new homonormativity: The sexual politics of neoliberalism. In R. Castronovo & D. Nelson (Eds.), *Materializing democracy: Toward a revitalized cultural politics* (pp. 175–194). Durham, NC: Duke University Press.

Egale Canada. (2011). Ontario marriage challenge. Profile of the parties. http://www.egale.ca/index.asp?menu=22&item=288

Eskridge, W.N. (1996). The case for same-sex marriage. http://www.simonsays.com/titles/0684824043/sameex1c.html

Evans Pritchard, E.E. (1974). *Man and woman among the Azande.* London: Faber and Faber.

Flaks, D.K., Ficher, I., Masterpasqua, F., & Joseph, G. (2004). Lesbians choosing motherhood: A comparative study of lesbian and heterosexual parents and their children. In A. Sullivan (Ed.), *Same-sex marriage: Pro and con* (pp. 246–249). New York: Vintage Books.

Gettleman, J. (2011, January 27). Ugandan who spoke up for gays is beaten to death. *The New York Times.* http://www.nytimes.com/2011/01/28/world/africa/28uganda.html

Green, A.I. (2010). Queer unions: Same-sex spouses marrying tradition and innovation. *Canadian Journal of Sociology, 35*(3), 399–436.

Gullo, K. (2012, February 21). California gay marriage ban supporters ask panel to reinstate voided law. *Bloomberg*. http://www.bloomberg.com/news/2012-02-21/california-gay-marriage-ban-supporters-seek-appeal-rehearing-1-.html

Haviland, W.A., Fedorak, S.A., & Lee, R.B. (2009). *Cultural anthropology* (3rd Cdn ed.). Toronto: Nelson Education, Inc.

Herskovits, M.J. (1937). A note on "woman marriage" in Dahomey. *Africa*, *10*(03), 335–341. http://dx.doi.org/10.2307/1155299

Josephson, J. (2005). Citizenship, same-sex marriage, and feminist critiques of marriage. *Perspectives on Politics*, *3*(2), 269–284. http://dx.doi.org/10.1017/S1537592705050206

Lahey, K., & Alderson, A. (2004). *Same-sex marriage: The personal and the political*. Toronto: Insomniac Press.

Layng, A. (2009, January). Where is marriage going? *USA Today*.

Li, C. (2010, February 24). Gay rights in China: Road to respect. *China Daily*. http://www.chinadaily.com.cn/china/2010-02/24/content_9492137.htm

Look, A. (2012, May 14). Obama's gay marriage endorsement not popular in Africa. *Voice of America*. http://www.voanews.com/content/obama_gay_marriage_endorsement_not_popular_in_africa/666370.html.

Macintosh, H., Elke, D., Reissing, E.D., & Andruff, H. (2010). Same-sex marriage in Canada: The impact of legal marriage on the first cohort of gay and lesbian Canadians to wed. *Canadian Journal of Human Sexuality*, *19*(3), 79–90.

McGough, J. (2004). Deviant marriage patterns in Chinese society. In A. Sullivan (Ed.), *Same-sex marriage: Pro and con* (pp. 24–28). New York: Vintage Books.

Pickett, B. (2002). Homosexuality. In E.N. Zalta (Ed.), *The Stanford Encyclopedia of Philosophy*. http://plato.stanford.edu/archives/fall2002/entries/homosexuality

Queers United. (2008, May 18). Open forum: Queer liberationist or gay assimilationist? http://queersunited.blogspot.mx/2008/05/open-forum-queer-liberationist-or-gay.html.

Roberts, A. (2013, May 18). French president Francois Hollande signs gay marriage law. *Bloomberg*. http://www.bloomberg.com/news/2013-05-18/french-president-francois-hollande-signs-gay-marriage-law.html

Robinson, B.A. (2012). Same-sex marriages (SSM) & civil unions. Ontario Consultants on Religious Tolerance. http://www.religioustolerance.org/hom_mar16.htm

Sina English. (2010, July 16). Argentina legalizes gay marriage in historic vote. Sina English. http://english.sina.com/world/p/2010/0715/329554.html

Smith, D. (2012, February 15). Ugandan minister shuts down gay rights conference. *The Guardian*. http://www.guardian.co.uk/world/2012/feb/15/ugandan-minister-gay-rights-conference

Stone, L.S. (2004, May). Gay marriage and anthropology. *Anthropology News*. http://faculty.usfsp.edu/jsokolov/2410gaymar1.htm

Sullivan, A. (2004). Introduction. In A. Sullivan (Ed.), *Same-sex marriage: Pro and con* (pp. xxii–xxx). New York: Vintage Books.

Vanguard. (2013, June 20). Nigerians support anti-same sex Bill – Poll. http://www.vanguardngr.com/2013/06/nigerians-support-anti-same-sex-bill-poll/

Vanita, R. (2010, July/August). Same-sex weddings, Hindu traditions and modern India. *Tikkun*. http://www.tikkun.org/nextgen/same-sex-weddings-hindu-traditions-and-modern-india-2

Walters, S.D. (2001). Take my domestic partner, please: Gays and marriage in the era of the visible. In M. Bernstein & R. Reinmann (Eds.), *Queer families, queer politics: Challenging culture and the state* (pp. 338–357). New York: Columbia University Press.

Weeks, J., Heaphy, B., & Donovan, C. (2001). *Same sex intimacies: Families of choice and other life experiments*. London: Routledge. http://dx.doi.org/10.4324/9780203167168

White, J.B. (2012, November 21). Same-sex marriage coming soon to US Supreme Court. *International Business Times*. http://www.ibtimes.com/same-sex-marriage-coming-soon-us-supreme-court-894956

Whittington, L., & Gordon, S. (2005, June 29). Canadian Commons votes to legalize same-sex marriage. *Toronto Star* Ottawa Bureau.

Williams, W.L. (1986). *The spirit and the flesh*. Boston: Beacon Press.

Wood, P., & Lewin, E. (2006). Gay and lesbian marriage: Should gays and lesbians have the right to marry? In W.A. Haviland, R.J. Gordon, & L.A. Vivanco (Eds.), *Talking about people: Readings in contemporary cultural anthropology* (pp. 134–142). Toronto: McGraw-Hill.

Chapter 8: Social Media: What is its role in socio-political revolution?

Ackerman, S. (2011, October 18). Egypt's top 'Facebook revolutionary' now advising Occupy Wall Street. *Wired*. http://www.wired.com/dangerroom/2011/10/egypt-occupy-wall-street/

Afify, H. (2011, December 27). Egypt court ends 'virginity' tests on female detainees. *Egypt Independent*. http://www.egyptindependent.com/news/egypt-court-ends-virginity-tests-female-detainees

The Amateur Computerist. (2011, Summer). The collected works of Michael Hauben: A new website. *Netizen News*, 2(2): 2–3. http://www.ais.org/~jrh/acn/

Borneo Post. (2011, December 7). 'Facebook revolution' big hit with Russians. http://www.theborneopost.com/2011/12/07/%E2%80%98facebook-revolution%E2%80%99-big-hit-with-russians/

Cave, D. (2011, September 24). Mexico turns to social media for information and survival. *The New York Times*. http://www.nytimes.com/2011/09/25/world/americas/mexico-turns-to-twitter-and-facebook-for-information-and-survival.html

Choudhary, A., Hendrix, W., Lee, K., Palsetia, D., & Liao, W. (2012, May). Social media evolution of the Egyptian revolution. *Communications of the ACM*, 55(5), 74–80. http://dx.doi.org/10.1145/2160718.2160736

Cohen, J. (2011, February 11). Google's Wael Ghonim thanks Facebook for revolution. *All Facebook: The unofficial Facebook blog*. http://www.allfacebook.com/googles-wael-ghonim-thanks-facebook-for-revolution-2011-02

Dahdal, S. (2011, March). How social media changed Arab resistance. *Newmatilda.com*. http://www.newmatilda.com/2011/03/04/how-social-media-changed-arab-resistance

Else, L. (2012). The revolution will be tweeted. *New Scientist*, 213(2850): n.p.

Etling, B., Faris, R., & Palfrey, J. (2010, Summer–Fall). *Political change in the digital age: The fragility and promise of online organizing*. The Berkman Center for Internet and Society at Harvard University. http://dash.harvard.edu/handle/1/4609956

Evangelista, B. (2011, February 13). Social revolution. *San Francisco Chronicle*.

Garcia, B. (2011, May 24). Citizens, audiences part of media revolution shaping with world. *Kuwait Times*. https://www.facebook.com/note.php?note_id=156607967738139

Gaworecki, M. (2011, Winter). Social media: Organizing tool and a "space of liberty" in post-revolution Egypt? *Social Policy*, 41(4), 66–69.

Gladwell, M. (2010, October 4). Small change: Why the revolution will not be tweeted. *The New Yorker*. http://www.newyorker.com/reporting/2010/10/04/101004fa_fact_gladwell

Grossman, L. (2010, December 15). Person of the year. *Time*. http://www.time.com/time/specials/packages/article/0,28804,2036683_2037183,00.html

Harry Ransom Center (2007). Gutenberg's legacy. The University of Texas at Austin. http://www.hrc.utexas.edu/educator/modules/gutenberg/books/legacy/

Hauben, R. (2011a, Summer). Netizens in Egypt and the republic of Tahrir Square. *The Amateur Computerist*, 20(2): 19–21. http://www.ais.org/~jrh/acn/

Hauben, R. (2011b). The need for netizen journalism and the ever evolving netizen – news – net symbiosis. *Netizen News*, 20(2): 9–11. http://www.ais.org/~jrh/acn/

Hirschkind, C. (2011, February 9). From the blogosphere to the street: The role of social media in the Egyptian uprising. *Jadaliyya*. http://www.jadaliyya.com/pages/contributors/7521

Hovesepian, N. (2011, February 9). The Arab pro-democracy movement: Struggles to redefine citizenship. *Jadaliyya*. http://www.jadaliyya.com/pages/index/588/the-arab-pro-democracy-movement_struggles-to-redef

Hutton, G., & Fosdick, M. (2011). The globalization of social media: Consumer relationships with brands evolve in the digital space. *Journal of Advertising Research*, 51(4), 564–570. http://dx.doi.org/10.2501/JAR-51-4-564-570

Ingram, M. (2011, March 29). Malcolm Gladwell: Social media still not a big deal. *Gigaom*. http://gigaom.com/2011/03/29/malcolm-gladwell-social-media-still-not-a-big-deal/

In Sight. (2011). Colombia groups. http://www.insightcrime.org/criminal-groups/colombia/farc/itemlist/tag/Manuel%20Marulanda.

Iskandar, A. (2013, July 2). Egypt's revolution hones its skills. *Al Jazeera*. http://www.aljazeera.com/indepth/opinion/2013/07/201372121622650964.html

Kelty, C. (2010, Winter). Introduction: Culture in, culture out. *Anthropological Quarterly, 83*(1), 7–16. http://dx.doi.org/10.1353/anq.0.0108

Mahmood, S. (2011, February 14). The architects of the Egyptian revolution. *The Nation.* http://www.thenation.com/article/158581/architects-egyptian-revolution

Martin, M. (2011, June 30). Khalid Said case postponed, police brutality persists in new Egypt. *Business Law.* http://www.ibtimes.com/khaled-saeed-said-egypt-postpone-delay-military-trial-police-brutality.htm

Miller, L. (1995). Women and children first: Gender and the settling of the electronic frontier. In J. Brook & I. Boal (Eds.), *Resisting the virtual life* (pp. 49–58). San Francisco: City Lights.

NPR staff. (2011, August 15). Internet: Road to democracy ... or elsewhere? NPR. http://www.npr.org/2011/08/15/139640456/Internet-road-to-democracy-or-elsewhere?

Peterson, M.A. (2011, May 3). Egypt's experimental moment: Contingent thoughts on media and social change. Media and Social Change. http://mediasocialchange.net/2011/05/03/egypts-experimental-moment-contingent-thoughts-on-media-and-social-change/

Postill, J. (2011, November 7). Democracy in the age of the viral reality: A media epidemiography of Spain's *indignados* movement. *Media anthropology blog.* http://johnpostill.com/2011/10/03/democracy-in-the-age-of-viral-reality-1/

Reardon, S. (2012, April 7). Was it really a Facebook revolution? *New Scientist, 214*(2859), 24. http://dx.doi.org/10.1016/S0262-4079(12)60889-6

Rheingold, H. (2003). *Smart mobs: The next social revolution.* Cambridge: Perseus Publishing.

———. (2008). Mobile media and political collective action. In J.E. Katz (Ed.), *Handbook of mobile communication studies* (pp. 225–237). Cambridge: Massachusetts Institute of Technology.

Rutledge, P. (2013, January 25). How Obama won the social media battle in the 2012 presidential campaign. *The Media Psychology Blog.* http://mprcenter.org/blog/2013/01/25/how-obama-won-the-social-media-battle-in-the-2012-presidential-campaign/

Shah, V. (2009, April 22). The psychology and anthropology of social networking. *Thought Economics.* http://thoughteconomics.blogspot.mx/2009/04/psychology-and-anthropology-of-social.html

Shirky, C. (2011, January/February). The political power of social media. *Foreign Affairs, 90*(1), n.p.

Shoichet, C.E. (2011, September 15). Latest battlefield in Mexico's drug wars: Social media. *CNN World.* http://www.cnn.com.

Sreberny, A. (2011, March 28). A social media revolution? Media and Social Change. http://mediasocialchange.net/2011/05/12/a-social-media-revolution/

Srinivasan, R. (2011, July 11). How the street and digital world speak to one another: From Egypt Blog. http://rameshsrinivasan.org/2011/07/11/how-the-street-and-digital-world-speak-to-one-another-from-egypt/

Suárez, S.L. (2011, March). Social media and regime change in Egypt. Campaigns and elections. http://www.campaignsandelections.com/magazine/us-edition/175972/social-media-and-regime-change-in-egypt.thtml

Suleiman, M. (2011, December 21). Debate over authenticity of assault on Egyptian woman intensifies. *Al-Arabiya Cairo.* http://www.alarabiya.net/articles/2011/12/21/183823.html

Technology Review. (2011, September/October). Key moments in the Arab Spring. http://www.technologyreview.com/files/68753/

Tomlin, J. (2011a, September 22). Iran, Sudan, Libya, Egypt: Social media helps give women a voice. *The Guardian.* http://www.wluml.org/news/iran-sudan-libya-egypt-social-media-helps-give-women-voice

———. (2011b, September 22). Social media gives women a voice in Iran. *The Guardian.* http://www.guardian.co.uk/lifeandstyle/2011/sep/22/social-media-women-iran

Tufekci, Z. (2011, August 30). New media and the people-powered uprisings. *Technology Review.* MIT. http://www.technologyreview.com/view/425280/new-media-and-the-people-powered-uprisings/

Watkins, S.C. (2011, February 18). Social movements in the age of social media: Participatory politics in Egypt. The Young and the Digital. http://theyoungandthedigital.com/2011/02/18/social-movements-in-the-age-of-social-media-participatory-politics-in-egypt/

Wu, D.D., & Mao, S. (2011). Editorial. Media discourses and cultural globalization: A Chinese perspective. *Cultural Arts: A South-North Journal of Cultural and Media Studies, 25*(1): 1–6. http://www.tandfonline.com/doi/pdf/10.1080/02560046.2011.552202

Zaks, D. (2011, August 16). How e-mail helped bring down the USSR. *Yahoo! News*. http://www.google.com/hostednews/afp/article/ALeqM5g98uUTVpjCzj2Wd7OWom-HZu6C7w?docId=CNG.f86f7de5aa4632fa5f9294df8b17a703.3e1

Zuckerman, E. (2011, June 27). Four questions about civic media. DML Central. http://dmlcentral.net/blog/ethan-zuckerman/four-questions-about-civic-media

Chapter 9: Global Nomads: Do Third Culture Kids own a national identity?

Amazon.com Reviews for Pollock, D. & R. van Reken. (2009). *Third culture kids: The experience of growing up among worlds*. http://www.amazon.com/Third-Culture-Kids-Experience-Growing/dp/1857882954

Appadurai, A. (1991). Global ethnoscapes: Notes on queries for a transnational anthropology. In R. Fox (Ed.), *Recapturing anthropology* (pp. 48–65). Santa Fe, NM: School of American Research Press.

Bikos, L.H., Kocheleva, J., King, D., Chang, G.C., McKenzie, A., Roenicke, C., Campbell, V., & Eckard, K. (2009). A consensual qualitative investigation into the repatriation experiences of young adult, missionary kids. *Mental Health, Religion & Culture, 12*(7), 735–754. http://dx.doi.org/10.1080/13674670903032637

Bowman, D.H. (2012, January 10). Identities blur for "third-culture kids." *Education Week*. Editorial Projects in Education. http://www.edweek.org/ew/articles/2001/05/09/34tck.h20.html

CBC News. (2009, October 29). Estimated 2.8 million Canadians live abroad. http://www.cbc.ca/news/canada/story/2009/10/28/canada-emigration-c.html

Cottrell, A.B. (1999). ATCKs have problems relating to their own ethnic groups. TCK world: The official home of Third Culture Kids. http://www.tckworld.com/useem/art4.html

———, & Useem, R.H. (1993a, September). TCKs experience prolonged adolescence. News/Articles Third Culture Kids: Focus of Major Study. http://www.tckworld.com/useem/art3.html

———, & Useem, R.H. (1993b). ATCKs maintain global dimensions throughout their lives. News/Articles Third Culture Kids: Focus of Major Study. http://www.tckworld.com/useem/art5.html

Eakin, F.B. (1998). According to my passport, I'm coming home. http://www.state.gov/documents/organization/2065.pdf

Erikson, E.H. (1970). Reflections on the dissent of contemporary youth. *International Journal of Psycho-Analysis, 51*(1), 11–22. Medline:5533527

Fechter, A.M. (2008). *Transnational lives: Expatriates in Indonesia*. Aldershot, UK: Ashgate.

Gould, J.B. (2002). Book review of *The Third Culture Kid experiences* by David C. Pollock and Ruth E. Van Reken (1999), and *Letters I never wrote* by R.E. van Reken (1986). *Journal of Loss and Trauma, 7*, 151–156.

Heyward, M. (2002). From international to intercultural: Redefining the international school for a globalized world. *Journal of Research in International Education, 1*(1), 9–32. http://jri.sagepub.com/cgi/content/abstract/1/1/9

Hill, B.V. (1986). The educational needs of children of expatriates. *Missiology: An International Review, XIV*, 326–346.

Just Landed. (2009). Expatriates worldwide: How many expats are there? Just Landed. http://www.justlanded.com/english/Common/Footer/Expatriates/How-many-expats-are-there

Kearney, M. (1995). The local and the global: Anthropology of globalization and transnationalism. *Annual Review of Anthropology, 24*(1), 547–565. http://dx.doi.org/10.1146/annurev.an.24.100195.002555

Kebshull, B., & Pozo-Humphries, M. (n.d.). Third culture kids/Global nomads and the culturally skilled therapist. http://clinicalsocialworksociety.org/docs/continuing_education/ThirdCultureKids.pdf

Keuss, J.F., & Willett, R. (2009). The sacredly mobile adolescent: A hermeneutic phenomenological study toward revising of the Third Culture Kid typology for effective ministry practice in a multivalent culture. *Journal of Youth Ministry, 8*(1), 7–24.

King, A.D. (Ed.) (1991). *Culture, globalization and the world-system: Contemporary conditions for the representation of identity*. Binghamton: State University of New York Press.

Klemens, M.J., & Bikos, L.H. (2009). Psychology well-being and sociocultural adaptation in college-aged, repatriated, missionary kids. *Mental Health, Religion & Culture, 12*(7), 721–733. http://dx.doi.org/10.1080/13674670903032629

Langford, M. (1998). Global nomads, third culture kids and international schools. In M. Hayden & J. Thompson (Eds.), *International education principles and practice* (pp. 28–43). New York: Routledge.

Nolan, R.W. (1990). Culture shock and cross-cultural adaptation: Or I was okay until I got here. *Practicing Anthropology, 12*(4), 2, 20.

Pollock, D.C., & Van Reken, R.E. (2009). *Third culture kids: The experience of growing up among worlds*. London: Nicholas Brealey & Intercultural Press.

Ridout, A. (2010). "The view from the threshold": Doris Lessing's Nobel acceptance speech. *Doris Lessing Studies, 29*(1), 4–8.

Uehara, A. (1986). The nature of American student re-entry adjustment and perceptions of the sojourner experience. *International Journal of Intercultural Relations, 10*(4), 415–438. http://dx.doi.org/10.1016/0147-1767(86)90043-X

Useem, R.H. (1993, January). TCK "mother" pens history of field. News/Articles Third Culture Kids: Focus of Major Study. http://www.tckworld.com/useem/art1.html

Van Reken, R.E., & Bethel, P.M. (2007). Third Culture Kids: Prototypes for understanding other cross-cultural kids. http://mkplanet.com/third-culture-kids-prototypes-for-understanding-other-cross-cultural-kids/

Vertovec, S. & Cohen, R. (Eds.). (2002). *Conceiving cosmopolitanism: Theory, context, and practice*. Oxford: Oxford University Press.

Ward, C., Bochner, S., & Furnham, A. (2001). *The psychology of culture shock* (2nd ed.). Philadelphia: Taylor & Francis Inc.

Chapter 10: Food Security: What are the economic and political determinants of food security and the global implications of world hunger?

Altieri, M., & Funes-Monzote, F.R. (2012). The paradox of Cuban agriculture: Monthly Review. Monthlyreview.org. http://monthlyreview.org/2012/01/01/the-paradox-of-cuban-agriculture

Avery, D.T. (2009). Cubans starve on diet of lies. http://cgfi.org/2009/04/cubans-starve-on-diet-of-lies-by-dennis-t-avery/

Bryant, C., & Kappaz, C. (2005). *Reducing poverty, building peace*. Bloomfield, CT: Kumarian Press.

Food and Agriculture Organization (FAO) (1996). Rome declaration on world food security and world food summit plan of action. World Food Summit, November 13–17. http://www.fao.org/docrep/003/w3613e/w3613e00.htm

_____ (2001). Agribusinesses and small farmers. Food and Agriculture Organization of the United Nations. Agriculture and Consumer Protection Department. http://www.fao.org/ag/magazine/0107sp.htm

_____ (2006 June). Food security. *Policy brief* 2: 1–4. ftp://ftp.fao.org/es/ESA/policybriefs/pb_02.pdf

_____ (2008). The state of food insecurity in the world 2008: High food prices and food security – Threats and opportunities. ftp://ftp.fao.org/docrep/fao/011/i0291e/i0291e00a.pdf

Funes-Monzote, F.R. (2008). *Farming like we're here to stay* (PhD dissertation). Wageningen University, Netherlands.

González, H. (2010). Debates on food security and agrofood world governance. *International Journal of Food Science & Technology, 45*(7), 1345–1352. http://dx.doi.org/10.1111/j.1365-2621.2010.02248.x

Harvard Business School (n.d.). Ray A. Goldberg. http://www.hbs.edu/faculty/Pages/profile.aspx?facId=12285

Hirschman, A.O. (1958). *The strategy of economic development*. New Haven, CT: Yale University Press.

Horrigan, L., Lawrence, R.S., & Walker, P. (2002). How sustainable agriculture can address the environmental and human health. Harms of industrial agriculture. *Environmental Health Perspectives*, *110*(5), n.p. http://www.organicconsumers.org/Organic/IndustrialAg502.cfm

Jenkins, J.C., Scanlan, J., & Peterson, L. (2007). Military famine, human rights, and child hunger: A cross-national analysis, 1990–2000. *Journal of Conflict Resolution*, *51*(6), 823–847. http://dx.doi.org/10.1177/0022002707308215

Kugelman, M., & Levenstein, S.L. (2012). *The global farms race: Land grabs, agricultural investment, and the scramble for food security*. Oakland, CA: Island Press.

Lallanilla, M. (n.d.). Let's chat about agribusiness and the factory farm. About.com Green Living. http://greenliving.about.com/od/healthyliving/a/environmental-impact-livestock-meat.htm

Lappe, F.M., & Collins, J. (1977). Why can't people feed themselves? In *Food First: Beyond the myth of scarcity*. New york: Random House. http://windward.hawaii.edu/facstaff/dagrossa-p/articles/WhyCantPeopleFeedThemselves.pdf

McMichael, P., & Schneider, M. (2011). Food security politics and the Millennium Development Goals. *Third World Quarterly*, *32*(1), 119–139. http://dx.doi.org/10.1080/01436597.2011.543818 Medline:21591303

Mihalache-O'Keef, A., & Li, Q. (2011). Modernization vs dependency revisited: Effects of foreign direct investment in food security in less developed countries. *International Studies Quarterly*, *55*(1), 71–93. http://dx.doi.org/10.1111/j.1468-2478.2010.00636.x

Norberg-Hodge, H., Merrifield, T., & Gorelick, S. (2013). Bringing the food economy home. International Society for Ecology & Culture. http://www.localfutures.org/publications/online-articles/bringing-the-food-economy-home

Novais, A. (2012). The Brazilian agribusiness. *The Brazil Business*. http://thebrazilbusiness.com/article/the-brazilian-agribusiness

Owens, E. (1976). *The right side of history*. Unpublished manuscript.

Poole-Kavana, H. (2006, Summer). 12 myths about hunger. *Food First Backgrounder*, *12*(2), 1–4. Retrieved from http://www.foodfirst.org/sites/www.foodfirst.org/files/pdf/BG%20SU06%2012%20Myths%20About%20Hunger.pdf

Pottier, J. (1999). *Anthropology of food: The social dynamics of food security*. Cambridge, MA: Cambridge Polity Press.

Radha, S. (1976). *Food and poverty*. New York: Holmes & Meier.

Ramalingam, B., Proudlock, K., & Mitchell, J. (2009). The global food price crisis: Lessons and ideas for relief planners and managers. ALNAP. http://www.alnap.org/pool/files/ALNAPLessonsFoodPriceCrisis.pdf

Rapetto, R., & Beliga, S.S. (1990). *Pesticides and the immune system: The public health risks*. Washington, DC: World Resources Institute.

Rocha, C., & Lessa, I. (2009). Urban governance for food security: The alternative food system in Belo Horizonte, Brazil. *International Planning Studies*, *14*(4), 389–400. http://dx.doi.org/10.1080/13563471003642787

Rodney, W. (1972). *How Europe underdeveloped Africa*. Washington, DC: Howard University Press.

Ryerson University (2013). Bela Horizonte wins major award Centre for Studies in Food Security. http://www.ryerson.ca/foodsecurity/projects/brazil/award.html

Sala-i-Martin, X., & Subramanian, A. (2003). *Addressing the natural resources curse: An illustration from Nigeria*. National Bureau of Economic Research Working Paper No. 9804, Cambridge, MA.

Samatar, A.I. (1993). Structural adjustment as development strategy? Bananas, boom, and poverty in Somalia. *Economic Geography*, *69*(1), 25–43. http://dx.doi.org/10.2307/143888

Union of Concerned Scientists. (2012). Industrial agriculture. http://www.ucsusa.org/food_and_agriculture/our-failing-food-system/industrial-agriculture/

Weisbrot, M. (2002). Globalism on the ropes. In R. Board (Ed.), *Global backlash: Citizens initiatives for a just world economy* (pp. 38–41). Lanham, MD: Rowman & Littlefield.

World Food Council (n.d.). *Celebrating the Belo Horizonte food security programme. Future Policy Award 2009: Solutions for food crisis*. http://www.futurepolicy.org/fileadmin/user_upload/PDF/Future_Policy_Award_brochure.pdf

Chapter 11: Ethnic Conflicts: What are the underlying reasons and the consequences of these conflicts?

Adam, G.A. (2008). Why has Darfur's indigenous population been put at risk? *Peace Review: A Journal of Social Justice, 20*(2), 158–165. http://dx.doi.org/10.1080/10402650802068051

AlertNet. (2011, April 19). At a glance. http://www.trust.org/spotlight/darfur-conflict

American Anthropological Association (2004, December). Statement on the humanitarian crisis in Darfur, Sudan. Draft copy. http://www.aaanet.org/committees/cfhr/stmt_darfur.htm

Apsel, J. (2009). The complexity of destruction in Darfur: Historical processes and regional dynamics. *Human Rights Review, 10*(2), 239–259. http://dx.doi.org/10.1007/s12142-008-0099-6

Avlon, J. (2011, February 20). A 21st-century statesman. *The Daily Beast.* World News. http://www.thedailybeast.com/newsweek/2011/02/20/a-21st-century-statesman.html

Bates, R.H. (1982). Modernization, ethnic competition, and the rationality of politics in contemporary Africa. In D. Rothchild & V.A. Olunsorola (Eds.), *State versus ethnic claims: African policy dilemmas.* Boulder, CO: Westview Press.

BBC News. (2006, December 6). Darfur conflict zones map. http://news.bbc.co.uk/2/hi/africa/6213202.stm

Boas, F. (1932, December 30). The aims of anthropological research. *Science, 76*(1983), 605–613. http://dx.doi.org/10.1126/science.76.1983.605 Medline:17730027

Bowen, J.R. (1996). The myth of global ethnic conflict. *Journal of Democracy, 7*(4), 3–14. http://dx.doi.org/10.1353/jod.1996.0057

Bringa, T. (1995). *Being Muslim the Bosnian way.* Princeton, NJ: Princeton University Press.

Brubaker, R. (2004). *Ethnicity without groups.* Cambridge, MA: Harvard University Press.

Burr, J.M., & Collins, R.O. (2006). *Darfur: The long road to disaster.* Princeton, NJ: Markus Weiner Publishers.

Caselli, F., & Coleman, W.J. (2011). *On the theory of ethnic conflict.* London: The Fuqua School of Business. http://faculty.fuqua.duke.edu/~coleman/web/ethnic.pdf

Cheney, B. (2000, October 28). *Ukrainian immigration.* http://faculty.fuqua.duke.edu/~coleman/web/ethnic.pdf

Crawford, B. (1998). The causes of cultural conflict: An institutional approach. In B. Crawford & R.D. Lipschutz (Eds.), *The myth of ethnic conflict: Politics, economics and "cultural" violence* (pp. 3–43). Berkeley: University of California.

Davis, J. (1992). The anthropology of suffering. *Journal of Refugee Studies, 5*(2), 149–161. http://dx.doi.org/10.1093/jrs/5.2.149

Davis, M.C. (2008). *Autonomy and ethnic conflict: The case of Tibet.* http://citation.allacademic.com/meta/p_mla_apa_research_citation/2/5/2/0/4/pages252041/p252041-1.php

De Vos, G.A. (1995). Concepts of ethnic identity. In L. Romanucci-Ross & G.A. De Vos (Eds.), *Ethnic identity, creation, conflict, and accommodation* (3rd ed., pp. 15–47). Walnut Creek, CA: Altamira Press.

Dreyer, J.T. (2003). Taiwan's evolving identity. Paper presented at Woodrow Wilson International Institute for Scholars, Washington, DC. http://formosafoundation.org/pdf/Taiwans%20Identity%20(J_Dreyer).pdf

D'Souza, F. (1981). *The Refugee Dilemma: International recognition and acceptance.* London: Minority Rights Group, No. 43.

Eller, J.D. (1999). *From culture to ethnicity to conflict: An anthropological perspective on international ethnic conflict.* Ann Arbor: The University of Michigan Press.

Fearon, J. (1995, August 30–September 2). *Ethnic war as a commitment problem.* Paper presented at the 1994 Annual Meetings of the American Political Science Association, New York. http://www.stanford.edu/~jfearon/papers/ethcprob.pdf

Fenton, S. (2003). *Ethnicity.* Cambridge: Polity Press.

Harrell-Bond, B.E. (1986). *Imposing aid: Emergency assistance to refugees.* Oxford: Oxford University Press.

_____, & Voutira, E. (1992). Anthropology and the study of refugees. *Anthropology Today, 8*(4), 6–10. http://dx.doi.org/10.2307/2783530

Henshaw, A. (2008, October 28) Trapped in Darfur refugee camp. BBC News. http://news.bbc. co.uk/2/hi/africa/7685248.stm

Human Rights Education Association. (n.d.). *Refugees and displaced persons.* http://www.hrea.org/ index.php?doc_id=418

Jerusalem Post. (2009). Refugees – A global issue. http://www.freerepublic.com/focus/news/838625/ posts

Markakis, J. (1998). Introduction. *Resource conflict in the Horn of Africa.* London: Sage Publications.

Mayroz, E. (2008). Ever again? The United States, genocide suppression, and the crisis in Darfur. *Journal of Genocide Research, 10*(3), 359–388. http://dx.doi.org/10.1080/ 14623520802305735

Miyares, I.M., & Airries, C.A. (2007). *Contemporary ethnic geographies in America.* Lanham, MD: Rowman & Littlefield Publishers, Inc.

Mulaj, K. (2008). *Forced displacement in Darfur, Sudan. Journal Compilation.* Oxford: Blackwell Publishing Ltd.

Omari, C.K. (1987). Ethnicity, politics and development in Tanzania. *African Study Monographs, 7,* 65–80.

Power, S. (2004, August 24). Dying in Darfur: Can the ethnic cleansing in Sudan be stopped? *The New Yorker,* 61.

Raghaven, S. (2004, July 31). Militias in Sudan are burning people alive, aid worker says. *Knight Ridder Newspapers.* http://www.freerepublic.com/focus/f-news/1182918/posts

Ter-Gabrielian, G. (1999). Strategies in "ethnic" conflict. *The Fourth World Journal.* http:// www.uni-muenster.de/Politikwissenschaft/Doppeldiplom/docs/CWIS%20-%20The%20 Fourth%20World%20Journal%20%20Strategies%20in%20Ethnic%20Confl.htm

UN News Centre. (2010, July 11). Darfur: Conflict claimed more than 200 lives in June, UN-African mission reports. UN News Service. http://www.un.org/apps/news/story.asp?NewsID =35290&Cr=darfur&Cr1

U.S. Department of State. (2007). *Darfur, Sudan: Confirmed damaged and destroyed villages.* Humanitarian Information Unit. http://hiu.state.gov

Wadlow, R. (2005, August 24). Darfur, Sudan: The overkill. *Toward Freedom.* http:// towardfreedom.com/home/content/view/557/63/

Welling, J.J. (2007, Spring). Non-governmental organizations, prevention, and intervention in internal conflict: Through the lens of Darfur. *Indiana Journal of Global Legal Studies, 14*(1), 147–179. http://dx.doi.org/10.2979/GLS.2007.14.1.147

Wolff, S. (2006). Introduction. Ethnopolitics: Conflict versus cooperation. *Ethnic conflict: A global perspective.* Oxford: Oxford University Press.

World Savvy Monitor. (2008, May). The situation in Sudan and the conflict in Darfur. http:// worldsavvy.org/monitor/index.php?option=com_content&view=article&id=65&Item id=934

World Without Genocide. (2011). Darfur genocide. World Without Genocide. At William Mitchell College of Law. http://worldwithoutgenocide.org/genocides-and-conflicts/ darfur-genocide

Chapter 12: Human Migration: What are the socio-economic and political implications of the transnational flow of people?

Alsvik, K. (2009, October 21–23). Integrating migrant rights and protection in migration and development policy and practice. *National workshop on ILO instruments for promotion and protection of the rights of migrant workers.* Harare, Zimbabwe. http://www.ilo.org/public/ lang--en/index.htm

Arnold, C., & Bertone, A. (2002). Addressing the sex trade in Thailand: Some lessons learned from NGOs. Part I. *Gender Issues, 20*(1), 26–52. http://dx.doi.org/10.1007/s12147-002-0006-4

Balakrishnan, T.R., & Hou, F. (1999). Residential patterns in cities. In S.S. Halli & L. Driedger (Eds.), *Immigrant Canada: Demographic, economic, and social challenges* (pp. 116–147). Toronto: University of Toronto Press.

Bales, K. (2005). *Understanding global slavery.* Berkeley: University of California Press.

Boswell, C. (2008). Combining economics and sociology in migration theory. *Journal of Ethnic and Migration Studies, 34*(4), 549–566. http://dx.doi.org/10.1080/13691830801961589

Butler, D. (2005, October 31). Immigrants threaten Canada's peace: Poll. *The Star Phoenix*, B1.

Byrne, C. (2010, October 8). Ontario family facing charges in 'modern day slavery' case. *thestar.com*. http://www.thestar.com/news/ontario/article/873022-ontario-family-facing-charges-in-modern-day-slavery-case

Castles, S. (2000). International migration at the beginning of the twenty-first century: Global trends and issues. *International Social Science Journal 52*(165), 269–281.

Chrisafis, A. (2010, November 16). Immigration: France sees tensions rise five years on from Paris riots. *The Guardian*. http://www.guardian.co.uk/world/2010/nov/16/france-racism-immigration-sarkozy

World Factbook, C.I.A. (2009). *Trafficking in persons*. http://www.cia.gov/library/publications/tje-world-factbook/docs/notesanddefs.html

Cross, T. (2012, May 6). Why did Sarkozy lose the French presidential election? RFI English. http://www.english.rfi.fr/economy/20120506-why-did-sarkozy-lose-french-presidential-election

Cruz, G.T. (2008). Between identity and security: Theological implications of migration in the context of globalization. *Theological Studies, 69*, 357–375.

CTV News. (2011, December 23). Landmark child trafficking case catches advocates' eyes. Ctvbc.ca. http://www.ctvbc.ctv.ca/servlet/an/local/CTVNews/20111223/bc_human_trafficking_reza_moazami_111223/20111223/

de Haas, H. (2010). The internal dynamics of migration processes: A theoretical inquiry. *Journal of Ethnic and Migration Studies, 36*(10), 1587–1617. http://dx.doi.org/10.1080/1369183X.2010.489361

_____, H. (2012, March 26). *Migration...it's the economy, stupid!* http://heindehaas.blogspot.mx/

Esquivel, P., & Becerra, H. (2012, April 24). Report finds wave of Mexican immigration to U.S. has ended. *Los Angeles Times*. http://articles.latimes.com/2012/apr/24/local/la-me-immigration-20120424

The Evangelical Fellowship of Canada (EFC). (2009). *Human trafficking: A report on modern day slavery in Canada*. http://files.efc-canada.net/si/Human%20Trafficking/HumanTraffickingReportApril2009.pdf.

Fitzgerald, D. (2006). Towards a theoretical ethnography of migration. *Qualitative Sociology, 29*(1), 1–24. http://dx.doi.org/10.1007/s11133-005-9005-6

General Assembly resolution 55/25 of 15 November 2000 in United Nations Office on Drugs and Crime (2004). United Nations Convention Against Transnational Organized Crime and the Protocols. New York: United Nations.

Fuga, A. (2008). Multiculturalism in France: Evolutions and challenges. Online working paper no. 12. Eurosphere. Diversity and the European public sphere. Toward a citizen's Europe. http://eurospheres.org/files/2010/08/Eurosphere_Working_Paper_12_Fuga.pdf

Halli, S.S., & Driedger, L. (1999). The immigrant challenge 2000. In S.S. Halli & L. Driedger (Eds.), *Immigrant Canada: Demographic, economic, and social challenges* (pp. 3–7). Toronto: University of Toronto Press.

Hamilton, K., Simon, P., & Veniard, C. (2004). Country profiles: The challenge of French diversity. Migration Information Service. http://www.migrationinformation.org/Profiles/display.cfm?ID=266.

Heyer, K.E. (2012). Reframing displacement and membership: Ethics of migration. *Theological Studies, 73*, 188–206.

Jennings, J. (2000). Citizenship, republicanism and multiculturalism in contemporary France. *British Journal of Political Science, 30*(4), 575–598. http://dx.doi.org/10.1017/S0007123400000259

Kamber, M., & Lacey, M. (2005, September 11). For Mali villagers, France is a workplace and lifeline. *The New York Times*, A6. http://www.infotrac.galegroup.com

Katseli, L.T., Lucas, R.E.B., & Xemogiani, T. (2006). Effects of migration on sending countries: What do we know? OECD Development Centre Working Paper No. 250. OECD Publishing. http://www.eric.ed.gov/PDFS/ED504069.pdf

Kymlicka, W. (2003). Immigration, citizenship multiculturalism. In S. Spencer (Ed.), *The politics of migration: Managing opportunity, conflict and change* (pp. 195–208). Malden, MA: Blackwell Publishing.

Li, P.S. (1988). *The Chinese in Canada*. Toronto: Oxford University Press.

Maclean's. (2005, October 13). Pettigrew says more immigrants needed to help augment dwindling labour force. http://www.macleans.ca/topstories/politics/news/shownews.jsp?content=n101351A

MailOnline. (2007, April). 'Global upheaval' will make Britain home to 69m by 2050. http://www.dailymail.co.uk/news/article-446993/Global-upheaval-make-Britain-home-69m-2050.html

Malik, K. (2012 June 4). What is wrong with multiculturalism? (Part 1). The Milton K.Wong lecture. http://kenanmalik.wordpress.com/2012/06/04/what-is-wrong-with-multiculturalism-part-1/

Massey, D.S., Arango, J., Hugo, G., Kouaouci, A., Pellegrino, A., & Taylor, J.E. (1993). Theories of international migration: A review and appraisal. *Population and Development Review, 19*(3), 431–466. http://dx.doi.org/10.2307/2938462

Moses, J. (2006). *International migration: Globalization's last frontier.* London: Zed Books.

Neuwirth, G. (1999). Toward a theory of immigrant integration. In S.S. Halli & L. Driedger (Eds.), *Immigrant Canada: Demographic, economic, and social challenges* (pp. 51–69). Toronto: University of Toronto Press.

Ng, W.C. (1999). *The Chinese in Vancouver, 1945–80: The pursuit of identity and power.* Vancouver: UBC Press.

Online Press Conference. (2010, October 12). Human trafficking expert Benjamin Perrin exposes hidden Canada tragedy. Online Press Conference—Campaign to End Modern-day Slavery. http://endmodernslaveryrelease.eventbrite.com/

Oosterman, J. (2010, June 17). Pursuing a culture of freedom: Combating modern-day slavery in Canada. *C2C Journal.* http://c2cjournal.ca/2010/06/pursuing-a-culture-of-freedom-combating-modernday-slavery-in-canada/

Perrin, B. (2010). *Invisible Chains: Canada's underground world of human trafficking.* Toronto: Viking Canada.

Randall, V. (1997, 2008). Racial discrimination: The record of France. Race, Racism, and the Law. Human Rights Documentation Center. http://academic.udayton.edu/race/06hrights/georegions/Europe/France01.htm

Reuters. (2013, June 24). Update 2: U.S. immigration bill passes key test vote in Senate. http://www.reuters.com/article/2013/06/24/usa-immigration-idUSL2N0F01YV20130624

Rosenblum, M.R., & Brick, K. (2011). US immigration policy and Mexican/Central American migration flows: Then and now. Migration Policy Institute. http://www.migrationpolicy.org/pubs/RMSG-regionalflows.pdf

Schauer, E., & Wheaton, E. (2006). Sex trafficking into the United States: A literature review. *Criminal Justice Review, 31*(1), 1–24.

Schiller, N.G. (2009). A global perspective on migration and development. *Social Analysis, 53*(3), 14–37. http://dx.doi.org/10.3167/sa.2009.530302

Simmons, A.B. (1999). Immigration policy: Imagined futures. In S.S. Halli & L. Driedger (Eds.), *Immigrant Canada: Demographic, economic, and social challenges* (pp. 21–50). Toronto: University of Toronto Press.

Smith, A.D. (2001). *Nationalism: Theory, ideology, history.* Cambridge: Polity Press.

Soria, M. (2005, September 19). Immigration is an asset, not a liability. *Business Record* (Des Moines), 301. http://www.infotrac.galegroup.com

Spencer, S. (2003). Introduction. In S. Spencer (Ed.), *The politics of migration: Managing opportunity, conflict and change* (pp. 1–24). Malden, MA: Blackwell Publishing.

Stirk, F. (2009, July 31). Salvation Army to help deter Olympics sex traffickers. http://www.salvationarmy.ca/2009/07/31/salvation-army-to-help-deter-olympics-sex-traffickers/

Tomasi, S. (2008). Migration and Catholicism in a global context. In S. Lefebvre & L. Carlos (Eds.), *Migration in a global world* (pp. 13–31). London: SCM Press.

UNODC (United Nations Office on Drugs and Crime). (2000, December 12). Address at the opening of the signing conference. *UNODC.* http://unodc.org/unodc/en/about-unodc/speeches/speech_2000-12-12_1.html

Well, P. (2004). A nation in diversity: France, Muslims and the headscarf. http://www.opendemocracy.net/faith-europe_islam/article_1811.jsp

Wheaton, E.M., Schauer, E.J., & Galli, T.V. (2010). Economics of human trafficking. *International Migration, 48*(4), 114–141. http://dx.doi.org/10.1111/j.1468-2435.2009.00592.x Medline:20645472

Wickramasekara, P. (2008). Globalization, international labour migration and the rights of migrant workers. *Third World Quarterly, 29*(7), 1247–1264. http://dx.doi.org/10.1080/01436590802386278

Chapter 13: Global Conflict: Is the world safer because of military intervention, and what are the consequences of militarism?

Ali, J. (n.d.). *The economic and environmental impact of the Gulf War on Kuwait and the Persian Gulf.* http://www1.american.edu/ted/KUWAIT.HTM/

Barnett, C. (2006). Oil, conflict and the future of global energy supplies. *Global Research.* http://www.globalresearch.ca/oil-conflict-and-the-future-of-global-energy-supplies/1781

Bulletin Staff. (2013, April 5). Interview with Siegfried Hecker: North Korea complicates the long-term picture. *The Bulletin.* http://thebulletin.org/interview-siegfried-hecker-north-korea-complicates-long-term-picture

Chandler, D. (2002). *From Kosovo to Kabul: Human rights and international intervention.* London/Sterling, VA: Pluto Press.

Chomsky, N. (2005). *Imperial ambitions: Conversations with Noam Chomsky in the post-9/11 world.* New York: Metropolitan Books.

_____. (2007). *Failed states: The abuse of power and the assault on democracy.* New York: Holt Paperbacks.

Democracy Now! (2010, October 29). U.S. life expectancy falls to 49th. http://www.democracynow.org/2010/10/29/headlines/us_life_expectancy_falls_to_49th

Du Boff, R.B. (1989). *Accumulation and power: An economic history of the United States.* Armonk, NY: M.E. Sharpe Publishers.

Eisenhower, D. (1961) Military-Industrial Complex Speech, Dwight D. Eisenhower, 1961. *Public Papers of the Presidents, Dwight D. Eisenhower, 1960* (pp. 1035–1040). http://coursesa.matrix.msu.edu/~hst306/documents/indust.html

Global Issues Overview. (n.d.). Overview of global issues. Peace, war and conflict. World Revolution.org. http://www.worldrevolution.org/projects/globalissuesoverview/overview2/PeaceNew.htm.

Goodman, M.A. (2013a). *National insecurity: The cost of American militarism.* San Francisco: City Lights Publishers.

_____. (2013b). American militarism: Costs and consequences. Truth Out.org. http://truth-out.org/progressivepicks/item/14926-american-militarism-costs-and-consequences

Greenwald, G. (2013, January 21). From the Guardian: MLK's vehement condemnations of US militarism are more relevant than ever. *The Guardian.* http://www.guardian.co.uk/commentisfree/2013/jan/21/king-obama-drones-militarism-sanctions-iran

Human Security Report Project (HSRP). (2012, December 24). Chapter 5: State-based armed conflict. http://www.isn.ethz.ch/isn/layout/set/print/content/view/full/24620?lng=en&id=156350

King, M.L. (1967). MLK: Beyond Vietnam. http://www.choices.edu/resources/documents/TAH_race4_1.pdf

Lindorff, D. (2012, September 24). American militarism. *Counter Punch.* http://www.counterpunch.org/2012/09/24/american-militarism/

Lobe, J. (2013, April 5). Libya intervention more questionable in rear view mirror. *Common Dreams.* http://www.commondreams.org/headline/2013/04/05-0

Masters, J. (2013, February 8). Targeted killings. Council on Foreign Relations. http://www.cfr.org/counterterrorism/targeted-killings/p9627

Nikolic-Ristanovic, V. (2008, June). Local conflicts and international interventions: Victimisation of civilians and possibilities or restorative global responses. *Contemporary Justice Review, 11*(2), 101–115. http://dx.doi.org/10.1080/10282580802057702

NPR staff. (2011, January 17). Ike's warning of military expansion, 50 years later. *NPR News.* http://www.npr.org/2011/01/17/132942244/ikes-warning-of-military-expansion-50-years-later

Parry, R. (2013, March 4). What has US militarism wrought? Consortiumnews.com. http://consortiumnews.com/2013/03/04/what-has-us-militarism-wrought/

Peters, C. (1992). *Collateral damage: The new world order at home and abroad.* Cambridge, MA: South End Press.

Project Ploughshares. (2013). 2012 armed conflicts report summary. *The Ploughshares Monitor, 33*(3), n.p. http://ploughshares.ca/pl_publications/2012-armed-conflicts-report-summary/

Shah, V. (2009, July). Global conflict: Causes and solutions for peace. *Thought Economics. Interviews with the world's leading thinkers.* http://thoughteconomics.blogspot.mx/2009/07/global-conflict-causes-and-solutions_16.html

Sirota, D. (2013). The blind theology of militarism. Creators.com. http://www.creators.com/opinion/david-sirota/the-blind-theology-of-militarism.html

Tadjbakhsh, S., & Chenoy, A.M. (2007). *Human security: Concepts and implications.* New York: Routledge.

Vidal, G. (2002). *Perpetual war for perpetual peace: How we got to be so hated.* New York: Nation Books.

Walt, S.M. (2011, April 14). Was intervention in Libya justified? Was it legal? *Foreign Policy.* Stephen M. Walt Blog. http://walt.foreignpolicy.com/posts/2011/04/14/more_to_read_about_libya

Welsh, M.J. (2002). From right to responsibility: Humanitarian intervention and international society. *Global Governance Boulder, 4,* 503–521.

Worldcentric.org. (2013). Militarism and conflicts. http://worldcentric.org/conscious-living/militarism-and-conflicts. http://worldcentric.org/conscious-living/militarism-and-conflicts

INDEX